To Lydia
Wishing you all the best as
you discover gender and security!

Jenny

Women, Peace and Security

This book provides a critical assessment of the impact of UN Resolution 1325 by examining the effect of peacebuilding missions on increasing gender equality within conflict-affected countries.

UN Resolution 1325 was adopted in October 2000, and was the first time that the security concerns of women in situations of armed conflict and their role in peacebuilding was placed on the agenda of the UN Security Council. It was an important step forward in terms of bringing women's rights and gender equality to bear in the UN's peace and security agenda. More than a decade after the adoption of this Resolution, its practical reality is yet to be substantially felt on the ground in the very societies and regions where women remain disproportionately affected by armed conflict and grossly under-represented in peace processes. This realization, in part, led to the adoption in 2008 and 2009 of three other Security Council Resolutions, on sexual violence in conflict, violence against women, and for the development of indicators to measure progress in addressing women, peace and security issues.

The book draws together the findings from eight countries and four regional contexts to provide guidance on how the impact of Resolution 1325 can be measured, and how peacekeeping operations could improve their capacity to effectively engender security.

This book will be of much interest to students of peacebuilding, gender studies, the United Nations, international security and IR in general.

'Funmi Olonisakin is Director of the Conflict, Security and Development Group at King's College London. She initiated the establishment of the African Leadership Centre to build the next generation of African scholars and analysts on peace and security. Prior to this, she worked at the United Nations. **Karen Barnes** is Gender Project Coordinator at the OECD Development Centre. Previously, Karen led the gender and peacebuilding team at International Alert and she is currently completing her PhD at the London School of Economics. **Eka Ikpe** is currently a Research Associate with the Conflict Security and Development Group, King's College London.

Contemporary Security Studies
Series Editors: James Gow and Rachel Kerr
King's College London

This series focuses on new research across the spectrum of international peace and security, in an era where each year throws up multiple examples of conflicts that present new security challenges in the world around them.

Women, Peace and Security

Translating policy into practice

**Edited by 'Funmi Olonisakin,
Karen Barnes and Eka Ikpe**

Routledge
Taylor & Francis Group

LONDON AND NEW YORK

First published 2011
by Routledge
2 Park Square, Milton Park, Abingdon, Oxon OX14 4RN

Simultaneously published in the USA and Canada
by Routledge
270 Madison Avenue, New York, NY 10016

Routledge is an imprint of the Taylor & Francis Group, an informa business

Typeset in Times by Wearset Ltd, Boldon, Tyne and Wear
Printed and bound in Great Britain by TJI Digital, Padstow, Cornwall

British Library Cataloguing in Publication Data
A catalogue record for this book is available from the British Library

Library of Congress Cataloging-in-Publication Data
Women, peace, and security : translating policy into practice / edited by
'Funmi Olonisakin, Karen Barnes, and Eka Ikpe.
p. cm.
1. Women and peace. 2. Women and war. I. Olonisakin, 'Funmi.
II. Barnes, Karen. III. Ikpe, Eka.
JZ5578.W667 2010
327.1'72082–dc22   2010022490

ISBN13: 978-0-415-58797-6 (hbk)
ISBN13: 978-0-203-83708-5 (ebk)

Dedicated to the masses of ordinary women around the world who dare to demand a more secure place to stand and, in so doing, chart the path for others to follow.

Contents

Contributors

Dr. 'Funmi Olonisakin is Director of the Conflict, Security and Development Group (CSDG) at King's College London. She initiated the establishment of the African Leadership Centre (ALC), which aims to build a next generation of African scholars generating cutting-edge knowledge on peace, security and development. Prior to this, she worked in the office of the United Nations' Special Representative of the Secretary-General for Children and Armed Conflict. She also serves on the international advisory boards of the Norwegian Foreign Ministry's Training for Peace (TfP) programme and of the Geneva Centre for Democratic Control of Armed Forces (DCAF). She is the West African Regional Coordinator of the African Security Sector Network (ASSN) and an Associate Fellow of the Geneva Centre for Security Policy (GCSP). She is the author of *Peacekeeping in Sierra Leone: The Story of UNAMSIL* (Lynne Rienner, 2008); co-author of *Global Development and Human Security* (Transaction, 2007); and co-editor of *Women and Security Governance in Africa* (Pambazuka, 2010) among a range of other publications.

Karen Barnes is Gender Project Coordinator for the OECD's Development Centre in Paris. Her expertise is at both policy and field level with a particular focus on West Africa, and her recent publications include papers on EU-level implementation of UNSCR 1325 and gender and security sector reform. She has a PhD in International Relations from the London School of Economics, focusing on gender issues and peacebuilding in Sierra Leone. Prior to joining the OECD, she led the gender and peacebuilding programme at International Alert where she was responsible for a multi-year, cross-regional programme around the implementation of UNSCR 1325.

Eka Ikpe is a Research Associate with the Conflict Security and Development Group, King's College London. In this role, she manages the CSDG Knowledge Building and Mentoring programme and the CSDG Women, Peace and Security project and edits the CSDG publication series, *Comments on Africa*. Eka has researched and published on state fragility, women, peace and security, donor-aid policy and security and justice provision to the poor. She is also completing a doctoral thesis at the Economics department of the School of Oriental and African Studies (SOAS), University of London.

Catherina H. Hall-Martin is a researcher and programme coordinator at the Conflict, Security and Development Group, King's College, London. She has obtained a Master's degree in Conflict, Security and Development from King's College, London.

Emma Njoki Wamai is a consultant with the Centre for Humanitarian Dialogue and a member of the Board of the Young Women's Leadership Institute (YWLI), Kenya. She is also a former Peace and Security Fellow, King's College, London.

Lesley Abdela is a partner in Eyecatcher Associates/Shevolution and is Chief Executive of Project Parity. Lesley has over 25 years of experience in the fields of gender and democratic development and has worked in over 40 countries as an expert advisor to governments, NGOs and the private sector. She is the recipient of the UK Woman Journalist of the Year Award (2009).

Kiri-Ann E. Richardson-Olney has been working in the field of international development for five years and has a Master's degree in Conflict, Security and Development from King's College, London. Having been awarded a postgraduate diploma in International Relations by LSE, Kiri-Ann began working for Refugees International in Washington, DC. From 2007 she worked for Oxfam GB before starting in her current role as Development Associate at St John's College, Oxford.

Gihan Eltahir-Eltom is a researcher with the Rift Valley Institute based in Sudan and a former Peace and Security Fellow, King's College, London.

Sumie Nakaya is a Political Affairs Officer in the Darfur Integrated Operational Team in the United Nations Department of Peacekeeping Operations. Prior to joining the UN Secretariat, Sumie worked with the Social Science Research Council and the United Nations Development Programme. Sumie holds a PhD. in Political Science from the City University of New York and an MA in Law and Diplomacy from the Fletcher School. Her publications include book chapters and journal articles on gender and peacebuilding, aid effectiveness, and post-conflict state building.

Bineta Diop is the founder and the Executive Director of Femmes Africa Solidarité, an NGO based in Geneva and Dakar. As Executive Director of FAS, she helped initiate the West African women's movement, the Mano River Women's Peace Network (MARWOPNET), which was awarded the UN Prize in the Field of Human Rights in 2003. Bineta is the Vice-President of the African Union Women's Committee, and she also chairs the Geneva-based United Nations Working Group on Peace, which is part of the NGO Committee on the Status of Women. She was appointed to co-chair the Civil Society Advisory Group that is tasked with advising the High-Level Steering Committee for the tenth anniversary of UNSCR 1325 and ensuring a coherent and coordinated approach by the UN system to implementing UNSCR 1325.

Awa Ceesay-Ebo is an independent consultant to several organizations, including USAID and Population Services International. She holds a BSc degree in Decision Sciences/Management Information Systems and International Relations. She was Communications and Information Officer at the International Action Network on Small Arms (IANSA) and a former Peace and Security Fellow, King's College, London.

Nyaradzo Machingambi-Pariola is a part-time lecturer at the Nelson Mandela University Law Faculty where she is also undertaking her Doctorate in International Human Rights Law and Gender Studies. She is also a former Peace and Security Fellow, King's College, London.

Preface

This book is the product of a research programme initiated in 2005 by the Conflict, Security and Development Group at King's College London. It aims to provide a critical assessment of the impact of United Nations Security Council Resolution 1325 (UNSCR 1325) in a number of national and regional contexts. When UNSCR 1325 was adopted in October 2000, it was hailed by policy analysts and international observers alike as a path-breaking step. It was the first time that the security concerns of women in situations of armed conflict and their role in peacebuilding were placed on the agenda of the UN Security Council. It was a significant milestone in the struggle for the advancement of women, bringing women's rights and gender equality to bear on the UN's peace and security agenda.

At the five-year mark in 2005, it became evident that greater attention was placed on celebrating this achievement than on the substance of implementation and application on the ground. This was understandable for a period given that UNSCR 1325 was in large part the product of sustained activism by the women's movement, particularly since the fourth World Conference on Women held in Beijing in 1995.

However, ten years after the adoption of this Resolution, its practical reality is yet to be substantially felt on the ground in the very societies and regions where women remain disproportionately affected by armed conflict and grossly under-represented in peace processes. This realization, in part, led to the adoption in 2008 and 2009 of three other United Nations Security Council Resolutions. UNSCR 1820 focuses on sexual violence in conflict, and UNSCR 1888 builds on this, proposing the appointment of a Special Representative on violence against women and also focusing on strengthening reporting, prevention and response mechanisms. UNSCR 1889 called for the development of indicators to measure progress in addressing women, peace and security issues and as requested by the Security Council in the resolution, the Secretary-General submitted a report on 6 April 2010 outlining the proposed set of indicators on women, peace and security.

All of these are welcome developments, and have strengthened the international community's women, peace and security agenda. However, the real challenge to be addressed is that there remains a serious gap in knowledge about the real difference that UNSCR 1325 has made in the lives of the most affected communities and regions; and what added value the new resolutions will bring. While research and anecdotal evidence about the implementation of UNSCR 1325 has proliferated over the past five years, understanding of the process whereby it is translated from a rhetorical commitment at the UN level into concrete progress on the ground is still lacking.

Until recently, the key focus of research on gender and peacebuilding issues has been either how to mainstream a gender approach or the operational and bureaucratic reasons behind the seemingly inevitable gap between policy and practice. While these analyses have provided important insights and have been used to inform the international community's efforts to implement gender-related programs within their peacebuilding activities, one of the main problems with the existing work in this area, and particularly in relation to UNSCR 1325, is that advocacy outweighs substance.

This book is the first to undertake a critical assessment of the impact of UNSCR 1325 across a broad range of countries and regions, compiled in one source. We believe the empirical evidence provided in this volume will be immensely relevant to scholars, analysts and policymakers as the United Nations takes stock of the situation of women in armed conflict ten years after the adoption of UNSCR 1325. In this regard, this book has several inter-related objectives. First, it intends to amend the gap in the literature, and to interrogate the assumptions on which UNSCR 1325 is based. Second, it questions the ability, and legitimacy, of external actors to bring about gender-related structural changes in conflict-affected countries. Given that gender relations are often thrown into flux during conflict, a critical window of opportunity can exist at such times to reform these relations along more equitable lines during the peacebuilding phase. Specifically, we ask whether having a peacekeeping mission and the framework of UNSCR 1325 actually make a difference in terms of advancing gender equality within conflict-affected countries. Third and last, the book examines the lessons that can be learned from the alternative local mechanisms that exist in these contexts.

The authors in this book share the experiences of eight countries and four regional contexts in which to explore these issues. The cases have been selected on the basis that they will provide a broad regional, thematic and contextual body of evidence from which to draw conclusions about the impact of peacekeeping missions on efforts to advance gender equality within conflict-affected countries. Most importantly, some countries have experienced a UN-mandated peacekeeping mission where others have not. Furthermore, the peacekeeping missions that have been carried out vary in terms of whether they were initiated and conducted prior to or after the critical turning point of October 2000 when the UN Security Council adopted UNSCR 1325. We also examine the role of a number of regional organizations in addressing the issues at the heart of the Resolution. These include the African Union (AU), Economic Community of West African States (ECOWAS), European Union (EU) and the Southern African Development Community (SADC).

The central focus of all of the case studies will be to explore the potential for using UNSCR 1325 to promote gender-related change at the national and regional levels. Three of the case studies were selected for further fieldwork – East Timor, Sierra Leone and Sudan. All cases in the study are also based, in part, on semi-structured interviews with UN and other practitioners and policy makers who are, or have been, involved in the conflicts, local officials who were involved in implementing UNSCR 1325 or related projects, as well as local men and women who are active in civil society or involved in gender-related issues. Two of the chapters – on the AU and Nepal – were also written by policy practitioners with the experience of working on women, peace and security issues in the field with the UN; and through regular engagement with the AU.

This in-depth exploration of eight, mostly conflict-affected countries will make an important contribution to the literature on gender and peacebuilding, as well as the growing body of critical research around conflict, security and development issues. This study also aims to have direct policy relevance, particularly in terms of identifying strategies for moving from ad hoc interventions to the kind of systematic transformation envisaged by UNSCR 1325. Bridging theory and practice, or developing a praxis to guide future responses by the international community in the area of gender and peacebuilding is one of the underlying goals of this investigation.

This book has global significance – it speaks directly to the international community's efforts to achieve a qualitative shift in the lives of women worldwide. It provides valuable empirical data for the academic community and a tool for evidence-based policy for the policy makers globally and regionally. It will also serve as a useful guide to practitioners seeking to learn lessons from the application of UN commitments such as UNSCR 1325 in various contexts. Furthermore, the book is timely. The year 2010 (the time of writing) is an important one for the world as the United Nations and the women's movement worldwide embarks on a review of the impact of UNSCR 1325 after ten years.

It would not have been possible to successfully complete this book without the important partnerships that developed on several levels and at crucial stages. One was the support provided to the Conflict, Security and Development Group by the Norwegian Ministry of Foreign Affairs, which enabled us to commission a number of country studies and for which we are profoundly grateful. Another was the collaboration that developed between the three editors and their commitment to build on the initial study by undertaking additional work to take the research findings to the publication stage. We are particularly grateful to Catherina Hall-Martin for providing additional research support and undertaking the painstaking work of fact checking during a lengthy editing process in addition to the Kosovo country study. Most importantly, we would like to thank the country and regional case study contributors through whom we have gained a great deal of insight.

The views expressed in this volume are those of the authors alone. They do not represent the views of the various institutions to which they are affiliated.

The Editors

Abbreviations

50/50	The Fifty-Fifty Group
AFELL	Association of Female Lawyers in Liberia
AMIS	African Union Mission in Sudan
APG	Associate Parliamentary Group
APRM	African Peer Review Mechanism
APSA	African Union Peace and Security Architecture
ASF	African Standby Force
AU	African Union
AUGD	African Union Gender Directorate
AUWC	African Union Women's Committee
AWCPD	African Women Committee on Peace and Development
AWIC	African Women in Crisis
CA	Comprehensive approach
CA	Constituent Assembly
CAT	Convention against Torture
CAVR	Commission for Reception, Truth and Reconciliation
CCC	Concerned Christian Community
CDE	Convention Against Discrimination in Education
CEDAW	Convention on the Elimination of All Forms of Discrimination Against Women
CEWS	Continental Early Warning System
CIVPOL	UN Civilian Police Force
CNRT	National Congress for Timorese Reconstruction
CPA	Comprehensive Peace Agreement
CPN-M	Communist Party of Nepal – Maoist
CRC	Convention on the Rights of the Child
CS	Civil society
CSDE	Convention against Discrimination in Education
CSOs	Civil society organizations
CSW	Commission on the Status of Women
DDR	Disarmament, Demobilization and Reintegration
DDRR	Disarmament, Demobilization, Rehabilitation and Reintegration
DFID	Department for International Development

DG RELEX	Directorate-General for External Relations
DPA	Darfur Peace Agreement
DPKO	UN Department of Peacekeeping Operations
DRC	Democratic Republic of Congo
EC	European Commission
ECLAC	Economic Commission for Latin America and the Caribbean
ECOMIL	ECOWAS Mission in Liberia
ECOMOG	Economic Community Ceasefire Monitoring Group
ECOWAS	Economic Community of West African States
ECPF	ECOWAS Conflict Prevention Framework
EP	European Parliament
EPLO	European Peacebuilding Liaison Office
ERC	Equal Remuneration Convention
ESDP	European Security and Defence Policy
ESF	ECOWAS Standby Force
ESPA	Eastern Sudan Peace Agreement
EU	European Union
Falintil	Armed Forces of National Liberation of East Timor
FAS	Femmes Africa Solidarité
FAWE	Forum of African Women Educationalists
FCD	Foundation for Community Development
FGM	Female Genital Mutilation
FLS	Forward Looking Strategies
FOKUPERS	East Timorese Women's Communication Forum
Fretilin	Revolutionary Front for an Independent East Timor
GA	Gender advisor
GAD	Gender and development
GAPS	Gender Action for Peace and Security
GBV	Gender-based violence
GEMAP	Governance and Economic Management Assistance Programme
Gencap	Gender Standby Capacity
GEST	Gender Expert Support Team
GoNU	Government of National Unity
GoS	Government of Sudan
GoSS	Government of South Sudan
HIV/AIDS	Human Immunodeficiency Virus/Acquired Immune Deficiency Syndrome
IAC	Interim Administrative Council
IASC	Inter Agency Standing Committee
ICCPR	International Covenant on Civil and Political Rights
ICERD	International Convention on the Elimination of All Forms of Racial Discrimination
ICESCR	International Covenant on Economic and Social and Cultural Rights
ICGLR	International Conference on the Great Lakes Region

IDP	Internally Displaced Persons
IfP	Initiative for Peacebuilding
IGAD	Inter-Governmental Authority on Development
IHRICON	Institute of Human Rights Commission Nepal
ILO	International Labour Organization
INGO	International Non-Governmental Organizations
ISAF	International Security Assistance Force
JIAS	Joint Interim Administrative Structure
JNTT	Joint National Transition Team
KLA	Kosovo Liberation Army
KPS	Kosovo Police Service
KTC	Kosovo Transitional Council
KWI	Kosovo Women's Initiative
KWN	Kosovo Women's Network
LDK	Democratic League of Kosovo
LPA	Lomé Peace Agreement
LURD	Liberians United for Reconciliation and Democracy
LWI	Liberia Women Initiative
MAP	Monthly Action Plan
MARWOPNET	Mano River Women's Peace Network
Migeprofe	Ministry of Gender and Promotion of Women's Development
MINUSTAH	United Nations Stabilization Mission in Haiti
MONUC	United Nations Mission DR Congo
MSWGCA	Ministry of Social Welfare, Gender and Children's Affairs
NAP	National Action Plan
NARDA	New Africa Research Development Agency
NATO	North Atlantic Treaty Organisation
NCDJ	National Committee for Development of Janajatis
NDA	National Democratic Alliance
NEFIN	Nepal Federation of Indigenous Nationalities
NEPAD	New Partnership for Africa's Development
NGO	Non-Governmental Organization
NGOWG	NGO Working Group on Women, Peace and Security
NPFL	National Patriotic Front of Liberia
OAU	Organisation of African Unity
OCHA	Office for the Coordination of Humanitarian Affairs
ODIHR	Office for Democratic Institutions and Human Rights
OGA	Office of Gender Affairs
OHCHR	Office of the High Commissioner for Human Rights
ONUB	United Nations Operation in Burundi
OPMT	Popular Organization of Timorese Women
OSAGI	Office of the Special Adviser on Gender Issues
OSCE	Organisation for Security and Cooperation in Europe
PBC	Peacebuilding Commission
PBF	Peacebuilding Fund

PBSO	Peacebuilding Support Office
PEP	Post Exposure Prophylaxis
PfA	Beijing Platform for Action
PLA	People's Liberation Army
PSC	Peace and Security Council
PSWG 1325	Peace Support Working Group on UNSCR 1325
RECs	Regional Economic Communities
RH	Reproductive Health
RISDP	Regional Indicative Strategic Development Plan
RPF	Rwandan Patriotic Front
RUF	Revolutionary United Front
SADBRIG	Southern African Standby Brigade
SADC	Southern African Development Community
SADCC	Southern African Development Co-ordination Conference
SCAS	Supplementary Convention on the Abolition of Slavery, the Slave Trade and Institutions and Practices Similar to Slavery
SDGEA	Solemn Declaration on Gender Equality in Africa
SEGBVN	Sexual Exploration and Gender-Based Violence Network
SGBV	Sexual gender-based violence
SIPO	Strategic Indicative Plan for the Organ
SLWF	Sierra Leone Women's Forum
SLWMP	Sierra Leone Women's Movement for Peace
SPLM/A	Sudan People's Liberation Movement/Army
SRSG	Special Representative of the UN Secretary-General
SSR	Security sector reform
SuWEP	Sudanese Women's Empowerment Network
SWU	Sudanese Women's Union
TRC	Truth and Reconciliation Commission
TWGGI	Technical Working Group on Global Indicators
UN DPKO	United Nations Department of Peacekeeping Operations
UNAMID	United Nations–African Union Mission in Darfur
UNAMIR	United Nations Assistance Mission for Rwanda
UNAMSIL	United Nations Mission in Sierra Leone
UNAVEM	United Nations Angola Verification Mission
UNBiH	United Nations in Bosnia-Herzegovina
UNCT	UN Country Team
UNDP	United Nations Development Programme
UNECA	United Nations Economic Commission for Africa
UNESCO	United Nations Educational, Scientific and Cultural Organization
UNFPA	United Nations Population Fund
UNHCR	United Nations High Commission for Refugees
UNICEF	United Nations Children's Fund
UNIFEM	United Nations Development Fund for Women
UNIOSIL	United Nations Integrated Office in Sierra Leone
UNIPSIL	United Nations Integrated Peacebuildings Office in Sierra Leone

UNMIK	United Nations Interim Administration in Kosovo
UNMIL	United Nations Mission in Liberia
UNMIN	United Nations Mission in Nepal
UNMIR	United Nations Mission in Liberia
UNMIS	United Nations Mission in Sudan
UNMOZ	United Nations Operation in Mozambique
UNOCI	United Nations Operation in Côte d'Ivoire
UNOMIL	United Nations Observer Mission in Liberia
UNOSOM	United Nations Operation in Somalia
UNPROFOR	United Nations Protection Force Yugoslavia
UNSCR 1325	United Nation Security Council Resolution 1325
UNTAC	United Nations Transitional Authority in Cambodia
UNTAET	United Nations Transitional Administration in East Timor
UNTAG	United Nations Transition Assistance Group
VAW	Violence against women
VPU	Vulnerable Persons' Unit
WACSOF	West African Civil Society Forum
WANEP	West African Network for Peacebuilding
WAPPDCA	Women's Alliance for Peace, Power, and the Constituent Assembly Democracy
WCSNP	Women's Civil Society Network for Peace
WFP	World Food Programme
WGDD	Women Gender Development Directorate
WID	Women in development
WILPF	Women's International League for Peace and Freedom
WIPNET	Women in Peacebuilding Network
WIPSEN-Africa	Women Peace and Security Network – Africa

Part I

Introduction

1   Introduction

Karen Barnes and 'Funmi Olonisakin

Background

In October 2000, the United Nations Security Council adopted Resolution 1325 (UNSCR 1325) on Women, Peace and Security, which was an important step forward in terms of bringing women's rights and gender equality to bear on the UN's peace and security agenda.[1] It calls on member states to ensure that gender is mainstreamed throughout all conflict prevention and peacebuilding activities, and reaffirms women's rights to be involved in decision-making and to access and take on leadership positions. This Resolution was the outcome of a long process of advocacy from civil society and several member states that were particularly committed to these issues, and it continues to be supported by an active, vibrant and extensive network of activists, researchers and practitioners. UNSCR 1325 has since been further strengthened by other gender-related policies adopted by the various UN bodies involved in conflict and security issues, as well as by other Resolutions including UNSCR 1820, 1880 and 1889. This forms the framework for bringing gender issues to the front and centre of conflict prevention and peacebuilding initiatives, including peacekeeping operations.

Until recently, the key focus of research on gender and peacebuilding issues was either how to mainstream a gender approach or the operational and bureaucratic reasons behind the seemingly inevitable gap between policy and practice. While these analyses provide important insights and have been used to inform the international community's efforts to implement gender-related programs within their peacebuilding activities, one of the main problems with the existing work on gender and peacebuilding, and particularly UNSCR 1325, is that advocacy outweighs substance.

What has not been explored is the *impact* that UNSCR 1325 has had since it was passed in 2000, and whether or not it has made a difference at the national and regional level. While some positive changes have been made in terms of making token references to gender mainstreaming in peacekeeping mission mandates and setting up gender offices on the ground, much remains to be done. It is not clear that any real changes have occurred beneath the surface, or that gender issues have been brought into the mainstream of the international community's security and development agendas. While it can be difficult to measure the impact of such changes quantitatively, especially given the long period of time that it can take for gender equality-related ideas to filter through organisations and society as a whole, it should be possible to identify qualitative shifts in attitude and organisational practice. These shifts should then have an impact in terms of the way that peacekeeping operations are conducted and gender-related change is brought about.

This book intends to amend this gap, and to question the assumptions on which UNSCR 1325 is based, as well as the ability, and legitimacy, of external actors to bring about gender-related structural changes in conflict-affected countries. Given that gender relations are often thrown into flux during conflict, a critical window of opportunity can exist at such times to reform these relations along more equitable lines during the peacebuilding phase. There are certain assumptions that the existence of UNSCR 1325, and other frameworks to promote gender equality and, by extension, the presence of a UN peace support operation and other external actors to implement it, will permit, or at the very least increase the chances of this process of reformulation. However, no research has yet explored these assumptions to determine whether or not, and if so, how, this is the case.

Furthermore, local initiatives to promote gender equality within conflict-affected contexts are often overlooked or overshadowed by UN-led peace operations, and the insights and mechanisms they provide can be lost or undermined. Little attention has been focused on the interaction between the 'formal' peacebuilding process that exists within and is directed by UN structures and the more organic, 'informal' parallel processes that are being carried out by women's organisations and other actors. While the amount of research and anecdotal evidence about the implementation of UNSCR 1325 has proliferated over the past ten years, understanding of the process whereby it is translated from a rhetorical commitment at the UN level into concrete progress on the ground is still lacking. In recognition of this need, this book seeks to address whether having a peacekeeping mission and the framework of UNSCR 1325 actually make a difference in terms of advancing gender equality within conflict-affected countries, and what lessons can be learned from the alternative local mechanisms that already exist in these contexts.

The lack of empirical evidence of the impact of peacekeeping missions and UNSCR 1325 in advancing gender equality at the various national, regional and international levels is a major shortcoming of the literature on gender and peacebuilding issues. Without a more detailed understanding of this impact it is impossible to determine whether the ongoing marginalisation of women from conflict prevention and peacebuilding is a case of flaws in implementation or approach, or whether in fact the Resolution itself and the mechanisms in which to apply it are ill-matched for the objectives and structural changes that it tries to bring about. This differentiation is in turn important in terms of improving the UN's capacity to engender security and promote an equitable, sustainable peace.

Some of the latest research has begun to probe the discourse of gender mainstreaming that underlies UNSCR 1325 and other related initiatives, to determine whether or not they are compatible with UN peacekeeping operations and the broader goals of peacebuilding.[2]

This volume seeks to build on these ideas to examine how (and indeed if) UNSCR 1325 can be used strategically to drive systemic change at the national and regional levels, and whether the presence of a peacekeeping mission helps or hinders this process. Two sets of questions provide the broad guidance for the book. First, what is the relationship between formal peacekeeping structures and informal local structures? And how do the various mechanisms to promote gender issues adopted in each sphere interact? Do peacekeeping operations undermine or reinforce local initiatives? Second, how does UNSCR 1325 drive change at the national and regional level and how do the different domestic and regional actors use it? Does the presence of international actors make a difference in terms of advancing gender equality?

As feminist theorists have argued, 'the traditional privilege bestowed upon the military-political security of the state has effectively excluded the acknowledgement of gendered security problems.'[3] While UNSCR 1325 provides the illusion that this is beginning to change, it is not at all clear that efforts to mainstream a gender perspective into peacekeeping operations have been successful on the ground in terms of bringing these gendered security problems to the fore. However, UN peace support operations do not enter countries in a vacuum, and peacekeeping only constitutes one part of the picture, albeit an important one. Local initiatives for building peace and promoting gender equality have usually been in place for a long time, often prior to the conflict itself. These initiatives are generally thought to fall within the 'informal' sphere and do not necessarily overlap or merge with the more 'formal' (i.e. UN-mandated) initiatives once the peace mission arrives. A crucial question then becomes what happens to these locally based initiatives? Could linking up with these grassroots processes help the UN to become more effective in its efforts to incorporate women's rights in peacebuilding? By providing the first systematic attempt to analyse the impact of the international community's attempts to support and advance gender equality within the framework of UNSCR 1325, it is hoped that this study will provide important insights to the academic and policy communities interested in the challenges of engendering security and empowering women in conflict-affected contexts.

Key themes explored in this book

While each conflict and peace support operation is unique, certain broad questions can be applied to all these different contexts. In exploring the central research questions outlined above through eight in-depth country case studies, this study will draw from and build on a broad range of literature and inter-related themes linked to contemporary debates around gender, conflict and security, as well as the prospects for gender mainstreaming within UN peace operations. We will outline some of these themes here, tying them to the volume's objectives and research questions.

Security as a gendered concept

Since the end of the Cold War there has been a slow progression from the emphasis on 'national security' to a broader, more holistic idea of security, which places the individual at the centre of security concerns, or what has come to be known as 'human security'.[4] Despite being a contested and somewhat cloudy concept, human security has been unofficially adopted by the UN in a number of important policy statements, and has become integrated into the foreign policy of several countries. Theoretically, the focus on the individual offers an important opportunity to broaden the scope of what is considered relevant to security debates, and it has contributed to the expansion of the range of activities that are considered to fall within the domain of UN peace operations.[5] However, in practice, human security is also problematic in two key respects, and security continues to be a gendered concept.

First, while focusing attention on the individual it can also risk masking gender-differentiations in what it means to be secure. For example, while refugee camps aim to provide security to men and women fleeing conflict, if the women are too afraid to use the toilets at night for fear of sexual attacks can we say that they are secure? Similarly, the insecurity that men and boys can experience in refugee camps because the concentration of the population in one place makes them susceptible to recruitment or abduction by armed gangs must be acknowledged. Therefore, security as a concept or experience is mediated by gender, but these differences are rarely reflected in security policy.[6] Indeed, research by feminist critical security scholars demonstrates that

> girls and women experience human insecurity differently from men and are subject to gender hierarchies and power inequities that exacerbate their insecurity [and] because of their lower status, girls and women are less able to articulate and act upon their security needs, as compared with boys and men.[7]

Despite this reality, the security discourse within peace operations rarely recognises these differences and tends to treat security as a phenomenon experienced at the group level.

Second, it is not clear that the UN-directed understanding of any kind of security, including human security, that is incorporated into UN policies and programs in fact matches local perceptions of security. The objective of human security is supposedly universal, but in reality it is a highly subjective concept that varies greatly depending on the context and the individuals in question. According to critical security theorists, ideas about what it is to be secure and what 'matters' to security are defined discursively by the dominant actors within a given situation. Therefore, during peace operations it is generally the external actors, principally the UN, who determine the point at which the security of a population has been achieved. Rarely do peacekeepers or those involved in peace operations consult with the local populations to attain a better understanding of how they define their own (in)security nor do they often recognise that there is diversity among the insecure. The result is that externally imposed notions become the standard points of reference. The assumption that peace operations are able to provide security to local communities, particularly women, must be destabilised. Furthermore, the presence of the peace mission can impact on gender relations and by extension security in negative ways, as witnessed by the many well-publicised recent examples of sexual exploitation and abuse at the hands of peacekeepers around the world.

Understanding what security means and how it can be achieved is central to the success of peace support operations, and to the implementation of UNSCR 1325. However, as this study demonstrates, security is a problematic and contingent concept, and understanding the way it is conceptualised and operationalised within peace operations is fundamental to understanding the kind of impact that these missions are able to have. UNSCR 1325 calls on the UN and member states to ensure that women and girls are protected from all forms of violence in situations of armed conflict and that their needs and rights are taken into account, but can this be achieved if security is a gender-blind concept? Indeed, what are the security implications of the fact that women and children are frequently marginalised from power and resources during and in the aftermath of conflict? Exploring the idea of security as a gendered concept at the conceptual level, and then tying this into the different country case studies will provide a key theoretical basis for the study.

Transmitting UNSCR 1325 from headquarters to the field-level and to the national context

Similar to other Security Council Resolutions, UNSCR 1325 is a framework that is explicitly designed to operate within the mechanisms of the UN system, and this is reflected in the language and strategies that it draws on. However, at the same time, it is also envisaged as a driver of change at the national and regional levels, where the strategies contained within the Resolution can be translated to any given domestic context to result in positive gender-related outcomes. Thus in achieving its ends, UNSCR 1325 needs to go through two phases of transmission. First, UN headquarters establish policies and guidelines that theoretically incorporate UNSCR 1325, which are transmitted to the field-level for implementation in peacekeeping operations. Given that the concept of gender equality has not been effectively institutionalised or mainstreamed throughout the UN system, it is possible that the understanding and internalisation of UNSCR 1325 that occurs in the field-level contexts may take on a different character to that intended in the original policy documents. Second, actors at the field-level must then transmit the ideas within UNSCR 1325 to the national context where governments hold ultimate responsibility for advancing gender equality. Linking into the previous theme, this raises several questions about whether or not Western, top-down approaches to advancing gender equality can be transplanted onto fragile national contexts where governments can lack the capacity, resources and political will to implement UNSCR 1325, particularly in the complex aftermath of civil conflict. Furthermore it assumes a certain level of gender awareness and training among field-level staff that does not always, or in fact rarely, exists.

While bridging these three levels (headquarters, field-level and national context) is an issue for most peacebuilding and development policies, UNSCR 1325 is unique in the sense that it is related to a third level of transmission that could potentially present an alternative method of advancing gender equality. Although the passing of the Resolution is the product of high-level policy-making at the UN Security Council, the process initially gained its momentum from an active and vibrant global civil society movement. These actors had been advocating for the recognition of women's right to participate in and contribute to peacebuilding processes for many years, and an extensive network of resources and expertise existed at the grassroots level even prior to 2000.

Therefore, in addition to the two phases of transmission described above, there is also a third, locally rooted diffusion of gender equality goals from domestic actors to the national government and international actors, even though these ideas may not be couched in the language of the actual Resolution. Therefore, while the official discourse on women, peace and security has been immortalised within the Resolution, several alternative, 'unofficial' discourses may exist on the ground. While these may have been informed by UNSCR 1325 to a certain extent, it is likely that they are also based on local understandings of 'security', 'gender equality' and 'peace' that may differ from UN interpretations, and may offer important alternative mechanisms for achieving the same goals as those advocated by the Resolution.

This book is interested in exploring these competing understandings of UNSCR 1325 and gender equality within the context of peacemaking, peacekeeping and peacebuilding, and whether they undermine or reinforce each other. Indeed, more attention should be paid to the need to integrate these different levels and processes of transmitting UNSCR 1325 from the international to the local, national and regional contexts. As indicated above, central to exploring these questions is understanding the process whereby UNSCR 1325 filters down and is implemented from the headquarters to the field level, and then from there is interpreted and applied within the local context. These connecting layers are by no means automatic and there is tremendous scope for reinterpretation, misinterpretation and cooption by the different actors involved in peace operations. Indeed, how the language of UNSCR 1325 is interpreted can have quite radical consequences for the achievement of gender equality and the ways in which the actors at the different levels interact.

Peace operations and SCR 1325 in action: the impact on the ground[8]

Following on from the theme of how UNSCR 1325 is interpreted and implemented by different actors both within peace missions and outside of it, this study also intends to explore what the actual impact of these missions on the ground has been. Given the direct references to peacekeeping and associated activities such as demobilisation, disarmament and reintegration (DDR) contained within UNSCR 1325, it is clear that gender issues are extremely relevant to peace operations. This claim is supported by a solid body of academic and policy literature on gender and peacekeeping and it received formal acknowledgement with the establishment of a gender advisor within the UN Department of Peacekeeping Operations (DPKO) in 2004. Despite recent efforts to train peacekeepers and to provide comprehensive guidelines on how to integrate a gender perspective into peace operations, it remains one of the most difficult areas in which to incorporate the provisions of UNSCR 1325. Linking in with the discussion around security as a gendered concept, this volume explores the challenges and opportunities of advancing gender equality within the highly militarised and patriarchal environment of UN peacekeeping missions, and the impact that these missions have on the ground.

The impact of peace missions on the ground will be examined from three perspectives. First, the volume will explore how UNSCR 1325, and gender equality more broadly, is understood within peace missions. The 'tyranny of the urgent' is a frequent dimension of peace operations, where the ending of overt violence between primarily male actors is seen as the most important priority. While not doubting that this is a necessary step in the peacekeeping process, failing to consider how gender inequalities sustain the conflict and the various roles that men, women, boys and girls are playing in carrying out the violence could compromise the achievement of stability. Gender equality is generally seen as a long-term ideal that can be postponed until more immediate concerns have been dealt with, and gender issues are frequently marginalised within the peacekeeping operation. Arguably, there is still a failure to see women as legitimate actors and gender as a legitimate subject. However, given that some peace missions now have gender advisers or gender units the case studies may indicate that some progress in this respect has been made.

Second, the impact of the peace mission on gender relations and gender equality within the local context will be examined. Even where peace support operations are gender-blind they inevitably have an impact, whether intended or not, on the gender relations of the host country.[9] One important question to ask is whether peace operations actively seek to influence local actors or to transfer principles, structures and methods for advancing gender equality? If so, is UNSCR 1325 used in the process and are these efforts successful? In the cases where a peacekeeping mission is present, is the local population more aware of and sensitive to UNSCR 1325 than they were prior to the arrival of the UN? Which actors does the UN engage with, particularly in the context of fragile states where capacity for implementing UNSCR 1325 is low or non-existent?

Clearly, the relationship is not unidirectional, and therefore the third perspective is how, if at all, local realities and knowledge influence the conduct of peace operations. The nature of externally driven peacebuilding and development initiatives often leads to a 'one size fits all' approach, where little effort is made to adapt structures and processes to the needs of different contexts. However, in the case of advancing gender equality it is clear that local traditions, dynamics and power relations will play an important role in influencing how successful these efforts can be. Does the existence of UNSCR 1325 then enhance the likelihood that peacekeepers will be able to bridge the gap between the external and internal initiatives by emphasising the importance of involving women in all peacekeeping and peacebuilding initiatives? Or do the militaristic and masculinist culture of peacekeeping and the tokenism of gender mainstreaming within these environments inhibit efforts to incorporate local and external mechanisms for advancing gender equality? In asking these questions this book diverges from the majority of literature on the subject that fails to question whether or not it is possible to integrate gender equality into peace missions, but rather assumes this as given, and again places all emphasis on *how to* rather than *why* or *to what end*. It is to the latter two questions, why and to what end, that this volume addresses itself.

Alternative strategies for implementing UNSCR 1325

A brief survey of the literature around gender and peacebuilding confirms that much of what has been achieved in the past in terms of empowering women and promoting gender equality has been done at the informal, grassroots level. Women have long mobilised at the community level to oppose conflict within their societies, and many examples exist of where they have built bridges across ethnic or religious divides. However, when a peace mission enters a country little effort is made to link up with these informal efforts and they are often marginalised or overwhelmed by official, externally led projects to mainstream gender. For example, some of the most qualified women gain employment within the peacekeeping missions themselves or with the international non-governmental organisations (INGOs) that invariably flood in to deal with the aftermath of civil conflict. While this is important in ensuring that gender balance and gender expertise are realised within the peacekeeping operation, it also has the negative consequence of reducing local capacities to advance gender equality even more.

In promoting gender equality within peacebuilding, the UN tends to advocate for measurable, visible and quick-impact results such as requiring that 30 per cent of all parliamentary positions go to women. While not seeking to diminish the importance of these goals, they are not the only ways to ensure that women have access to decision-making roles and political and socio-economic resources. Women can wield influence and power in less overt ways that are not captured by the UN focus on the 'formal' sphere or quantifiable results. Without conscious effort to foster and incorporate the alternative strategies that women use to advance gender-related objectives, valuable knowledge and insight is lost. While UNSCR 1325 may not necessarily be directly relevant to traditional structures and capacities, it still acts as an important tool that local actors can draw upon and they should be supported in adapting the Resolution to their needs.

Of key interest to this volume is the question of whether these 'informal', alternative (meaning those existing outside of UN peacekeeping structures) strategies and discourses are lost in the push to institutionalise the 'formal' UN approach to gender mainstreaming in peacekeeping and peacebuilding operations, and if so, why does this occur? Is this something that is acknowledged by the different stakeholders or is it merely an unintended consequence of the presence of a peacekeeping mission? Do the different stakeholders consider the UN efforts to be more important or effective than local approaches? Can the impetus for advancing gender equality be successful if it originates from somewhere other than a UN peace mission? Because this study broaches conflicts where peace support operations have and have not been deployed, it provides a unique opportunity to comparatively assess both indigenous and externally driven efforts to advance gender equality.

Methodology

This book compares the experiences of eight conflict-affected countries in which to explore the themes set out above. In addition to the country case studies, we also examine the role of a number of regional organisations in addressing the issues at the heart of UNSCR 1325. These include the African Union (AU), the Economic Community of West African States (ECOWAS), the European Union (EU) and the Southern African Development Community (SADC). The cases have been selected on the basis that they will provide a broad regional, thematic and contextual body of evidence from which to draw conclusions about the impact of peace missions on efforts to advance gender equality within conflict-affected countries. The central focus of all of the case studies will be to explore the potential for using UNSCR 1325 to promote gender-related change at the national and regional levels.

Ensuring accurate measurement of the real impact of UNSCR 1325 is beyond the scope of this book. Other processes have already begun, at the United Nations, to attempt to assess application and impact of UNSCR 1325. UNSCR 1889 aims to strengthen the UN's commitment to the implementation of the core elements of UNSCR 1325. In this regard, the Resolution requests the development of indicators to track and monitor the implementation of UNSCR 1325. Specifically, operational paragraph 17 of UNSCR 1889 of 2009:

> Requests the Secretary-General to submit to the Security Council within 6 months for consideration, a set of indicators for use at the global level to track the implementation of its resolution 1325 (2000), which could serve as a common basis for reporting by relevant United Nations entities, other international and regional organizations, and Member States, on the implementation of resolution 1325 (2000) in 2010 and beyond.

The UN system had organised itself to develop these indicators by the close of 2009. A Technical Working Group on Global Indicators (TWGGI) was

Table 1.1

Country	Presence of a peacekeeping mission	Peacekeeping mission present before or after passing of UNSCR 1325
East Timor	UN Transitional Authority in East Timor (UNTAET). This was succeeded in 2002 by the United Nations Mission of Support in East Timor (UNMISET) established by UN Resolution 1410	UNTAET was established on 25 October 1999. By mid-2000 a special Gender Affairs Unit was established.
Kosovo	United Nations Mission in Kosovo (UNMIK).	UNMIK was established as a transitional administration in 1999 by UN Resolution 1244. The UNMIK Office of Gender Affairs was established as an advisory unit on gender affairs and derives its mandates from international resolutions such as UNSCR 1325 and CEDAW.
Liberia	United Nations Mission in Liberia (UNMIL).	UNMIL was established by Security Council resolution 1509 in 2003. The Office of the Gender Advisor works toward implementation of UNSCR 1325 in UNMIL and special attention was given to women during the DDR process.
Nepal	United Nations Mission in Nepal (UNMIN).	UNMIN was established in 2007 by the passing of UN Resolution 1740 and is mandated to remain in Nepal until 15 May 2010.
Nigeria	Nigeria has never had a UN peacekeeping mission. However, it is a major troop contributing country.	
Rwanda	United Nations Assistance Mission for Rwanda (UNAMIR) was originally established to assist with the implementation of the Arusha Accords.	UNAMIR was established by Security Council Resolution 872 in October 1993 and lasted until March 1996.
Sierra Leone	United Nations Mission in Sierra Leone (UNAMSIL). Upon completion of its mandate, UNAMSIL was succeeded by the United Nations Integrated Office for Sierra Leone (UNIOSIL).	UNAMSIL was established in 1999 with the passing of Security Council Resolution 1270 in order to assist with the implementation of the Lomé Peace Agreement. Its mandate was considered complete in 2005. UNIOSIL was established in accordance with Resolution 1620 in 2005 to succeed UNAMSIL.
Sudan	Preceded by the United Nations Advance Mission in Sudan (UNAMIS), the United Nations Mission in Sudan (UNMIS) was established. This was followed by the United Nations-African Union Hybrid Operation in Darfur.	UNMIS was established in 2005 after the passing of Resolution 1590. In 2006 the United Nations-African Union Hybrid Operation in Darfur (UNAMID) was established via Resolution 1769 in an effort to stabilize the Darfur region.

established by the UN Task Force on Women, Peace and Security coordinated by the Office of the Special Adviser on Gender Issues (OSAGI) at the UN. OSAGI and the United Nations Development Fund for Women (UNIFEM) in collaboration with the Task Force on Women, Peace and Security provided technical lead for a process of indicators' development. By March 2010, a set of potential indicators had been submitted to a UN High-Level Steering Committee as part of a process of ensuring accountability for implementation of UNSCR 1325.

The cases explored in the book will invariably complement such efforts by highlighting the general trends observed in the way UNSCR 1325 is impacting women's lives in different national and regional contexts. What types of trends, for example, are observable in terms of changes in the status of women in the affected regions? Are these trends due to a transfer of UNSCR 1325 principles from the UN – from headquarters and field-levels to local contexts? Or are they the results of other efforts at the regional level or indeed the outcome of local efforts? These case studies discussed in this book lend themselves to an assessment of the impact of UNSCR 1325 along these lines. However, there is some variability among the cases investigated here. Table 1.1 gives an indication of the variability in the country case studies.

Some countries have experienced a UN-mandated peace operation where others have not. Furthermore, the peace operations that have been carried out vary in terms of whether they were initiated and conducted prior to or after the critical turning point of October 2000 when UNSCR 1325 was adopted by the Security Council. All the cases however present an opportunity to explore the local dynamics in order to understand the degree of local engagement with the issues at the heart of UNSCR 1325 and what influence, if any, the UN presence on the ground might have had on these local dynamics. Collectively, these cases present a picture of the degree to which UNSCR 1325 has made a difference across different national and regional contexts. The chapters that follow discuss these national and regional experiences and assess how UNSCR 1325 was experienced from the particular perspective of each country or regional organisation.

Notes

1 United Nations (2000) Security Council Resolution 1325 on Women, Peace and Security. S/Res/1325.
2 For example, see Sandra Whitworth, *Men, Militarism and UN Peacekeeping: A Gendered Analysis*. London: Lynne Rienner Publishers, 2004.
3 Lene Hansen and Louise Olsson, 'Guest Editors' Introduction', *Security Dialogue*, Vol. 35 (4), 2004, p. 405.
4 The term 'human security' first appeared in: United Nations Development Programme, *Human Development Report, 1994*. New York: Oxford University Press, 1994.
5 The 'Brahimi Report' released in 2000 demonstrates this expanded notion of peacebuilding and 'human security'. See United Nations (2000a) 'Report of the Panel on United Nations Peace Operations', UN Doc. A/55/305-S/2000/809, 21 August. New York: United Nations.

6 While many other factors such as ethnicity, religion or class can compromise an individual's access to security, this study focuses specifically on the gender dimensions of security.
7 Susan McKay, 'Women, Human Security and Peace-building: A Feminist Analysis' in H. Shinoda and H.W. Jeong (eds) *Conflict and Human Security: A Search for New Approaches of Peace-building*, IPSHU English Research Report Series No. 19, 2004, p. 153. Available at: http://home.hiroshima-u.ac.jp/heiwa/Pub/E19/Contents.htm. Also see Gunhild Hoogensen and Svein Vigeland Rottem, 'Gender Identity and the Subject of Security', *Security Dialogue*, Vol. 35 (2), 2004, pp. 155–171; and Lene Hansen, 'The Little Mermaid's Silent Security Dilemma and the Absence of Gender in the Copenhagen School', *Millennium*, Vol. 29 (2), 2000, pp. 285–306.
8 This theme only applies to those case studies where a peacekeeping operation is, or has been, present.
9 For example see Louise Olsson *et al., Gender Aspects of Conflict Interventions: Intended and Unintended Consequences*. Oslo: International Peace Research Institute, 2004.

2 The evolution and implementation of UNSCR 1325

An overview

Karen Barnes

Introduction

United Nations Security Council Resolution (UNSCR) 1325 on Women, Peace and Security is the most frequently cited policy framework in relation to gender and peacebuilding issues. The adoption of the Resolution was the first time that the UN Security Council had devoted its consideration exclusively to issues related to the role of women in peace and security processes. UNSCR 1325 did not emerge spontaneously, rather it was the culmination of ongoing advocacy, research, activism and field-based evidence that argued for the need to recognise the myriad and complex ways in which gender relations affected and were affected by armed conflict and efforts to build a sustainable peace. To provide some context for the subsequent country and regional case studies, this chapter offers a brief overview of the evolution of UNSCR 1325 as well as its implementation at the national, regional and international levels. It concludes with the recent adoption of UNSCRs 1820, 1888 and 1889.

The evolution of UNSCR 1325

Although women and gender issues have been historically marginalised from peace and security issues, bodies of the UN such as the Commission on the Status of Women (CSW) and the General Assembly have taken on the advancement of women as a critical concern from the organisation's earliest stages, albeit in an ad hoc and limited way. The four UN global conferences on women held between 1975 and 1995 played a particularly important role in raising awareness about gender inequality and creating important networks advocating for women's empowerment at the national and international levels.[1] At the end of the 1980s, feminist International Relations scholars were also challenging the conventional discourse around peace and conflict, thereby exposing some of the gendered power dynamics that underpin war and peacebuilding.[2]

The early advocates of women, peace and security issues were able to draw on advances made in other fields such as human rights and development. Approaches to women in development (WID) and gender and development (GAD) had been informing policy and practice on gender issues, and important tools such as the Convention on the Elimination of All Forms of Discrimination Against Women (CEDAW) provided a framework for thinking about women's rights. Nevertheless, policies and initiatives to address women's needs and interests remained at the margins of peace and security, and according to Carey, 'institutional responses [...] developed slowly in the 1990s. Approaches were ad hoc and isolated. As peacekeeping operations faltered, gender issues were erroneously considered peripheral or ignored.'[3]

However, by the mid-1990s, some degree of change was becoming evident, even if this was not reflected in the peace and security reform agendas put forward during that decade by former UN Secretary-Generals Boutros Boutros-Ghali and Kofi Annan.[4] The UN Fourth World Conference on Women held in Beijing in 1995 was the largest ever conference organised by the UN, and the parallel forum for non-governmental organisations (NGOs) attracted more than 30,000 women from around the world. The outcome document of the conference, the Beijing Declaration and Platform for Action (PfA), addressed 12 critical areas of concern and included strategic objectives and recommendations. One of these 12 'Platforms for Action' (Platform E) was dedicated to women and armed conflict.[5] The preamble to the strategic objectives of this platform explicitly linked peace to gender equality and recommended that a gender perspective be mainstreamed into all policies and programs.[6]

Following on from Beijing, in 1996 the UN Educational, Scientific and Cultural Organisation (UNESCO) launched its 'Women's Contribution to a Culture of Peace' project. The aims of this initiative were the empowerment of women and support for their peace initiatives, as well as gender-sensitisation with a focus on fostering an ethos of non-violence.[7] In 1998, the African Women's Report published by the United Nations Economic Commission for Africa (UNECA) was devoted to presenting a gender perspective of post-conflict reconstruction in Africa.[8] This report affirmed the importance of applying a gender perspective to conflict and the need to recognise that 'women in post-conflict situations are not mere passive sufferers and aid-dependent beneficiaries specially vulnerable to abuse, but have been and should be very much part of the solution.'[9]

However, while these reports and declarations were all important in terms of advocacy and awareness raising, their impact on the mainstream of conflict and security issues at the UN was negligible. Considerable resistance to gender issues was still evident within the UN, donors and the governments of conflict-affected countries, and this was reflected in their early forays into peacebuilding. International actors consistently failed to consider how stereotypical conceptualisations of men, women and gender relations shaped their actions in conflict zones, and rarely conducted any kind of gender analysis of their programs.[10]

The advocacy of women's groups throughout the previous decade and the increased level of public awareness about gender issues due to the large-scale crises in Rwanda and Bosnia gathered pace at the end of the 1990s. At the same time, the failure to fulfil the various objectives of declarations such as the PfA became increasingly evident, and the voices of feminists and others who were critiquing gender-blind approaches to addressing conflict became louder. It was at a debate on Platform E of the PfA during the annual CSW meeting in March 1998 that the group of NGOs working together as the Women and Armed Conflict Caucus started to discuss the possibility of getting these issues on the table of the Security Council.[11] Furthermore, academics and policy-makers were also beginning to recognise that gender relations and power dynamics influenced the effectiveness (in terms of design, delivery and impact) of humanitarian assistance in emergency and conflict situations, and that women's needs were often overlooked in aid programs.[12]

Building on these early discussions, in 1999, International Alert, a London-based peacebuilding NGO launched a global campaign, *Women Building Peace: From the Village Council to the Negotiating Table.*[13] Through this campaign, a coalition of 200 civil society organisations supported by key actors at the UN such as the United Nations Development Fund for Women (UNIFEM), advocated for the adoption of a Security Council Resolution on women, peace and security to address the absence of women and gender perspectives from peacekeeping, peace negotiations, justice and reconciliation and post-conflict reconstruction.

At this time, the first gender units were also being established in two peacekeeping missions, namely in Kosovo in June 1999 and in East Timor in October 1999.[14] These units represented a significant step forward for the UN Department of Peacekeeping Operations (DPKO) which had historically paid little attention to gender issues. In March 2000, Ambassador Anwarul Chowdhury of Bangladesh, president of the UN Security Council at the time, used the opportunity of International Women's Day to make a statement linking the role of women to conflict prevention and peacebuilding. In his statement, Ambassador Chowdhury said that Security Council members,

> affirm that the equal access and full participation of women in power structures and their full involvement in all efforts for the prevention and Resolution of conflicts are essential for the maintenance and promotion of peace and security [. . . .] Members of the Council note that although women have begun to play an important role in conflict resolution, peacekeeping and peace-building, they are still under-represented in decision-making in regard to conflict. If women are to play an equal part in security and maintaining peace, they must be empowered politically and economically, and represented adequately at all levels of decision-making, both at the pre-conflict stage and during hostilities, as well as at the point of peacekeeping, peace-building, reconciliation and reconstruction.[15]

NGOs were able to draw on this powerful statement issued by the Security Council as efforts to get women, peace and security issues on the table intensified throughout 2000. The Women and Armed Conflict Caucus continued to ensure these issues were part of the agenda of Beijing +5,[16] and at the end of the CSW in March 2000, six of the members formally came together to establish the NGO Working Group on Women, Peace and Security (NGOWG).[17] This network was initially established to advocate for an open debate and Resolution on women, peace and security issues at the UN Security Council. Cohn has documented the crucial role played by NGOs, in particular the NGOWG, in laying the groundwork for the eventual adoption of UNSCR 1325.[18] For example, they provided relevant literature and references and 'agreed language' from previous UN documents and statements, met with Security Council members, and enabled women from conflict-affected areas to share their stories with them.

Further momentum came from the Windhoek Declaration and Namibia Plan of Action of 31 May 2000 that was issued following a seminar on 'Mainstreaming a Gender Perspective in Multidimensional Peace Support Operations' hosted by the Government of Namibia and the Lessons Learned section of DPKO. This declaration highlighted the need to include a gender perspective in all aspects of peace support operations, making recommendations in areas such as training, leadership, structure of the missions and procedural issues.[19] The 23rd special session of the General Assembly from 5–9 June 2000 was devoted to discussions on 'Women 2000: Gender Equality, Development and Peace for the Twenty-First Century', also known as Beijing +5.[20] All of these forums provided important opportunities for women's civil society advocates from around the world, including from conflict-affected contexts, to push for change within the corridors of the UN.

Given that it had hosted the Windhoek meeting earlier that year, the Namibian government was perceived as a possible supporter of the proposed resolution on women, peace and security. It was therefore approached to consider holding an open session on these issues under its presidency of the UN Security Council during October 2000.[21] In advance of this open debate in the Security Council an 'Arria formula'[22] meeting was held on 23 October 2000, during which members of the Security Council heard testimonies from four women from conflict-affected areas.[23] The Namibian presidency of the Security Council subsequently sponsored a special debate on Women, Peace and Security on 24–25 October 2000, ultimately leading to the unanimous adoption of Resolution 1325 on women, peace and security to applause in the chamber of the UN Security Council on 31 October 2000.[24] According to Anderlini, 'this Resolution marked a watershed. It provides a critical legal and political framework through which, for the first time in history, women worldwide can claim their space and voice their views on peace and security matters.'[25]

Along with certain NGOs and UN agencies, the five governments that are considered to have been critical to the adoption of UNSCR 1325 are Bangladesh, Jamaica, Canada, the Netherlands and the UK.[26] Canada's presence on the UN Security Council during the time of the adoption of UNSCR 1325 was particularly critical, as its focus on human security issues was able to influence the discussions in the Council,[27] and Jamaica had one of the few female ambassadors to the UN at the time. According to observers and participants in the process leading up to the adoption of UNSCR 1325, it was outsiders rather than those working within the UN who saw and acted upon the opportunity to bring about the Resolution. Many on the inside felt that the timing was not right to raise these issues on the floor of the Security Council, but in the end, the Ford Foundation who provided resources to fund the networking and advocacy of NGOs and a few non-permanent members of the Security Council enabled these actors to push for the Resolution to happen.[28]

The main provisions of UNSCR 1325

UNSCR 1325[29] signalled a real change in the donor community in the sense that it sought to make gender relevant and mainstreamed in all aspects of peace operations, placing responsibility (in theory at least) squarely on the shoulders of the international community. The Resolution recognises the 'important role of women in the prevention and Resolution of conflicts and in peace-building, and stress[es] the importance of their equal participation and full involvement in all efforts for the maintenance and promotion of peace and security.'[30] However, not only does it acknowledge the vital role that women can play in peacebuilding and suggests that their inclusion is an important dimension of these processes, it also recognises that it is their *right* to participate.[31] Women and gender perspectives have historically been marginalised from the security sphere, despite the gender hierarchies inherent within the concept of security and the different ways in which men and women experience in/security.[32] Similarly, the Security Council has historically been, and to an extent still remains, 'an overwhelmingly male and masculinized preserve'. [33] This makes the adoption of UNSCR 1325 by the Security Council an even more significant achievement.

The text of the Resolution begins with a reiteration and reaffirmation of previous Security Council Resolutions and other commitments and declarations made by the international community which are relevant to women, peace and security. The 18 operational paragraphs of the Resolution cover a wide range of issues, ranging from women's roles in decision-making for the prevention, management and resolution of conflict, to recognising the needs of women and girls during repatriation and the need for consultation with local and international women's groups.[34] The provisions of UNSCR 1325 have often been summarised into the '3 Ps': the protection of women, the prevention of conflict, and the increased participation of women. The integration of a gender perspective into all aspects of peacebuilding and reconstruction is also a key component of the Resolution, and along with prosecution or punishment for crimes of sexual violence, has sometimes been included as a priority area by advocates of UNSCR 1325.

Although it is almost certainly a reflection of the necessary compromises that were made among the Member States to arrive at a document that was universally acceptable, the language used in UNSCR 1325 is somewhat ambiguous. This ambiguity opens up the Resolution to a myriad of different interpretations, a problem that is even further exacerbated by the failure of the UN and its Member States to specify priorities among the different recommendations. It covers a much broader range of potential interventions than can realistically be implemented, and it is not clear where donors should invest their limited commitment and resources in furtherance of these objectives.

The lack of accountability mechanisms, although not unique to this Security Council Resolution, also renders it impotent to a considerable extent.[35] UNSCR 1325 succeeds in raising a number of important issues and highlights the disproportionate effect that conflict can have on women, their right to be involved in decision-making around peace and security issues and the important role they play in peacebuilding, particularly at the community level. But at the same time, it fails to challenge some of the more entrenched, fundamental constructs linked to notions of masculinity, military/ised power and gender inequalities that are tied up in the discourse of international peace and security institutions.[36] UNSCR 1325 can appear to reinforce the notion of women as peacemakers, with the implicit opposite of men as aggressors.

While the eventual adoption of UNSCR 1325 was a sign of progress, it is important to note that at the same time, negotiations were under way on a number of key issues related to peacebuilding, and that there was little to no cross-over of the gender-related issues into the more 'mainstream' policy-making processes.[37] For example, there is no mention of gender at all in the *Agenda for Peace*, the 1992 UN report that first coined the term 'post-conflict peacebuilding', and women only feature once in the report in their traditional place of being lumped with children as the 'more vulnerable group' in society.[38] Gender equality is also absent from the list of 'essential complements' to effective peacebuilding in the *Report of the Panel on United Nations Peace Operations*, more commonly known as the Brahimi Report, and indeed the word 'gender' features only eight times in the 74 pages. Seven of these times it was in reference to the need to ensure 'fair geographical and gender distribution' in the various UN operations, and once was to emphasise that all UN personnel should be sensitive to gender and cultural differences.[39]

As another indication of the marginalisation of gender issues from the UN's broader peace and security policy, despite the existence of UNSCR 1325, of the 264 country-specific and thematic reports of the Secretary-General to the UN Security Council from January 2000 to September 2003, 67 per cent made no reference or only one reference to women and gender issues.[40] Furthermore, only 14.7 per cent of all Security Council Resolutions from January 2000 to September 2003 included any language on women or gender issues. Therefore, while UNSCR 1325 was a significant achievement, it still existed on the periphery of peace and security policy at the UN.

The adoption of the Resolution finally provided the international community with a concrete framework that could be adapted and incorporated into existing peacebuilding policies and programs, and theoretically brought gender issues into the mainstream. In addition to forming the basis of donor policies related to gender and peacebuilding, UNSCR 1325 has also played an important role in awareness-raising, education and advocacy, and has become the centre of a global civil society movement dedicated to promoting the inclusion of women in building peace around the world. UNSCR 1325 is an important part of the growing international legal framework that recognises the particular rights and protection needs of women and girls. As such, it can be used as an important tool to persuade a range of actors such as UN agencies, Member States, parties to armed conflict, NGOs, peacekeepers and others to place increased priority on the inclusion of gender issues within their policies and programs. As Cohn points out, 'although "gender mainstreaming" has been official UN policy since 1997, Resolution 1325 represents the first time that gender has been mainstreamed in the *armed conflict and security* side of the UN.'[41] The next section of this chapter will explore the implementation of UNSCR 1325 in more detail, providing some examples of progress made as well as the ongoing challenges in turning the Resolution into a reality.

Implementing UNSCR 1325

The adoption of UNSCR 1325 led to a plethora of policy recommendations, conferences and global networking between women's organisations. This section will outline some of the steps that have been taken to implement the Resolution at the international, regional and national levels. Despite being a United Nations resolution, UNSCR 1325 has largely continued to be driven and owned by civil society organisations, and so the section will conclude by highlighting some of these initiatives. It must be noted that policies, activities and networks to support the implementation of UNSCR 1325 have increased exponentially over the past few years. It is therefore not possible to cover all these initiatives exhaustively, but rather this section aims to give only some examples to illustrate the scope and possibilities for taking action on women, peace and security issues at different levels.

Implementation at the international level

Following the adoption of UNSCR 1325, in 2002, UNIFEM appointed two special representatives to conduct an in-depth assessment into women, peace and security issues. As part of this research, Ellen Johnson Sirleaf (who later became president of Liberia) and Elisabeth Rehn (a former Finnish defence minister) travelled to several conflict-affected countries around the world, gathering evidence and testimonies from women active in building peace at the community level. Their report, *Women, War, Peace*, covers various thematic issues linked to UNSCR 1325 such as violence against women, peace operations, and justice and accountability, providing an overview of the key challenges and anecdotal evidence of the ways in which women around the world are affected. It also provides a number of detailed recommendations, finding that

> it is indisputable that, despite numerous UN Resolutions passed by consensus by governments from around the world, the UN system still needs to improve staff capacity, organizational practices and systems, and high-level commitment to more effectively address the gender dimensions of war and peace.[42]

The Secretary-General also commissioned a study, *Women, Peace and Security*, which was published in 2002, and takes a similar thematic approach but with an emphasis on how the various UN agencies have integrated gender into their peacebuilding work.[43]

Since 2000, the Security Council has also issued annual reports that provide an update on actions taken by the different agencies of the UN to implement the Resolution, and annual debates are held in the Security Council on the anniversary of the Resolution at the end of October of each year. While these debates ensure that the UN takes stock of implementation each year, turning UNSCR 1325 into a once-a-year event risks allowing it to be placed at the bottom of the list of priorities for the rest of the year. Implementation at the UN is coordinated and monitored by the Interagency Taskforce on Women, Peace and Security, and is overseen by the Office of the Special Adviser on Gender Issues (OSAGI). A UN System-wide Action Plan on Women, Peace and Security was first released in 2005, providing a detailed outline of activities undertaken by each UN entity working on issues related to women, peace and security. This plan was updated in 2008, and provides a useful overview of progress that has been made and the specific actions that have been taken by each entity.[44]

Most UN agencies now have policy statements on women, peace and security issues, and several also have dedicated staff or focal points working on these issues. For example, the UN Peacebuilding Commission (PBC) was established by the UN on 20 December 2005 and, since its creation, has been an important body in mobilising and coordinating actors around a peacebuilding framework for the countries on its agenda. There has been some success in getting gender on its agenda, including in its original mandate, which can be attributed by ongoing advocacy by women's advocates and the fact that shortly after its establishment, a UNIFEM official was seconded to the Peacebuilding Support Office (PBSO).[45] The integration of gender issues into early recovery and post-conflict reconstruction processes has been slow, but since 2008, the PBC and PBSO have played increasingly important roles in mobilising support in this area.

However, overall, the amount of resources allocated to the implementation of UNSCR 1325 is still insufficient, reflecting the overall marginalisation of gender issues within the UN. While there is more reporting, information-sharing and data available on women, peace and security issues than there was in 1999 prior to UNSCR 1325, almost ten years later this is still not systematic. Between 1948 and 2008, only 17 women have ever held the position of Special Advisor to the Secretary-General. Despite various country-specific projects funded by UN agencies and the efforts of UNIFEM and OSAGI to spur action at the UN level, there is still no systematic monitoring of the implementation of UNSCR 1325. Women's advocates have also repeatedly critiqued the lack of leadership and accountability within the UN system for implementation, citing it as one of the major obstacles to effective action on women, peace and security issues at the UN level.[46]

Implementation at the regional level

Conflicts have regional dynamics, and they necessarily need regional solutions, and regional bodies are increasingly playing a role in international peace and security issues. They often have their own set of policies that guide their member states in development and peacebuilding activities, and they can therefore be important actors in the implementation of UNSCR 1325. However, the regional level has been largely overlooked, with most governments focusing on either the UN or national level. This volume includes case studies of several regional organisations, which take a more detailed look at the process of regional-level implementation of UNSCR 1325 in the African Union (AU), European Union (EU), Economic Community of West African States (ECOWAS) and Southern African Development Community (SADC). However, there are other regional bodies that have over the past five years taken on board specific commitments in relation to UNSCR 1325.

For example, in 2009, NATO's Strategic Commanders released a military directive that outlines measures to implement UNSCR 1325 in NATO-led missions.[47] The organisation has also developed a Code of Behaviour for military personnel and created gender advisor positions to support the Provincial Reconstruction Teams and International Security Assistance Force (ISAF) commanders in Afghanistan. The Secretary-General of NATO has also given his own personal political support to the issue, which will increase the likelihood of the implementation of these new measures.[48]

In 2007, the gender office within the Office for Democratic Institutions and Human Rights (ODIHR) at the Organisation for Security and Cooperation in Europe (OSCE) funded trainings on UNSCR 1325 with government and civil society representatives in Central Asia. They also supported the development of a toolkit on integrating gender issues into security sector reform (SSR) which was one of the first resources to look at this issue.[49] Importantly, in April 2009, 17 OSCE member states agreed to report on implementation of UNSCR 1325 through the 'OSCE Forum for Security Cooperation's Code of Conduct on Politico-Military Aspects of Security'.[50] The OSCE has also worked with parliamentarians in countries such as Georgia to raise awareness and build capacity on addressing gender and security issues.

In Africa, the International Conference on the Great Lakes Region (ICGLR) has also played a vital role in supporting the implementation of UNSCR 1325 across the region, and particularly in the Democratic Republic of Congo (DRC), Rwanda, Burundi and Uganda. On 18 June 2008, the Member States of the ICGLR adopted the Goma Declaration on Eradicating Sexual Violence and Ending Impunity in the Great Lakes Region.[51] The Secretariat of the ICGLR has also been supporting efforts to develop a regional action plan on UNSCR 1325 by holding a workshop and developing a common agenda on this issue in March 2010.

Regional bodies are also recognising the value of using UNSCR 1325 as an entry point for increasing their collaboration, as well as to ensure the more strategic use of their limited resources and capacity. Under the framework of the Initiative for Peacebuilding (IfP), the UN delegations of the African Union and the European Commission collaborated for the first time ever at a joint round-table focusing on regional-level implementation of UNSCR 1325 in February 2009. The EU also co-hosted a conference on 27 January 2010 to focus attention on ending sexual violence during conflict. The regional level is therefore increasingly becoming a focal point for action on UNSCR 1325, although it remains to be seen if the plethora of policy commitments and rhetorical calls to action will result in real progress being made at this level.

Implementation at the national level

In addition to calling on the UN Security Council and other relevant UN agencies and bodies to take specific actions with regard to women, peace and security, UNSCR 1325 also makes specific mention of the role of member states. In 2004, the annual report of the Secretary-General to the Security Council on UNSCR 1325 called on member states to take more action to implement the Resolution at the national level.[52] Since then, many countries have adopted such plans beginning with Denmark in 2005. As of December 2009, 16 countries had developed National Action Plans (NAPs), and several more are in preparation.[53]

The countries with existing NAPs are Austria (August 2007), Belgium (February 2009), Chile (August 2009), Côte d'Ivoire (January 2007), Denmark (June 2005, updated in 2008), Finland (September 2008), Iceland (March 2008), Liberia (March 2009), the Netherlands (December 2007), Norway (March 2006), Portugal (August 2009), Spain (November 2007), Sweden (June 2006, updated in February 2009), Switzerland (March 2007), Uganda (December 2008) and the United Kingdom (March 2006). European countries have led action on UNSCR 1325 at the national level, but since 2009, more NAPs are being launched by conflict-affected countries.[54] Rather than developing NAPs, some countries such as Germany have opted to incorporate UNSCR 1325 into existing frameworks, although it is not clear that such attempts at mainstreaming these commitments are actually successful.

One strategy that has been proposed to encourage more countries to develop NAPs is the 'twinning' of donor and conflict-affected countries. Exactly what this process of twinning might entail and how mutual learning could be facilitated is not entirely clear, but the Irish government has been using this innovative approach, which it refers to as 'cross-learning', in collaboration with Liberia and East Timor. While the donor community and international actors are often perceived as the experts in relation to peacebuilding and the implementation of UNSCR 1325,[55] in fact many of the NAPs coming out of conflict-affected countries have been developed more inclusively and address issues of women, peace and security in a much more holistic way. Indeed, it is important that any such process avoids becoming donor-driven, and that any partnerships continue beyond the development of the plan on paper.[56]

Donor governments, especially within Europe, have also played an important role in supporting national-level implementation in third countries. For example, Italy and Austria were among the funders for the process that led to the development of the Liberian NAP, the Department for International Development (DFID) has supported women's access to justice in the Eastern DRC, and Denmark has funded networking and capacity-building and networking around UNSCR 1325 in the Mano River Union. These and many other projects are vitally important for supporting both government and civil society networks in conflict-affected contexts. One suggestion could be to use NAPs in conflict-affected contexts as a way of garnering and channelling resources from the donor community to support the integration of gender into the peacebuilding process.

European countries have also sought to learn from each others' experiences of national-level implementation, for example through a cross-learning workshop held in October 2009.[57] OSAGI also supported two High-Level Policy Dialogues on the national-level implementation of UNSCR 1325, one in collaboration with the Economic Commission for Latin America and the Caribbean (ECLAC) in Santiago, Chile, from 19 to 21 November 2007 and another in collaboration with UNECA in Addis Ababa, Ethiopia, from 6 to 8 February 2008.[58]

The creation of NAPs offers a potentially valuable tool for ensuring accountability of implementation by national governments. However, the content of these plans varies widely, and they face a number of shortcomings. For example, few plans include indicators or monitoring mechanisms, in some cases they were developed with little consultation among civil society, and too few resources are allocated for their implementation.[59] In September 2009, the Initiative for Peacebuilding brought together civil society representatives from 18 countries across Europe to discuss implementation of UNSCR 1325.[60] Following the workshop, the organisations released a set of recommendations that outline the minimum requirements that should be included in all NAPs and this provides a useful baseline for the development of future plans.[61] It is clear that while they are potentially useful tools for calling national governments to account on UNSCR 1325, unfortunately too few of the existing NAPs are backed by adequate resources, and the governments responsible for implementing them often suffer from what Anderlini terms 'the Triple-A Syndrome' of apathy, ad-hoc practice and amnesia.[62]

NAPs

The role of civil society in implementing UNSCR 1325

UNSCR 1325 would not have been adopted without the initial momentum from civil society, and NGOs, working at both the international and national levels, have continued to drive the agenda forward. Following the adoption of UNSCR 1325, the NGOWG consolidated its role as the key network of organisations working on these issues, and played an important role in providing expert advice and information to UN policy-makers and acting as a 'connector'. It provided a channel through which women peacebuilders were able to access the UN and get their voices heard through initiatives such as the annual Arria formula meetings on UNSCR 1325 held in advance of the Resolution's anniversary on 31 October each year. The NGOWG continues to provide guidance to the UN and its Member States, for example through delivering trainings in women, peace and security issues to Security Council members and issuing Monthly Action Plans (MAPs) that highlight actions that each presidency of the Security Council could take to support UNSCR 1325 throughout 2010.

The work of INGOs to implement UNSCR 1325 has been critical in providing important links from the ground up to the policy level and vice versa, and they have created space for women activists to address policy-makers directly. From 2000 onwards, INGOs such as International Alert have also published extensive policy research on issues relating to UNSCR 1325 that provides useful insight into how implementation could be strengthened both in-country as well as at a global level.[63] Alert and other NGOs such as Femmes Africa Solidarité have also prioritised documenting and drawing attention to women's voices and experiences in relation to peacebuilding. The UN office of the Women's International League for Peace and Freedom (WILPF) established the PeaceWomen website as a resource for policy-makers and practitioners, providing links, analysis and documentation on issues related to the implementation of UNSCR 1325 and gender and peacebuilding more broadly.

In addition to action taken by governments, civil society groups have also emerged at the national level with the central purpose of lobbying their governments to include women in their peacebuilding and foreign policy agendas more broadly. These organisations conduct research at the grassroots level to build up knowledge in the area of gender and peacebuilding and to provide multilateral and bilateral donors with proven strategies to improve their capacities in this field.

For example, Gender Action for Peace and Security (GAPS) is a UK-based network of 13 organisations and individuals dedicated to promoting UNSCR 1325 and gender issues in the conflict, peace and security work of the UK government.[64] GAPS has a permanent coordinator and in 2009 it published the *Global Monitoring Checklist*, a resource that provides data and analysis on the situation of women and extent of implementation of UNSCR 1325 in five conflict-affected countries.[65] GAPS also initiated and is a member of the Associate Parliamentary Group (APG) on Women, Peace and Security which is a forum for parliamentarians, civil servants and civil society to meet to discuss and push forward the implementation of UNSCR 1325 in the UK, including through monitoring of the UK National Action Plan on Resolution 1325.

Other examples of national-level civil society networks focusing on UNSCR 1325 are the Dutch Working Group 1325 in the Netherlands,[66] Operation 1325 in Sweden,[67] and the Gender and Peacebuilding Working Group in Canada.[68] These types of networks are also increasingly emerging in conflict-affected countries such as Burundi and Nepal and are playing a key role in supporting their governments to implement the Resolution at the national level. In Kosovo, although there is no NAP, the Kosovo Women's Network (KWN) has drafted a shadow report assessing the implementation of UNSCR 1325,[69] and other NGOs in South-Eastern Europe are following suit by pushing for action by their governments.[70] In the Pacific region, NGOs such as FemLINK Pacific are creating networks, sharing information and developing innovative strategies to raise awareness around UNSCR 1325 and ensuring women's voices are heard.[71]

In addition to civil society organisations working with local communities and at the grassroots level, there are also some initiatives that target the very highest levels of policy dialogue. These organisations and foundations benefit from very high-profile directors and patrons, and have at times succeeded in pushing UNSCR 1325 to the top of international policy agendas. Realizing Rights and the Council of Women Leaders are two groups that have brought together key decision-makers and experts in a variety of different forums, thereby giving greater visibility and coherence to efforts to promote UNSCR 1325. Many women's organisations have also been active, and successful, in advocating for women's rights to participate in peace negotiations in countries such as Liberia and Somalia.

Civil society organisations therefore play a vital role in filling the gaps and focusing attention on priority areas linked to UNSCR 13235, from those working at the grassroots level in conflict-affected contexts all the way up to those that focus their energies on the corridors of the UN headquarters. Many of these organisations struggle to raise funds to support their work, and more efforts could be made to reduce duplication and increase collaboration, particularly at the regional and global levels where a coordinated voice is needed. As is often pointed out by advocates of the Resolution, UNSCR 1325 is one of the few Security Council Resolutions that has a global constituency of civil society organisations behind it.

UNSCRs 1820, 1888 and 1889

While UNSCR 1325 remains the central and over-arching articulation of the women, peace and security agenda, the international community recently renewed its commitment to these issues with the adoption of three new Security Council resolutions: UNSCR 1820 (2008), 1888 (2009) and 1889 (2009). One of the most obvious impacts of violent conflict on women is the high rate of sexual violence, and in particular rape, that they have to endure.[72] Some women's rights advocates felt that UNSCR 1325 did not adequately address the issue of sexual violence, and almost eight years later in June 2008, the UN Security Council adopted Resolution 1820 on sexual violence in conflict.[73]

UNSCR 1820 reaffirms UNSCR 1325 and places sexual violence on the agenda of the UN Security Council, recognising it as a tactic of war and a security issue that demands a security response. The Resolution furthermore recognises sexual violence as a war crime, crime against humanity and constituent act of genocide, which can therefore be referred to the UN sanctions committee. UNSCR 1820 focuses on prevention of and response to sexual violence in conflict settings, as well as calling for an end to impunity for these crimes and demands that parties to armed conflict prevent and punish sexual violence. The resolution also aims to improve data collection around sexual violence in conflict.

With the adoption of UNSCR 1820, the Security Council has a clear mandate to intervene and respond to the widespread sexual violence that occurs in conflict-affected contexts around the world, including through sanctions and empowering field staff. Nevertheless, there was some controversy around the adoption of UNSCR 1820, with some NGOs worrying that it would focus too much attention on women as victims of conflict rather than their agency to promote peacebuilding, as well as take vital resources and political will away from the broader mandate within UNSCR 1325.[74] The negotiation of UNSCR 1820 required diplomatic agility, as China and Russia in particular opposed some of the substance of the proposed text.[75] A progress report on UNSCR 1820 was released by the UN Secretary-General on 15 July 2009, making several recommendations on how implementation could be strengthened and highlighting the lack of data and information on sexual violence in conflict-affected contexts, among other issues.[76]

UNSCR 1888 was adopted on 30 September 2009 with Hillary Clinton presiding over the meeting in the Security Council, indicating the strong support the Resolution received from the US Administration.[77] This Resolution makes several additional requests in relation to addressing sexual violence in conflict, most importantly calling for the appointment of a Special Representative of the UN Secretary-General (SRSG) to provide leadership and coordination in UN efforts to address sexual violence. It also urges that issues related to sexual violence be considered in the context of peace processes, particularly in relation to justice and reparations, and requests more systematic monitoring and reporting of incidences of conflict-related sexual violence. As a direct result of these two resolutions, the position of SRSG on Sexual Violence was established on 1 March 2010.[78] Many advocates of UNSCR 1325 had been calling for the creation of an SRSG position on women, peace and security issues for years, and despite its narrower mandate on sexual violence, this appointment was still seen as a significant step forward and a sign of greater political will within the UN.

Finally, on 5 October 2009, the UN Security Council adopted UNSCR 1889, which reoriented some of the focus back onto the issue of women's participation.[79] This resolution reaffirms the important roles that women can play in peacebuilding and post-conflict reconstruction and the need to ensure that their needs are addressed in these processes. It calls for better reporting and mobilisation of resources in support of gender equality, and most significantly, for the development of a set of indicators applicable at the global level to track implementation of UNSCR 1325. Subsequently, a Technical Working Group on Global Indicators (TWGGI) was established with a mandate to take forward the development of the indicators and to propose a shortlist to the Secretary-General within six months. The working group is led by the UN's Assistant Secretary-General and Special Adviser on Gender Issues and the Advancement of Women and is composed of 15 UN and international entities. Civil society is represented on TWGGI by the NGOWG. In April 2010, after a review of global indicators and an inclusive and lengthy consultation process, TWGGI narrowed down the list of more than 2,500 indicators to a shortlist of only 26 comprehensive indicators on women, peace and security issues.[80] These indicators fall under four thematic pillars of prevention, participation, protection and relief and recovery.

All of these resolutions are mutually reinforcing, and should be seen as a collective body of commitments on women, peace and security issues, and it is important that the ever-growing number of resolutions does not dilute the core issues at stake. While UNSCR 1820 and 1888 highlight the specific and important issue of protecting women from conflict-related sexual violence, the emphasis on women's participation is maintained. Conflict prevention, peacebuilding and post-conflict reconstruction will be much less sustainable if women are not empowered to play constructive roles in these processes, and all the resolutions, particularly UNSCR 1325 and 1889, are important contributions towards this end.

The remainder of this volume will explore the implementation of the resolutions on women, peace and security from a variety of perspectives. The case studies drawn from across the globe illustrate progress at the national level, including activities being undertaken by civil society as well as governments. There are also four regional case studies which demonstrate the importance of coherent and decisive action at this level. After the in-depth analysis within the case studies, the book will conclude with an assessment of the main ongoing challenges and obstacles in integrating women, peace and security commitments into peacebuilding policy and practice around the world, as well as some recommendations to guide future action as we look forward to the landmark tenth anniversary of UNSCR 1325 in October 2010.

Notes

1 Devaki Jain, *Women, Development and the UN: A Sixty-Year Quest for Equality and Justice*. Indianapolis: Indiana University Press, 2005, p. xv.

2 For example, see Jean Bethke Elshtain, *Women and War*, New York: Basic Books, 1987; Spike V. Petersen (ed.), *Feminist (Re)Visions of International Relations Theory*, Boulder, CO: Lynne Rienner Publishers, 1992; J. Ann Tickner, *Gender in International Relations: Feminist Perspectives on Achieving Global Security*. New York: Columbia University Press, 1992; Cynthia Enloe, *The Morning After: Sexual Politics at the End of the Cold War*, Berkley: University of California Press, 1993; Christine Sylvester, *Feminist International Relations: An Unfinished Journey*. Cambridge: Cambridge University Press, 1994.

3 Henry F. Carey, 'Women and peace and security': The politics of implementing gender sensitivity norms in peacekeeping', *International Peacekeeping*, Vol. 8, No. 2, 2001, p. 57.

4 For an overview of how gender and peacebuilding policies have evolved at the UN, see Karen Barnes, *Reform or More of the Same? Gender Mainstreaming and the Changing Nature of UN Peace Operations*, YCISS Working Paper No. 41, 2006. www.yorku.ca/yciss/whatsnew/documents/WP41-Barnes.pdf.

5 United Nations, *Beijing Declaration and Platform for Action*. New York: UN/ Division for the Advancement of Women, 1995. Available online at: www.un.org/ womenwatch/daw/beijing/platform/.

6 UN, 1995, op. cit., paras. 131 and 141.
7 See www.unesco.org/cpp/uk/projects/wcpinfo.htm. For a more detailed discussion of the objectives of this initiative, see *Report of the Expert Group Meeting on Women's Contribution to a Culture of Peace*, UNESCO Consultative Committee on Women, Manila, 25–28 April 1995.
8 United Nations Economic Commission for Africa, *Post-conflict Reconstruction in Africa: A Gender Perspective*, African Women's Report 1998, Addis Ababa: UNECA, 1998.
9 UNECA, 1998, op. cit., p. v.
10 For example, see Chris Corrin, *Gender Audit of Reconstruction Programmes in South Eastern Europe*, New York: Women's Commission for Refugee Women and Children and Urgent Action Fund, 2000. Available online at: www.gla.ac.uk/centres/ icgws; Eugenia Date-Bah, *Evaluation of Gender Mainstreaming Work and Impact of United Nations Assistance Mission in Sierra Leone (UNAMSIL)*, New York: UN DPKO, 2006; Donna Pankhurst, 'The "sex war" and other wars: towards a feminist approach to peacebuilding' in Haleh Afshar and Deborah Eade, (eds) *Development, Women and War: Feminist Perspectives*, Oxford: Oxfam, 2004, pp. 17–20.
11 C. Cohn, 'Mainstreaming gender in UN security policy: a path to political transformation?' in Shirin M. Rai and Georgina Waylen (eds), *Global Governance: Feminist Perspectives*, Basingstoke, UK: Palgrave Macmillan, 2008, p. 187.
12 B. Byrne with S. Baden, *Gender, Emergencies and Humanitarian Assistance*, Report commissioned by the WID desk, European Commission, Directorate General for Development, Strasbourg: BRIDGE, 1995; GTZ, *Gender-aware Approaches to Relief and Rehabilitation: Guidelines*, Eschborn: Deutsche Gesellschaft für Technische Zusammenarbeit, 1996; M. Turshen and Clotilde Twagiramariya (eds), *What Women Do in Wartime: Gender and Conflict in Africa*, London: Zed Books, 1998; J. Vickers, *Women and War*, London: Zed Books, 1993.
13 For a description of some of this work see Sanam B. Naraghi-Anderlini, *From the Beijing Platform for Action to UN Security Council Resolution 1325 and Beyond: Achievements and Emerging Challenges*, London: International Alert, 2001. Available online at: www.international-alert.org/publications/getdata.php?doctype=Pdf&id=106.
14 Carey, 2001, op. cit., p. 58.
15 United Nations, 'Peace inextricably linked with equality between men and women says Security Council, in International Women's Day statement', Press release, SC/6816, 8 March 2000. www.un.org/News/Press/docs/2000/20000308.sc6816.doc.html.
16 E. Porter, *Peacebuilding: Women in International Perspective*, Abingdon: Routledge, 2007, p. 14.
17 The original founding members of the NGOWG were: International Alert, Women's International League for Peace and Freedom, Amnesty International, Hague Appeal for Peace, Women's Commission for Refugee Women and Children, and Women's Caucus for Gender Justice.
18 Cohn, 2008, op. cit., pp. 187–9.
19 Declaration   at   www.un.org/womenwatch/osagi/wps/windhoek_declaration.pdf. Accessed 13 August 2008.
20 See United Nations General Assembly (2000) www.un.org/womenwatch/daw/followup/ress233e.pdf.
21 F. Hill, M. Aboitiz and S. Poehlman-Doumbouya, 'Nongovernmental Organizations' Role in the Buildup and Implementation of Security Council Resolution 1325', *Signs: Journal of Women in Culture in Society*, Vol. 28, No. 4, 2003, pp. 1258–9.
22 Arria formula meetings are named after Ambassador Arria of Venezuela who used the mechanism for the first time in 1992 to enable a Bosnian priest to speak to members of Security Council. The aim of Arria formula meetings is to provide an informal space for Security Council members to hear from civil society representatives on issues or from contexts of interest to the Council's work. This formula for meetings

has been used repeatedly by those working on women, peace and security issues to advance specific advocacy messages with Security Council members in advance of the annual open debate.

23 The four women who addressed the Security Council were: Inonge Mbikusita-Lewanika from the Organisation of African Unity African Women's Committee on Peace and Democracy, Isha Dyfan from WILPF-Sierra Leone, Luz Mendez from the National Union of Guatemalan Women, and Faiza Jama Mohamed, a Somali from the Africa Office of Equality Now in Kenya. Hill, Aboitiz and Poehlman-Doumbouya, 2003, op. cit., p. 1259.

24 S. Anderlini, *Women Building Peace: What They Do, Why It Matters*, London: Lynne Rienner Publishers, 2007, p. 7.

25 Ibid.

26 F. Hill, C. Cohn and C. Enloe, *U.N. Security Council Resolution 1325 Three Years On: Gender, Security and Organizational Change*, Centre for Gender in Organizations, Simmons School of Management, 20 January 2004, p. 4. www.genderandsecurity.org/HCE.pdf (accessed 2 September 2008).

27 C. Cohn, S. Gibbings and H. Kinsella interviewing Felicity Hill, Maha Muna and Isha Dyfan, 'Women, Peace and Security: Resolution 1325', in *International Feminist Journal of Politics*, March 2004, Vol. 6, No. 1, pp. 130–40.

28 Hill, Cohn and Enloe, op. cit., p. 8.

29 United Nations (2000a) Security Council Resolution 1325 on Women, Peace and Security S/Res/1325.

30 UN, 2000a, op. cit.

31 C. Cohn, 'Feminist Peacemaking', *The Women's Review of Books*, Vol. 21, No. 5, 2004, p. 8.

32 See J. Ann Tickner, *Gendering World Politics: Issues and Approaches in the Post-Cold War Era*, New York: Columbia University Press, 2001, pp. 36–64; Gunhild Hoogensen and Svein Vigeland Rottem, 'Gender Identity and the Subject of Security', *Security Dialogue* Vol. 35, No. 2, 2004, pp. 155–71; Prasenjit Maiti, *Discoursing on a Gendered Security*, Burdwan University, India, 2001. Available online at: www.justlawlinks.com/NEWSLETTER/newsletter/art-01-06.htm.

33 C. Cohn and C. Enloe, 'A Conversation with Cynthia Enloe: Feminist Look at Masculinity and the Men Who Wage War', *Signs: Journal of Women in Culture and Society*, Vol. 28, No. 4, 2003, pp. 1189–90.

34 UN, 2000a, op. cit.

35 T. Magwaza, 'Counting the cost and listing the gains: Is the United Nations Security Council Resolution 1325 responsive to Africa's challenges?', *Conflict Trend*, No. 3, 2003, pp. 34–8.

36 Cohn, 2008, op. cit., pp. 197–8.

37 Karen Barnes, *Reform or More of the Same? Gender Mainstreaming and the Changing Nature of UN Peace Operations*, YCISS Working Paper No. 41, 2006. www.yorku.ca/yciss/whatsnew/documents/WP41-Barnes.pdf; Sandra Whitworth, *Men, Militarism and UN Peacekeeping: A Gendered Analysis*. London: Lynne Rienner Publishers, 2004, p. 127.

38 United Nations, *An Agenda for Peace: Preventive Diplomacy, Peacemaking and Peace-keeping*, A/47/277-S/24111, New York: United Nations, 1992, para. 81.

39 United Nations, *Report of the Panel on United Nations Peace Operations*, A/55/305-S/2000/809, 21 August, New York: United Nations, 2000b. These references occur on pages 11, 32, 33, 39, 41, 62, 71, and 72.

40 I. Dyfan, K. Haver and K. Piccirilli, *No Women, No Peace: The Importance of Women's Participation to Achieve Peace and Security*, Paper by the NGO Working Group on Women, Peace and Security submitted to the UN High-Level Panel on Threats, Challenges and Change, upon the invitation of the UN Foundation, 2004. www.peacewomen.org/un/ngo/ngopub/NoWomenNoPeace.pdf.

41 Cohn, 2008, op. cit., p. 185.
42 Elisabeth Rehn and Ellen Johnson Sirleaf, *Women, War and Peace: The Independent Experts' Assessment on the Impact of Armed Conflict on Women and Women's Role in Peace-building*. New York, UNIFEM, 2002, p. 5.
43 Link to report: www.un.org/womenwatch/daw/public/eWPS.pdf.
44 For details of each UN agency's commitments under the *2008–2009 UN System-Wide Action Plan on Security Council Resolution (2000) 1325 on Women, Peace and Security*, please see www.un.org/womenwatch/ianwge/taskforces/wps/actionplan20082009/pdfs/OCHA%202008-2009%201325.pdf.
45 For example, see Gina Torry (ed.), *Six Years On Report: SCR 1325 and the Peace-building Commission*, New York: NGO Working Group, 2006.
46 For example, see Gwendolyn Beetham and Nicola Popovic, *Putting Policy into Practice: Monitoring the Implementation of UN Security Council Resolutions on Women, Peace and Security*, background paper for an International Conference on Indicators for Monitoring 1325 and 1820, Oslo, pp. 11–13, November 2009.
47 NATO, *Bi-SC Directive 40-1: Integrating UNSCR 1325 and Gender Perspectives in the NATO Command Structure Including Measures for Protection During Armed Conflict*, Bi-SC Directive 40-1, September 2009. www.nato.int/nato_static/assets/pdf/pdf_2009_09/20090924_Bi-SC_DIRECTIVE_40-1.pdf.
48 A. Fogh Rasmussen, 'Women's rights: A matter of peace and stability', *Huffington Post*, 8 March 2010. www.huffingtonpost.com/anders-fogh-rasmussen/womens-rights-a-matter-of_b_489629.html.
49 M. Bastick and K. Valasek (eds), *Gender and Security Sector Reform Toolkit*, Geneva: DCAF, OSCE-ODIHR, UN-INSTRAW, 2008.
50 See OSCE Information Note, 18 June 2009. www.osce.org/documents/odihr/2009/06/38227_en.pdf.
51 For a copy of the text of the Goma Declaration, see www.womenwarpeace.org/webfm_send/1634.
52 United Nations, *Report of the Secretary-General on Women, Peace and Security*, S/2004/814, 13 October 2004. http://daccess-dds-ny.un.org/doc/UNDOC/GEN/N04/534/14/PDF/N0453414.pdf?OpenElement.
53 Sierra Leone and the Philippines both launched their NAPs in March 2010, and among other countries, Rwanda, Burundi and DRC have drafted plans but they are not yet publicly available.
54 For a comparison of NAPs in EU member states, see Andrew Sherriff with Karen Barnes, *Enhancing the EU Response to Women and Armed Conflict with Particular Reference to Development Policy*, ECDPM Discussion Paper 84, Maastricht: ECDPM, 2008, pp. 109–11.
55 O. J. Sending, 'Why Peace Builders are "Blind" and "Arrogant" and What to Do About It', *Policy Brief 3*, Oslo: NUPI, 2009, p. 3.
56 Dutch Working Group 1325, *Partnership on UNSCR 1325*, no date. www.cordaidpartners.com/uploads/documents/768/original/24235_Twinning_korr1.pdf.
57 For a report of this meeting, see Council of the European Union, *Implementation of UN Security Council Resolutions 1325 and 1820 on Women, Peace and Security: Elaboration and Implementation of UNSCR 1325 National Action Plans*, Brussels, 2 October 2009. https://ue.eu.int/uedocs/cmsUpload/09-10-02-NAP_Meeting_final_report.pdf.
58 For the background documents and reports of these meetings, see www.un.org/womenwatch/osagi/cdrom/start.html.
59 K. Valasek with K. Nelson, *Securing Equality, Engendering Peace: A Guide to Policy and Planning on Women, Peace and Security*, Santo Domingo: UN INSTRAW, 2006; Sherriff and Barnes, op. cit., pp. 60–6.
60 The Initiative for Peacebuilding is a consortium of ten NGOs led by International Alert and funded by the European Commission. Its purpose is to harness international

knowledge and expertise in the area of conflict prevention and peacebuilding. Gender issues are one of the six thematic focus areas of the consortium. See www.initiative-forpeacebuilding.eu/gender.php.

61 M. Lyytikainen and S. Tielemans (eds), *Civil Society Recommendations on the Implementation of UN SCR 1325 in Europe*, London: Initiative for Peacebuilding, 2009. www.gaps-uk.org/docs/Recommendations%201325%20in%20Europe.pdf.

62 Anderlini, 2007, op. cit., pp. 213–23.

63 See www.international-alert.org/gender.

64 See www.gaps-uk.org.

65 GAPS, *Global Monitoring Checklist on Women, Peace and Security*, London: GAPS, 2009. www.reliefweb.int/rw/RWFiles2010.nsf/FilesByRWDocUnidFilename/MYAI-84T4Q5-full_report.pdf/$File/full_report.pdf.

66 In 2008, the Dutch Working Group 1325 carried out a one-year evaluation of the NAP. Herman Majoor and Megan L. Brown, *Evaluating the Dutch National Action Plan on UNSC Resolution 1325 After One Year of Implementation*, 2008. www.ifor.org/WPP/Newsitems/Final_Report_Eval_NAP_1325_12Dec2008.pdf.

67 For more information on Operation 1325, see www.operation1325.se/content/view/30/42/.

68 For more information on the Gender and Peacebuilding Working Group, see www.peacebuild.ca/work-groups-gender-pb-e.php.

69 Kosovo Women's Network, *Monitoring Implementation of UNSCR 1325 in Kosovo*, Executive Summary, no date. www.unifem.at/pdfs/KWN_UNSCR1325.pdf.

70 A. Lukatela, *Drafting and Adopting National Action Plans for the Implementation of Resolution 1325 in the Countries of Southeast Europe*, Policy brief No. 3, no date. www.iknowpolitics.org/files/3.1325NAPs.pdf.

71 For more information on FemLINK's work, see www.femlinkpacific.org.fj/.

72 It is important to recognise that men and boys can also be, and are, victims of sexual violence during conflict, however the scale on which women experience rape during conflict far exceeds this. Sexual violence should also be understood as a form of patriarchal violence.

73 United Nations, *Resolution 1820*, Adopted by the Security Council at its 5916th meeting on 19 June 2008, S/RES/1820.

74 M. Achuthan and R. Black, *United Nations Security Council Resolution 1820: A Preliminary Assessment of the Challenges and Opportunities*, New York: International Women's Tribune Centre, 2009, p. 7. www.iwtc.org/1820blog/1820_paper.pdf.

75 Ibid: pp. 9–10.

76 United Nations, *Report of the Secretary-General Pursuant to Security Council Resolution 1820*, S/2009/362, 2009a. www.iwtc.org/1820blog/1820_screport.pdf.

77 United Nations, *Resolution 1888*, Adopted by the Security Council at its 6195th meeting, on 30 September 2009, S/RES/1888, 2009b. http://daccess-dds-ny.un.org/doc/UNDOC/GEN/N09/534/46/PDF/N0953446.pdf?OpenElement.

78 Margot Wallström, former vice-president of the European Commission, has been appointed to this position for an initial two-year term.

79 United Nations, *Resolution 1889 on Women, Peace and Security*, adopted by the Security Council at its 6196th meeting, on 5 October 2009, S/RES/1889, 2009c. http://daccess-dds-ny.un.org/doc/UNDOC/GEN/N09/542/55/PDF/N0954255.pdf?OpenElement.

80 United Nations, *Report of the Secretary-General on Women, Peace and Security*. S/2010/173, 6 April 2010. www.reliefweb.int/rw/RWFiles2010.nsf/FilesByRWDocUnidFilename/MYAI-84T4Q5-full_report.pdf/$File/full_report.pdf.

Part II
Country case studies

3 Gendered violence and UNSCR 1325 in Kosovo

Shifting paradigms on women, peace and security

Catherina H. Hall-Martin

Introduction

This chapter discusses the role played by Kosovar women to mitigate conflict, as well as to press for gender justice and recognition in the highly patriarchal institutions of their country before, during and after the war. The analysis is done against the backdrop of United Nations Security Council Resolution 1325 (UNSCR 1325).[1] In stages, the paper explores how Kosovo women engaged in informal non-violent activism to bring about a semblance of peace to their war-torn country before the intervention of the North Atlantic Treaty Organisation (NATO) and the United Nations Interim Administration in Kosovo (UNMIK). It also analyses how the presence of UNMIK impacted on and influenced the activism of women; and how, if at all, UNMIK peace initiatives took consideration of the women's civil action. The paper also looks at the impact of UNSCR 1325 on the women's informal activism and how its presence shaped the work of the women and also of UNMIK.

Women's leadership, perspectives and skills acquired during conflict and post-conflict reconstruction are invaluable in working toward sustainable peace. But as Mehren argues, and as the case of Kosovo illustrates, policy-makers persist in limiting negotiations to men, neglecting to recognise the grassroots work carried out by women across ethnic divides.[2] This perpetuates the archaic image of women as primarily victims, ignoring their contributions towards security and peace in many spheres and indeed even as combatants.

In order to study the cycle of conflict in Kosovo (war, reconstruction and status negotiations), one needs to consider the gender dimension and its close relationship with post-conflict reconstruction and peacebuilding. As Arino and de la Morena (2008) argue, although women have traditionally been excluded from the conflict discourse and the 'heterogeneity of needs' of both men and women in this process has been neglected, both sexes have played an array of roles. These include peacebuilding roles assumed by women in an attempt to develop an inclusive society. Furthermore, collaborations between the international community and local actors needed to be engendered in an attempt to overcome the patriarchal social hierarchies which define Kosovan society. Of particular significance is the fact that Kosovo's status as an international protectorate also provided an environment rich in possibility for the implementation of UNSCR 1325.[3] The particular needs, risks and experiences faced by the women of Kosovo during the conflict have earned them inclusion in the peacebuilding process. Their inclusion allows for a broader perspective on these processes 'by addressing issues specific to women'.[4]

Beginning with a brief description of pre-war Kosovo, the chapter looks at the women's initiatives which were extant before the war and the development of these organisations during the war. Women's civil society has been vital in advocating for women's rights and indeed can be seen to be more constructive than UNMIK contributions. In terms of utilising UNSCR 1325, civil society has been highly effective in its application in spite of the fact that UNMIK has failed by and large to seriously address gender mainstreaming through the structures outlined in UNSCR 1325.

Context of the war

In 1974, the Yugoslav Federation granted sovereign status and federal representation to Kosovo which was previously part of Serbia.[5] This level of self-government was crucial in Kosovo, where Albanians were an overwhelming majority of the population. During the early 1980s the Serbian government granted Kosovo more freedoms, as illustrated with the establishment of an Albanian university in Pristina and allowing the Albanian flag to be flown as a national emblem. Women's participation in political and civic spheres increased as reflected by the founding of various women's organisations. However, perceived discrimination against Serbians resulted in a demand for a return to pre-1974 conditions.[6]

In 1988, Slobodan Milosevic, then Yugoslavian president, proposed a constitutional amendment to revoke the autonomous status of Kosovo. The Kosovan Assembly, under extreme pressure, granted the amendment in 1989.[7] Consequently, Kosovars lost control of many of their institutions including the police and schools. The revocation of autonomy saw a corresponding rise in human rights abuses and harassment against ethnic Albanians. In an attempt to gain independence, the Kosovo Liberation Army (KLA), led numerous attacks against Serbian police forces.[8] Kosovo Albanians withdrew from the Kosovo government and in 1991 via a referendum, proclaimed the Republic of Kosovo and elected Ibrahim Rugova as president in 1992. This parallel government catered to the needs of ethnic Albanians and for the following eight years attempted to claim independence through a non-violent resistance movement.[9]

As in many theatres of conflict and instability, women are vital components in maintaining a semblance of functionality in society. Apart from remaining the traditional caregivers, Kosovar women became active in economic production, women's organisations working toward a peaceful resolution of the conflict and the provision of support to local women, especially through advocacy work on legislation dealing with violence against women.[10]

One of the alarming trends during the Kosovo conflict was the high level of rape and gender based violence (GBV)[11] resulting in severe psycho-social trauma. As the violence escalated during the early 1990 pre-war years, thousands of Albanian women fell victim to rape and ethnic cleansing. Rape in these situations was used as a weapon of war. A United Nations Development Fund for Women (UNIFEM) report, published in 2000, details how groups of Albanian women were separated from their husbands and families, detained by Serbian men and paramilitary forces and 'were subject to rape and torture'. The report further details how the majority of rapes were 'gang rapes, and the rape was associated with placing Serbian nationalist symbol tattoos on victims' bodies'.[12] Grassroots women's networks such as the Kosovo Women's Initiative (KWI) were found to be highly effective in decreasing suffering of victims and providing support to vulnerable women. Vocational training projects were also initiated, allowing women to come together and gain respite from the trauma that characterised their daily lives.[13]

In the period 1998–1999, the Kosovan war was characterised by expulsions and human rights abuses perpetrated by Serbians against Albanians. This was coupled with the Serbian refusal to sign the Rambouillet Accords,[14] eventually provoking an international response that culminated in the NATO bombing campaigns against Serbia in 1999.[15] Milosevic eventually capitulated with the signing of a ceasefire agreement leading to the withdrawal of Serb forces. Kosovo was placed under international administration with the adoption of UNSCR 1244.[16]

Women's organisations and security before the war

Although women were highly active in civil society in pre-war Kosovo, there are numerous traditions inhibiting the full emancipation of women. Many of these customary laws are formulated on the *Kanun*, historical Albanian laws regulating all moral and social spheres such as family hierarchy, marriage and inheritance. Primarily relating to the patriarchal nature of traditional Kosovar society, this largely prevented women from owning property, living independently or earning an income.[17] However, from the 1970s the position of women was strengthened under Communist rule, especially with regard to their increased access to education. In particular, the possibility of instruction in Albanian at the University of Pristina enabled this access at the vital tertiary level.[18]

Further pre-war initiatives came from women's civil society movements such as the Centre for the Protection of Women and *Motrat Qiriazi*,[19] providing basic services and humanitarian relief. Numerous women's organisations that had been active in Kosovo before the war were usually aligned along the separate Albanian and Serbian ethnic lines. The first political initiative undertaken by women in Kosovo involved the Platform for Action upon which the Albanian Women's League and the women's association of the Democratic League of Kosovo (LDK) were formed. During the years of parallel structures, the LDK was the main political party, thus the women's association became a vital part of women's participation in political and civil spheres.[20]

Both these spheres (political and civic) constituted an aspect of women's empowerment in pre-war Kosovo, although occurring in a national context which was not particularly focused on gender mainstreaming. However, they also served to strengthen the women's movement during the post-war reconstruction process, although this highlighted the dearth of experienced women, often resulting in a lack of sustainability.[21] The parallel structures extant in Kosovo before the war are considered to have given Kosovo-Albanians a head start in establishing a civil society. Albanian women's groups formed a vital part of this structure, becoming active in both the pre and post-war phases.

United Nations mission in Kosovo – good intentions but hollow application

As authorised by UNSCR 1244, UNMIK was established as a transitional administration until a permanent political resolution could be found. Pending this, the Kosovo Transitional Council (KTC) was created in preparation for the first phase of self-governance. The highest political consultative body, the KTC included representatives from most ethnic groups within Kosovo[22] and as such represented a microcosm of Kosovo's political, ethnic, civil and religious communities, but without a single female representative.[23]

In December 1999, the Joint Interim Administrative Structure (JIAS) was established. At that time, the KTC was also enlarged and consequently consisted of 17 per cent female representation. By February 2000, all previous parallel administrative and security structures had been replaced by the JIAS.[24] Following this, the Special Representative of the Secretary-General's (SRSG) main consultative body became the Interim Administrative Council (IAC), resulting in a loss of status for the KTC, once again relegating Kosovar women to the outskirts of the decision-making processes.[25] Although the IAC was able to discuss regulations and make public statements, the extent of the Council's power was limited in comparison to the SRSG. The KTC acts as a consultative forum on policy issues.

Up until the arrival of UNMIK in Kosovo, much of what had been done in the past in terms of empowering women and promoting gender equality in peacebuilding had been done at the informal, grassroots level, with women mobilising at the community level to oppose conflict within their societies, in turn building bridges across ethnic and religious divides. However, these indigenous peacebuilding efforts were quickly overshadowed when UNMIK took over administration of the country. Little effort was made to harness both the informal and formal peacebuilding structures and efforts for the common good.

This grassroots dialogue has much to contribute to the peace process although the amount of structured access that it had to the peace negotiations remained limited. As noted by Joanne Sandler, Executive Director of UNIFEM, 'despite the promises of 1325, peace tables remain the province of those who made the conflict rather than those who have the greatest motivation for ending it'.[26] This being said, one notes that what is most remarkable in the UNMIK terms of reference is the absence of a gender-specific component in its outline. UNMIK's presence in Kosovo, as already noted above, failed to transcend the orthodox definitions and strategies for peacekeeping and started its work from an inaccurate assumption that security and peacebuilding are gender-neutral activities. As a result of this oversight, UNMIK's work has long been criticised for excluding women from all its planning and implementation, and for failing to take care of women's specific security needs.[27] UNMIK did not include the previous peace-building efforts by women's groups on its agenda, and failed to engage them in dialogue in order to learn from their best practices to enhance its planning and implementation purposes.[28]

Ultimately UNMIK is characterised by a lack of coordination between institutions such as United Nations High Commission for Refugees (UNHCR), UNIFEM, the Office of Gender Affairs (OGA) and the Organisation for Security and Cooperation in Europe (OSCE). Few women were appointed to positions and none were involved in the first Kosovo Transitional Council (KTC). The lack of female representation in UNMIK undermines its legitimacy in Kosovo, causing concern as to lack of accountability and political participation.[29] Local willingness to assist UNMIK has been further undermined by the cumbersome bureaucratic processes, duplication of efforts and the rapid turnover of international staff frustrating local efforts to develop sustainable working relationships.[30] UNMIK authorities have also been criticised for failing to make democratic structures visible within UNMIK itself, thus impoverishing its potential as a democratic example.[31]

Engendering the rehabilitation process

There are two focal areas in the study of Kosovo from a gendered perspective: the prominent role, played by gender (in terms of GBV) during the conflict and post-conflict periods and the unique occasion created by Kosovo's transitional status. In effect, Kosovo became a 'gender laboratory' where pledges toward gender equality could be translated into practice. Both the aforementioned factors are vital in forging a sustainable peace.[32] Thus in effect, Kosovo provided a blank canvas for the application of UNSCR 1325 with UNMIK in a prime position to lead this process of gender mainstreaming. One of the impediments that arose in this process, however, is the varied understanding of 'security' between UNMIK and women's organisations, with UNMIK adopting a more traditionalist approach. While the former focused on the protection of the state from external threats, the latter was more concerned with human security and the differing security needs of individuals. Consequently, human security allows a more gendered approach when addressing security concerns as well as seeking to empower women through education and access as gender equality is a necessary precondition to peace and security.[33] More specifically, taking a gendered perspective on security is important in creating mechanisms to provide for the security needs of both men and women and addressing the ways in which both domestic and international factors are enhancing the risks faced by women.[34]

Neglecting the gender perspective in post-conflict processes translates into a gap in the creation of an inclusive peace, because reconstruction is not gender neutral. Gender dynamics are pervasive throughout the conflict cycle with the consequence that men and women experience the effects of violence and concomitant opportunities for peace, differently. In the same vein, violence during the conflict took on a gender dimension illustrated in the sexual violence carried out against women from both ethnic groups by Serbian and Kosovo Albanian security forces.[35]

After conflict, wounded male combatants are often viewed as heroes and warriors. Women suffering from the aftereffects of war, such as rape and GBV suffer from the stigmatisation and are most often ostracised from their communities. This situation was prominent in the post-conflict phase in Kosovo as rape had been such a prevalent occurrence. Women are seen to be perennial victims in war, rather than agents of peace and partners to the post-conflict reconstruction process. By failing to comprehensively apply UNSCR 1325, UNMIK and the international community in general served to delegitimise women's voices in the political process.

Kosovo is a society characterised by an entrenched patriarchal system. Up until its recent independence in February 2008, women were doubly disadvantaged. On the one hand was an international bureaucracy frequently bypassing women's rights in favour of wider ethnic stability, on the other was the aforementioned domestic patriarchy, largely non-accepting of women in politics. Although there had been a strong culture of women's activism since before the war, criticism had been levelled against UNMIK for lack of consultation with these women's groups.[36] There has been progress in women's issues since the cessation of hostilities but it is widely felt that UNSCR 1325 has had little impact on women in Kosovo.[37] On average across Kosovo, women have a lower per capita income and remain less educated than men and 69 per cent of women are not employed in the labour force.[38]

However, according to the Agency for Gender Equality, located in the Prime Minister's office, Resolution 1325 is being utilised in Kosovo to the advantage of local women's groups and has been used to raise awareness among authorities. These activities include organised protests, organising media debates and meeting with decision-makers as well as networking for the advancement of women, regionally and internationally.[39] UNIFEM has played a vital role in the implementation of UNSCR 1325 as well as increasing awareness among civil society through capacity building of local women's organisations and support for the Office for Gender Equality. It has also been key in bringing together government and civil society to prepare a Plan of Action for the Advancement of Gender Equality.[40] In spite of this, the question of implementation of 1325 results in opposing answers. Whereas women's NGOs in Kosovo have actively engaged with Resolution 1325, government institutions such as the Agency for Gender Equality have by and large ignored the issues raised by women's groups, resulting in 'their insignificant influence in the security sector'.[41]

Disjuncture between theory and practice

Additionally, there have been challenges with support from international actors. An example is the situation where Kosovo was flooded with aid following the tentative peace agreement that was signed in 1999. Among these sums was a US$10 million US government grant for the Kosovo Women's Initiative (KWI), modelled on the successful Bosnian Women's Initiative. The KWI aimed at addressing gender issues and assisting the recovery of women in post-war Kosovo. Although this form of reconstruction was necessarily long-term, donors required that all funds be spent within one year.[42] The imposition of such conditionalities often had a negative impact on sustainability of any gains made.[43]

Initially international organisations played a dominant role in the KWI, with the aim of gradually transferring responsibility to local women's organisations. Within KWI, women's groups prepared project proposals to be presented to the UNHCR which had the mandate to make funding decisions. Within the context of Kosovo's reconstruction process and through the activities of women's organisations, the emphasis was always on local ownership.[44] However, very few women's groups were involved in the planning stages of the KWI. Also, the KWI was modelled on the programme developed for Bosnia, suggesting that no adequate assessment was done on the ground in Kosovo. Furthermore, even though UNHCR had initially attempted to facilitate the participation of local women in the programme design, this was not wholly successful due to inter-ethnic tensions.[45]

A monitoring project carried out by the Kosovo Women's Network (KWN) concluded that many women in Kosovo have a superficial understanding of UNSCR 1325. This is reflected in an absence of political will among the international community to promote gender equality even though Kosovar women have been using UNSCR 1325 directly and indirectly to enhance their contribution to decision-making since its promulgation in 2000. Regrettably gender mainstreaming, as foreseen by human rights treaties such as the 1979 Convention on the Elimination of All Forms of Discrimination Against Women (CEDAW) and 1325, lack realistic application. Furthermore, the 2007 Head of OGA reported a lack of engagement with local actors and inefficient communication infrastructure between international institutions.[46]

Real advances or mere quota-based equality?

Although measures have been put in place to rectify the shortcomings of UNMIK and the application of UNSCR 1325 in Kosovo, they originate from a foundation biased against women as indicated in their perpetual absence from decision-making processes. This has resulted in an environment where these measures have either failed or had little positive impact.[47]

Two organisations that are leading the way in the integration of women and the implementation of UNSCR 1325 are the International Civilian Police (CIVPOL) and the Kosovo Police Service (KPS). According to the OSCE, inclusion of women in this organisation is relatively high in comparison to other Eastern European countries. Representation of women is around 14 per cent.[48] The CIVPOL Gender Advisor has also maintained crucial cross-institutional dialogue and is dedicated to increasing the number of women serving. Gender-focused training is provided to all incoming staff in an attempt to ensure accountability in terms of decision-making affecting women and issues within UNMIK's mandate pertaining to gender. However, there is still a gap in implementing adequate training, as the KPS requests to the SRSG to promote training in UNSCR 1325 for people stationed in Kosovo has gone largely unheeded.[49]

In general, UNMIK is considered to have persistently failed to address gender inequalities, particularly related to trafficking and domestic violence. In light of the establishment of the Gender Equality Laws, this illustrates how much remains to be achieved in the advancement of women in Kosovo.[50] However, one of the programmes implemented by UNMIK is a quota for parliamentary elections intended to increase female representation in parliament. This has allowed for up to 30 per cent female representation although there are still no programmes to sustain gender mainstreaming in politics and women remain marginalised within party structures.[51] Consequently mere numbers still do not equate to participation. Very often the political structures in place are neither democratic nor inclusive of women. Thus, as Corrin stipulates with regard to Kosovo, 'participation involves being heard and having what your views are taken into account'.[52]

The 2007 elections saw a slight improvement with the election of two women into ministerial positions and a further two elected as deputy ministers. However, most noteworthy was the absence of any women from the Kosovar Negotiation Team, leading the negotiations on Kosovo's final status. This failure is considered by many Kosovar women to be indicative of their inability to gain access to the highest echelons of decision-making.[53] The exclusion of women from the negotiations relating to Kosovo's final status is wholly contrary to UNSCR 1325's mandate calling for all actors in negotiations to adopt a gendered perspective including 'measures that support local women's peace initiatives ... and that involve women in all the implementation mechanisms of the peace agreement'.[54]

Final status negotiations

UNSCR 1325 Article 1 states that it: '*Urges* Member States to ensure increased representation of women at all decision-making levels in national, regional and international institutions and mechanisms for the prevention, management, and resolution of conflict'. By excluding women from the final status talks it was difficult for a gendered perspective to be adopted by participants. This gendered perspective is called for in Article 8 of the Resolution and calls for the involvement of women 'in all the implementation mechanisms of the peace agreements' and to provide 'measures that ensure the protection of and respect for human rights of women and girls, particularly as they relate to the constitution, the electoral system, the police and the judiciary'.[55]

Thus although UNSCR 1325 promotes female involvement in post-conflict negotiations, the mandate remains largely ignored by male leaders within Kosovo's political sphere, as well as by international actors active in the country. This is considered to be one of UNMIK's major shortcomings in Kosovo. As the primary interim decision-maker in the country it is expected by the local population to set an example by executing the requirements of UNSCR 1325 in the final status negotiations.[56] In reality, UNSCR 1325 is being expressly implemented only by women's groups as part of their operational basis. This is particularly evident in the work carried out by the KWN.

Adopting a gendered approach to reconstruction efforts

UNMIK: institutional shortcomings as stimulus for civil society

UNMIK established the Office of Gender Affairs (OGA) as part of its mandate, in mid-2003 to facilitate a gender-based approach to UNMIK's work. This is to be carried out via the UNMIK Implementation Plan of UNSCR 1325.[57] Subsequently, the OGA was expanded to include Kosovar women representatives of political parties and NGOs. The OGA has three priority areas: enabling women to actively participate in Kosovo's economic recovery; enhancing women's stake in the decision-making procedure with regard to reconstruction and peacebuilding processes; and addressing issues of violence against women.[58] The Gender Office has allowed for a heightened awareness of the necessity to operate on the basis of gender sensitivity regarding governance in the future Kosovo. This awareness touches on all aspects of society including: women's representation in elected bodies; the inclusion of a gender equality approach in policies, programmes and services; and the eradication of GBV including domestic violence and trafficking.[59] According to its mandate, UNMIK OGA aims to mainstream gender in its mandate and comprehensively address issues raised by UNSCR 1325.[60] However, in a survey carried out by the KWN, respondents noted the inconsistencies in UNMIK's administration and that UNSCR 1325 'is not being systematically or sustainably implemented within the work of internationals and is hence a negative example to local government and civil society'.[61]

Under the UNMIK Pillar 3, the OSCE is responsible for gender equality within the operational framework of the interim administration. However, as a result of the prioritisation of other political matters, gender issues are often subordinated and inadequate training is provided on gender mainstreaming issues arising from UNSCR 1325.[62] This lack of progress in gender issues is highlighted by the fact that there are no women in senior management positions nor has there been a female Head or Deputy Head of Mission.[63]

UNMIK's strategies for peacebuilding, as well as its definitions of security, fell into the mainstream as the mission focused more on reawakening and strengthening the previous institutions of governance, without deviating much from the Serbian way of viewing security. By so doing, UNMIK indirectly perpetuated the oppression and exclusion of women from the development scenario.

Noting the manner in which UNMIK was sidelining their efforts and excluding them from peacebuilding plans and initiatives, the women realised the need to strengthen their activism, and thus formed the Women's Peace Coalition in 2006.[64]

Shaping their future: Kosovo women's civil societies

Membership of the Women's Peace Coalition[65] comprised the Kosovo Women's Network and the Women in Black Network Serbia. Operating across ethnic, religious and national precincts, the Coalition is an independent citizen's project founded on women's solidarity. The Kosovo Women's Network, as noted above, is a network of local women's groups, comprising groups which have over ten years' experience of community development, as well as new groups founded since the arrival of the UN in Kosovo. The Women's Peace Coalition works towards a just and lasting peace, and the inclusion of women as equal partners in the peacebuilding process. Advocating for the effective implementation of UNSCR 1325 the Coalition operates on the principle that women are not only victims of war, but active participants in the peace movement and thus with a stake in post-conflict reconstruction.[66]

The Women's Coalition continues to be most active in peacebuilding, reconciliation and transitional justice processes, and to develop relationships of solidarity and mutual support. It encourages networking and joint activities between women-led organisations with similar political missions in Serbia and Kosovo, and women provide a variety of community services to vulnerable people.[67] These services include training, aid and psychological support, as well as gender-specific issues like violence against women and girls, trafficking, enrolment of girls in schools and universities, provision of clean water and cooking gas to women, to mention but a few. Grassroots women are also trained by the coalition to build their capacity to work effectively on behalf of their communities in peacebuilding initiatives.[68]

Indeed grassroots women's organisations are the only ones consistently addressing UNSCR 1325 as an operational principle. In 2007, KWN initiated a series of talks with the Kosovo Force[69] with regard to the importance of the Resolution in their mission. However, overall advancement is undermined due to insufficient cooperation from national institutions and the international community.[70]

Continued marginalisation of Kosovo's women

According to World Bank estimates, women's situation in post-war Kosovo society has deteriorated on numerous fronts, characterised by a return to the traditions espoused by *Kanun* law, which strictly regulates public and private life.[71] The situation with regard to women's safety is dire. GBV and sexual harassment are illustrative of the poor economic conditions and post-war trauma but KWN has been highly active in promoting awareness and campaigning for women's rights.[72] Further manifestations are reported to be unequal access to employment and increased trafficking of women and children.[73] For instance, Kosovo is a prime source, transit and destination point for women trafficked for prostitution.[74] According to an Amnesty International report, it was found that the presence of UNMIK and other international organisations exacerbated problems related to trafficking and that the international military force, led by NATO, was unable to effectively protect local women.[75]

As has been mentioned, post-war Kosovo still exhibits the marginalisation of women from decision-making positions. On this front, education remains a major obstacle for the advancement of women in Kosovo, illustrated by the 81 per cent dropout rate for females across all levels of education.[76] Clear strategies need to be implemented in order to address this and train women to enter various levels of politics and civil society. In October 2004, the second National Assembly elections were held, culminating in the election of 33 women parliamentarians to the 120-seat Assembly (27.5 per cent). However, the 30 per cent gender quota has had little real impact as most key decision-making positions are held by men.[77]

Although not implemented by UNMIK, the National Action Plan (NAP), formulated in 2002–2003, was key to enhancing gender mainstreaming in Kosovo. Under the leadership of UNIFEM, the NAP assesses critical areas of concern relating to women and is linked with the Beijing Declaration, the Platform of Action and CEDAW. It is considered to be a solid step in gender mainstreaming and incorporating UNSCR 1325 in policy formulation.[78] The NAP established the Law on Gender Equality, promulgated by the SRSG in UNMIK Regulation 2004/18.[79] The Law on Gender Equality allowed for numerous institutional mechanisms to be implemented at the national and local level, in order to accomplish gender equality. These include an Agency for Gender Equality within the Office of the Prime Minister, officers for gender equality in various ministries as well as municipalities.[80]

Conclusion

This chapter has analysed the implementation, or lack thereof, of UNSCR 1325 within post-war Kosovo. It has looked at the role local women's initiatives have played prior to the conflict and the largely positive impact they have had on strengthening the position of women within a highly patriarchal society. The work of the KWN has and is proving to be invaluable for the advancement of women's rights and UNSCR 1325 is often utilised as the framework for their operations.

Regrettably, the level of application and success of this vital Resolution is remarkable more in its absence than in the progress it has achieved in the years since its promulgation in 2000. The promotion of gender equality and the application of UNSCR 1325 occur predominantly within grassroots civil movements. Although progress is being made within civil society, it is the lack of awareness and training within the directives on the Resolution for Women's Peace and

Security in the government structures, which is limiting the impact it could have in Kosovo.

As a country under interim administration, Kosovo could have been an excellent opportunity to serve as a laboratory for the application of UNSCR 1325. Instead, starting from the Rambouillet Accords, the Transitional Council and the final status negotiations, the absence of women in the decision-making process is evident. This disparity with the aims of UNSCR 1325 was reinforced by UNMIK, whose priorities seemed to lie more with creating a stable ethnically inclusive environment at the expense of gender mainstreaming. This perpetuated the marginalisation of Kosovar women of all ethnic groups.

Although UNSCR 1325 is a vast improvement on the pre-war situation in that it advanced the position of women in peace and security, adequate mechanisms need to be implemented to ensure that its directives are effectively operationalised. In the case of Kosovo this would require, among other factors, increased training and awareness in the Resolution, and education for women to allow them equal opportunities to decision-making positions. While government institutions appear to have a basic knowledge of UNSCR 1325, there is a disconnect in application of the Resolution. Although mechanisms for implementation have been set in place articulation into policy is not occurring. This could be due to financial constraints but also a lack of political will. This needs to be addressed in order to ensure that the implementation of UNSCR 1325 remains firmly in the political and social spotlight.

Notes

1 Unanimously adopted on 31 October 2000, the Resolution is the first attempt at addressing the disproportionate and unique impact of conflict on women and girls, their under-utilised contribution to peacebuilding and conflict resolution and highlights the importance of their full participation as active agents of peace and security.

2 E. Mehren, 'Female Peacemakers Strategise How to Make Peace', 2003, www.womensenews.com/article.cfm/dyn/aid/1606 (accessed 13 July 2009).

3 A. Arino and G.R. de la Morena, *An Approach to the Kosovo Post-War Rehabilitation Process from a Gender Perspective*, Barcelona: School for a Culture of Peace Studies, 2008, p. 5.

4 S. Halimi, *Monitoring Security in Kosovo from a Gender Perspective*. Report by Kosovar Gender Studies Unit, 2007, www.kgscentre.org (Accessed 23 October 2009).

5 The Yugoslavian Constitution created Kosovo as an autonomous region within Serbia in 1946.

6 Women for Women International, *Stronger Women, Stronger Nations*, Kosovo Report: Amplifying the Voices of Women in Kosovo, Report Series, 2007, p. 10.

7 A. Kalungu-Banda, 'Post-Conflict Programmes for Women: Lessons from the Kosovo Women's Initiative', in C. Sweetman (ed.) *Gender, Peacebuilding and Reconstruction*, Oxford: Oxfam Publishers, 2005, p. 32.

8 Ibid.

9 Arino and de la Morena, op. cit., p. 7.

10 I. Rizvanolli, L. Bean and N. Farnsworth, *Kosovar Civil Society Report to the United Nations on Violence against Women in Kosovo*. Report prepared for the Kosovo Gender Studies Centre, Prishtina, 2005. Available at: www.un.org/womenwatch/daw/

vaw/ngocontribute/Kosovarper cent20Genderper cent20Studiesper cent20Center.pdf (accessed 23 June 2009).

11 The term gender-based violence has been defined as 'an umbrella term for any harm that is directed against a person on the basis of gender or sex, resulting from power imbalances that exploit distinctions between males and females, as also among males and females.' See Jeanne Ward, *If Not Now, When? Addressing Gender-based Violence in Refugee, Internally Displaced and Post-conflict Settings – A Global Overview*, Reproductive Health for Refugees Consortium (RHRC), April 2002.

12 R. Wareham, 'No Safe Place: An Assessment of Violence Against Women in Kosovo', United Nations Development Fund for Women, 2000. Available at www.unifem.org/attachments/products/NoSafePlace_Kosovo.pdf (accessed 12 January 2010).

13 J.M. Baker and H. Haug, 'Final Report. Independent Evaluation of the Kosovo Women's Initiative', United Nations High Commissioner for Refugees, 2002. Available at. www.unhcr.org/cgi-bin/texis/vtx/home (accessed 23 January 2010).

14 On 6 February 1999, representatives of the Yugoslav Federation and the Serbian government, on one side, and representatives of Kosovo, on the other, met in Rambouillet to engage in negotiations, co-chaired by Hubert Vedrine and Robin Cook, and under the direct auspices of the Contact Group. On 18 March, the proposed agreement was signed by the Albanian side, but was rejected by the Serbian party.

15 A. Kalungu-Banda, 'Post-Conflict Programmes for Women: Lessons from the Kosovo Women's Initiative', in Sweetman, op. cit., p. 32.

16 Ibid.

17 B. Von Glutz, 'Women in Kosovo between Tradition and Emancipation', South East Europe Review for Labour and Social Affairs, 2004, Issue 1, p. 131.

18 A. Lyth, *Getting it Right: A Gender Approach to UNMIK Administration in Kosovo*, Stockholm: The Kvinna Till Kvinna Foundation, 2001, p. 10.

19 A grassroots network of rural women activists focused on education, training and psycho-social assistance, established in 1995.

20 Lyth (ed.) op. cit., p. 11.

21 Arino and de la Morena, op. cit., p. 5.

22 Although Kosovo Albanians constitute 88 per cent of the population, 12 per cent is made up of Serbs, Roma, Ashkali, Bosniaks and Gorani. www.cia.gov/library/publications (accessed 30 November 2009).

23 Baker and Haug, op. cit.

24 Lyth (ed.) op. cit., p. 11.

25 Ibid.

26 J. Sandler, 'Towards Coherent and Effective Implementation of Security Council Resolution 1325 (2000)', Statement to the Security Council Open Debate on Women, Peace and Security, 2007. Available at www.peacewomen.org/un/7thAnniversary/Open_Debate/UNIFEM.pdf (accessed 27 January 2009).

27 Lyth (ed.), op. cit., p. 11.

28 C. Corrin, *Gender Audit of Reconstruction Programmes in South Eastern Europe*, Report for the Urgent Action Fund and Women's Commission for Refugee Women and Children, New York, 2000, p. 12.

29 V. Ingimundarson, 'Under Patriarchy and Peacekeeping: Women in Kosovo since the War', The Centre for Women's and Gender Studies at the University of Iceland, 2004. Available at www.hi.is/page/RIKK-womeninkosovo.html (accessed 30 November 2008).

30 Corrin, op. cit., p. 12.

31 Ibid.

32 Arino and de la Morena, op. cit., p. 11.

33 K. Haq, 'Human Security for Women', in M. Tehranian (ed.) *Worlds Apart: Human Security and Global Governance*, London: I.B.Tauris Publishers, 1999, p. 96.

34 Halimi, op. cit., p. 32.
35 Arino and de la Morena, op. cit., p. 11.
36 Ingimundarson, op. cit.
37 Ibid.
38 M. Haskuka, L. Malazogu, N. Luci and I. Dugolli, *The Rise of the Citizen: Challenges and Choices*, Human Development Report, Pristina: United Nations Development Programme, 2004, p. 34.
39 Halimi, op. cit., p. 32.
40 United Nations Development Fund for Women, Country Profile, 2006, www.unifem.sk/index.cfm?module=project&page=country&CountryISO=KS.
41 Halimi, op. cit., p. 31.
42 Similar programmes have been implemented in Bosnia and Rwanda. In both cases it remains unclear how economic projects targeting the most vulnerable groups of women address wider inequalities in gender relations.
43 A. Kalungu-Banda, 'Post-Conflict Programmes for Women: Lessons from the Kosovo Women's Initiative', in Sweetman, op. cit., p. 31.
44 Ibid. p. 36.
45 Ibid. p. 36.
46 L. Alice, *Monitoring Implementation of UNSCR 1325 in Kosovo, Executive Summary*. Pristina: Kosova Women's Network, 2007a. pp. 1–2. Available at www.peacewomen.org/resources/Kosovo (accessed 10 February 2009).
47 Lyth (ed.) op. cit., p. 8.
48 Halimi, op. cit., p. 32.
49 Alice, op. cit. 2007a, p. 3–4.
50 Ibid.
51 Ibid.
52 C. Corrin, 'Developing Democracy in Kosova: From Grassroots to Government', *Parliamentary Affairs* 2002, no. 55, p. 101.
53 R.L. Vuniqi, *Women's Role in Independent Kosovo*, Pristina: Kosovo Gender Studies Centre, 2008, p. 8.
54 UNSCR 1325 (2000); Alice, op. cit., 2007a, p. 3–4.
55 UNSCR 1325.
56 Alice, op. cit., 2007a, p. 8.
57 UNMIK Implementation Plan of UNSCR 1325 for 2004–2006, p. 2. Available at http://officeofgenderaffairs.unmikonline.org/ (accessed 7 June 2009).
58 Office of Gender Affairs, 'Terms of Reference: Conference on Gender Equality Mechanisms', 2004, p. 1. Available at www.officeofgenderaffairs.unmikonline.org/english/documents/inaction/ToRper cent20-%20Gender%20Equality%20Mechanisms%20Conference.pdf (accessed 20 November 2009).
59 Ibid.
60 M. Pezzotti, 'UNMIK Office of Gender Affairs Places Gender Concerns at the Top of the Peacekeeping Political Agenda in Kosovo'. Available at www.peacewomen.org/resources/Peacekeeping/UNMIKOGAOct04analysis.pdf (accessed 30 October 2009).
61 Ibid.
62 Alice, op. cit., 2007a, p. 2.
63 Ibid., p. 3.
64 Women's Peace Coalition, *Through Women's Solidarity to a Just Peace*. A Report based on the Women's Peace Coalition Second Annual Conference, Macedonia, 2007, p. 1. Available at www.womensnetwork.org/images/pdf/Womens%20Peace%20Coalition%20Report.pdf.
65 The Women's Peace Coalition was founded in March 2006 as an independent citizen's initiative based on women's solidarity. Initial advocacy efforts focused on monitoring the negotiations on Kosovo's final status.
66 Women's Peace Coalition, op. cit., 2007, p. 1.

67 L. Alice, 'Monitoring Implementation of United Nations Security Council Resolution 1325 in Kosovo', Pristina: Kosovo Women's Network, 2007b. Available at www.womensnetwork.org/images/pdf/KWN%20Report%201325.pdf (accessed 12 April 2010).

68 Global Fund for Women, 'Balkan Women Build Bridges for Peace', 2007. Available at www.globalfundforwomen.org/cms/blog-archive/blog-archive/balkan-women-build-bridges-for-peace.html.

69 Part of the NATO-led peace and support mission, KFOR entered Kosovo on 12 June 1999 after the adoption of UNSCR 1244. Today 10,000 troops, provided by 31 countries remain. Following the 2008 Declaration of Independence, the Alliance reaffirmed the continued presence of KFOR in Kosovo on the basis of the original mandate as stipulated in Resolution 1244. For further reading please see the North Atlantic Treaty Organisation website. Available at www.nato.int/cps/en/natolive/topics_48818.htm.

70 Alice, op. cit., 2007b, p. 32.

71 G. La Cave *et al.*, 'Conflict and Change in Kosovo: Impact on Institutions and Society', World Bank, Environmental and Socially Sustainable Working Paper, 2001, no. 31, p. 32.

72 Alice, op. cit., 2007a, p. 10.

73 La Cave, op. cit., 2001, p. 32.

74 US Department of State *2005 Trafficking in Persons Report*, www.state.gov/g/tip/rls/tiprpt/2005/46616.htm.

75 Amnesty International, 'Kosovo/Kosova (Serbia and Montenegro) The March Violence: One Year On', 2005. Available at www.amnestyusa.org/document.php?id=802 56DD400782B8480256FC700462AC7&lang=e.

76 Alice, op. cit., 2007a, p. 11.

77 Ibid.

78 W. Kusuma, 'Kosovo Action Plan for the Achievement of Gender Equality', Prishtina: United Nations Development Fund for Women, 2003, p. 32.

79 Office of Gender Affairs, 'Terms of Reference: Conference on Gender Equality Mechanisms', Pristina. Available at www.officeofgenderaffairs.unmikonline.org/english/documents/inaction/ToR20-%20Gender%20Equality%20Mechanisms%20Conference.pdf.

80 Vuniqi, op. cit., p. 6.

4 UNSCR 1325 implementation in Liberia

Dilemmas and challenges

Emma Njoki Wamai

Introduction

The Liberian context presents a major opportunity to advance the objectives of United Nations Security Council Resolution (UNSCR) 1325 for two key reasons. First, the United Nations Mission in Liberia (UNMIL) was the first UN peacekeeping mission with an explicit mandate to mainstream UNSCR 1325. Second, women with the political will to mainstream the resolution were appointed and elected, namely the Special Representative of the UN Secretary-General (SRSG) Ellen Margrethe Løj from Denmark and Africa's first elected female President Ellen Johnson Sirleaf. This chapter will explore whether these factors have made any difference to the implementation of UNSCR 1325 in Liberia.

UNMIL was established on 1 October 2003 after the UN Security Council Resolution 1509 (2003) on 19 September 2003, which had four mandates. First, to support the implementation of the ceasefire by deploying 15,000 peacekeepers; second, to protect UN staff, property and civilians; third, to assist humanitarian and human rights efforts; and, finally, to support security sector reform through the implementation of the Disarmament, Demobilization, Rehabilitation and Reintegration (DDRR) process, including combatants with special needs such as children, women and non-Liberian combatants. To date, UNMIL has concluded the implementation of the ceasefire and the DDRR process and is now mainly involved in supporting the government and peacebuilding efforts, including mainstreaming UNSCR 1325.

UNSCR 1325 calls for implementation in several areas: increased participation of women in decision-making at all levels; protection of women and girls from gender-based violence (GBV) during and after the conflict; and increased efforts to support women's role in conflict prevention, especially through local women's peacebuilding initiatives. Nevertheless it is evident that women have been largely ignored despite their roles in both contributing to and resisting conflict, due to security decisions associated with masculinity.[1] Further, throughout the various stages of peacemaking, peacekeeping and peacebuilding, local women's perspectives are largely ignored. As a result, women's views and aspirations in a new post-conflict environment are rarely heard, leading to an unsustainable agreement and more often than not a resumption of violence.[2]

Additionally, the failure to consult with local women's organizations after the establishment of a peacekeeping mission has far-reaching implications for the successful implementation of the peace agreement and transition to the peace-building phase.

In Liberia, where local women's organizations were not consulted in implementation of the DDRR programme, female ex-combatants who had not been disarmed and demobilized effectively sold their arms to male ex-combatants for a fee.[3] During the DDRR process over 101,000 former combatants were disarmed including 22,000 women and 11,000 children.[4] The Liberian case study has important lessons to teach us in ensuring that local women's gender perspectives inform the peacebuilding agenda such as in implementation of the DDRR programmes.

UNMIL failed to capitalize on local women's knowledge and experiences in implementing UNSCR 1325 in peacebuilding programmes such as DDRR in Liberia. This chapter examines the dilemmas and challenges that UNMIL faced in implementing UNSCR 1325 and the lessons that have been learnt. The chapter begins with a background to the Liberian conflict followed by a contextual analysis of gender and security in Liberia and the role of local women's organizations before the conflict in Liberia. It then explores the factors that could have influenced UNMIL's failure to capitalize on local women's perspectives. Finally, it draws lessons from UNMIL's experience and engagement in the Liberian context and assesses the extent to which UNMIL has made a difference through the advancement of UNSCR 1325.

Background to the Liberian conflict

The Liberian civil war lasted more than 14 years and came to an end after the seventeenth peace agreement signed in Accra in August 2003.[5] The eventual collapse of the Liberian state in the 1990s was the result of a long history of exclusion and poor governance by the Liberian elite. About ten rebel factions fought in the civil war in which 250,000 Liberians were killed and over 1 million went to exile.[6] A number of factors were identified as the main causes of this conflict by various commentators on Liberia.[7] They include exclusion of non-Americo-Liberians from socioeconomic opportunities, corruption, impunity and systematic human rights abuses by the Americo-Liberian ruling elite. This impunity and corruption further weakened the judicial institutions leaving Liberians with no formal conflict resolution mechanisms leading to lack of faith in the rule of law and reliance on vigilantes and violence. Mismanagement of the country's natural resource wealth including timber, gold, diamonds and rubber to benefit a few individuals further exacerbated the situation leading to the civil conflict from 1989 to 2003.

The civil war which began in December 1989 and ended in 2003 saw the intervention of several peacekeeping missions[8] beginning with the Economic Community Ceasefire Monitoring Group (ECOMOG; 1990–1998) under the auspices of the Economic Community of West African States (ECOWAS).

The other was the United Nations Observer Mission in Liberia (UNOMIL; 1993–1997) to provide support to ECOMOG and the Liberia National Transitional Government. The ECOWAS Mission in Liberia (ECOMIL; 2003) was deployed in mid-2003 after hostilities escalated in Liberia when the country degenerated into total mayhem. It had a mandate to institute a ceasefire and restore a semblance of security in the country until the Accra peace talks were concluded. The first two missions did not have the explicit mandate to implement UNSCR 1325 primarily because the resolution had not yet been adopted. UNMIL was established in 2003 and continues to operate in Liberia and, unlike ECOMIL, it was given an explicit mandate to implement UNSCR 1325.

Gender and security in Liberia

In a post-conflict transition, gender analysis demands that all the activities are analyzed critically to ensure perspectives of men and women inform the reconstruction process. The five strategic components of these transitions include security, governance, socioeconomic development, justice and reconciliation and resource mobilization and coordination. Gender analysis further demands attention to class, division of labour in the private and public spheres, access to and control over basic and strategic resources such as income, education, information, wealth and decision-making. It can also incorporate consideration of rural-urban divides and linkages as well as inter-generational hierarchies.

Looking at the place of Liberian women before the conflict, it is clear that they bore the brunt of a failing state that was characterized by exclusion, corruption, impunity and systemic human rights violations.[9] While recognizing that Liberian women are not homogenous and their position varies according to region, ethnic group and religion, it is important to note that the civil war had a profound impact on all women.[10] Conflict in Liberia increased the vulnerability of women and girls to sexual violence and HIV/AIDS, as noted by the Truth and Reconciliation Commission (TRC) among others.[11] After the civil war, higher prevalence rates of HIV/AIDS for women were reported compared to men.[12] Security in Liberia as in many African countries was perceived as the responsibility of men due to the customs and gender roles assigned to males and females.[13] These perceptions barred the various peacekeeping missions from engaging in formal consultation with local women's organizations. For example, during the Comprehensive Peace Agreement (CPA) in Accra in 2003, only 17 per cent of women were present as witnesses[14] compared to the men who participated actively as track one mediators, negotiators and advisors to the peace process. Additionally, women were not adequately demobilized, despite a gender perspective in DDR being called for in UNSCR 1325. This resulted in a further marginalization of women from the process.[15]

The results of the DDRR mid-term evaluation report of 2006 show that the process failed to acknowledge the role of Liberian women as combatants and non-combatants during the conflict. As a result, the structures failed to disarm, demobilize or reintegrate them effectively. To highlight this, the report cites the

United Nation's Children Fund's (UNICEF) DDRR process for child combatants as a success story compared to the experience of women combatants for two reasons. First, women lacked a comprehensive programme to address their specific needs and hence they were treated in much the same way as adult men, except for the fact that they were accommodated in separate cantonments. Second, there was no institution dedicated to addressing women's needs during the different phases of the DDRR programme. It is notable that the United Nations Population Fund (UNFPA) took leadership for the DD phase by forming a network of gender advisors from other institutions but the same network was non-existent during the reintegration phase, consequently losing on earlier gains made.[16]

However, with increased realization of the need for gender perspectives to the DDRR process, the participation of women increased. The excerpt from the mid-term evaluation report below shows how women's participation progressively increased in phase III of the DDRR process largely due to increased advocacy from UNPFA and UNMIL.

> During the first phase only 424 women disarmed and 1,404 children as compared to 11,296 adult men were disarmed. Percentage wise women represented only 3 per cent of 13,125 people disarmed, and children 11 per cent. In phase II with a total of 51,469 disarmed, the percentage of women rose to 21 per cent (with 5,310 children still representing around 10 per cent), and in phase III of a total of 38,425 women represented 29 per cent of the total number of people disarmed. From virtual exclusion in the first phase the number of women exploded to 29 per cent in the final phase, showing the inconsistencies of the screening process and the understanding of the eligibility criteria for women.[17]

Before UNMIL was established in 2003, a number of local women's organizations were already involved in peacebuilding activities that UNMIL could have benefited from. For instance, the Concerned Christian Community (CCC) was a grassroots church-related organization that operated in the south-western part of the country (Bomi County and the then lower Lofa County now called Gbarpolu County) by providing shelter and security for young women who had been sexually abused by rebels. By so doing, this organization addressed the protection component of UNSCR 1325 and UNMIL could have benefited from working with it given its role in the church and the access it had in the south-western part of the country. Another example is the Liberia Women Initiative (LWI) that was established in 1994. LWI sought to end the conflict by mobilizing women to popularize the disarmament of combatants by ECOMOG in 1996–1997, and later by mobilizing women to participate and vote for Ellen Johnson Sirleaf as the first female president of Liberia.[18] It is regrettable that the reintegration process did not harness local women's initiatives in the DDRR process more effectively. Successful reintegration is based on the community's acceptance of individuals, and this acceptance did not come easily for women combatants and other women involved in the war as, cooks and 'bush wives', who were often viewed as a source of dishonor to a community.[19]

Initially, UNMIL largely focused on mainstreaming UNSCR 1325 through partner agencies such as UNICEF and UNFPA among others. There was minimal focus on capacity building of local women's organizations to 'own' UNSCR 1325 or to adapt its implementation according to grassroots women's movements' perspective of peacebuilding. Hence, local women's organizations were left to continue with the activities they had been engaging in prior to the conflict, often with inadequate capacity to engage the DDRR process for sustainable peacebuilding and ownership of UNSCR 1325. These activities included, for example, HIV/AIDS projects, Girl Child Education and other forms of protection.[20]

Other women's organizations which were actively implementing UNSCR 1325 at a national and regional level before the establishment of UNMIL were the Mano River Women's Peace Network (MARWOPNET), the Women in Peacebuilding Network (WIPNET) which is a project of WANEP (West African Network for Peace) and the Association of Female Lawyers in Liberia (AFELL). Unlike the local women's organizations mentioned earlier, UNMIL partnered with these regional organizations albeit in an ad hoc manner in implementation of UNSCR 1325. The activities of these organizations are described briefly below.

MARWOPNET is a network of women's organizations from Guinea, Liberia and Sierra Leone (the Mano River countries) that was established in 2000 to ensure women's participation in peacebuilding efforts at the community, national and regional level. One of MARWOPNET's outstanding contributions was successfully bringing the Heads of State of the Mano River Union Basin (Lansanah Conté of Guinea, Charles Taylor of Liberia and Ahmed Tejan Kabbah of Sierra Leone) to the negotiating table in 2002 to discuss the security situation in the region, a feat that even the UN had not been able to accomplish. Second, in 2003 MARWOPNET participated as a witness in the Liberian peace talks in Accra between the government of President Charles Taylor and the rebel group, Liberians United for Reconciliation and Democracy (LURD). The organization was also a signatory to the Accra Peace Accords of 23 August 2003 that put into place the interim presidency of Charles Gyude Bryant thereby officially ending the 14-year Liberia civil war.

WIPNET was formed in 2002 as a project of WANEP to implement UNSCR 1325 for example through increasing women's participation in political decision-making and in security sector reform (SSR). So far, WIPNET has been involved in raising awareness at home and abroad about UNSCR 1325 and training women on the resolution. AFELL was established in the early 1990s to advocate for the protection and the advancement of the rights of women and children. AFELL was successful in mainstreaming legal protection of women from GBV in UNSCR 1325. However, despite the role played by women advocates[21] and the women's organizations, gross human rights violations against women such as rape continued unabated from 2003 to 2005.[22] This could be attributed to the fact that most of the organizations lacked capacity to ensure enforcement of protection laws for women's rights violations by security institutions and the lack of relevant domestic laws to prevent violations.

Challenges and dilemmas faced by UNMIL in mainstreaming UNSCR 1325

Despite the achievements UNMIL has made in working with formal regional women's organizations in implementing UNSCR 1325, it has been faced with challenges and dilemmas which have prevented it from effectively driving the change at the local level. The dilemmas it has faced can be grouped into coherence, duration, footprint dilemmas and accountability challenges.

Coherence dilemmas

First, UNMIL has been faced with two kinds of coherence dilemmas,[23] namely organizational coherence and normative coherence. According to Sisk, organizational dilemmas involve coordination challenges among many actors and normative dilemmas arise from inconsistencies in values and interpretation of norms such as UNSCR 1325. UNMIL has encountered both dilemmas in working with other UN Agencies and this has sometimes led to duplication of efforts and decreased impact. A case in point is the implementation of the DDRR process where different agencies were involved in uncoordinated efforts leading to a lesser involvement of women non-combatants in the process as earlier discussed. As previously mentioned the United Nations Population Fund (UNFPA) took leadership for the disarmament and demobilization phase by forming a network of gender advisors from other institutions but the same network was non-existent during the reintegration since a different agency with different modus operandi took over the next phase. Similarly, no system-wide data collection method exists to monitor trends such as sexual violence and other indicators for UNSCR 1325. Evaluations of UNMIL have also reported that not all UN agencies working in Liberia have a uniform interpretation or understanding of the mandate of UNSCR 1325, preventing coherent implementation of it.[24]

Duration dilemmas

UNMIL is still faced with a duration dilemma. This kind of dilemma arises from the contradiction which calls for longer-term state-building from the international community at the same time as a short stay to ensure that governance institutions can grow independently of UNMIL. Furthermore, residents tend to grow increasingly disillusioned with a prolonged peacekeeping mission that brings no meaningful change to their lives. In September 2009, UNMIL's mandate came under review by the UN Security Council (SC) which decided to extend UNMIL's mandate until September 2010 under UNSCR 1885 (2009).[25] This Resolution took note of the outcomes of the TRC and the progress made by

UNMIL in reforming the security sector. The SC also noted progress made in mainstreaming UNSCR 1325 and 1820 such as the development of the Liberia National Action Plan for the implementation of these resolutions. The SC called on UNMIL to continue its peacebuilding role especially as Liberia approaches its next general election in October 2011.

Though the prolonged presence of UNMIL has had an impact in increasing awareness of UNSCR 1325 among formal partners such as national non-governmental organizations (NGO), assessment reports[26] show that informal women's networks are still yet to own UNSCR 1325. This dilemma continues to trouble UNMIL and the Liberian government. The main dilemma that arises is whether UNMIL should continue with this mandate or whether the Liberian government should take leadership on the implementation of UNSCR 1325. On the other hand, the government still lacks sufficient capacity to mainstream UNSCR 1325 although it recently set up a national secretariat with responsibility for mainstreaming it in an attempt to resolve this dilemma.[27]

Another duration and sequencing dilemma faced by UNMIL was in the DDRR process. Originally, there were plans to implement the Disarmament, Demobilization, Reintegration and Rehabilitation process in this sequence. Successful reintegration requires a larger budget and programming targets where ex-combatants, after being disarmed in the short-term, can be reintegrated in the long-term. In Liberia, UNMIL failed initially by utilizing criteria that were too lax for the ex-combatants resulting in the disarmament of 105,000 people, thrice the expected number.[28] This further reduced the funds earmarked for reintegration and created insecurity in the region as the youths who had been insufficiently reintegrated preferred to trade their services to the next conflict rather than wait for UN promises. Hence, UNMIL faced a dilemma of either taking less time to disarm more youths or to disarm a lesser strategic group that can influence others while following the different stages in a consequential way to peacebuilding. The different stages include 'buying' the peace in the short-term, creating conditions or reintegration and job creation in peacebuilding. The failure to address reintegration needs successfully had a negative impact on the implementation of UNSCR 1325 as fewer funds were further earmarked for gender mainstreaming. Furthermore, although the reintegration of female ex-combatants needed greater attention as a result of stigma from their communities, there were also fewer funds available to support them.[29]

Footprint dilemmas

Third, UNMIL has been faced by footprint dilemmas, which arise from contradictions around the extent to which UNMIL's presence should be felt in the country. This has a direct effect on the implementation of UNSCR 1325. An intrusive UNMIL could end up usurping the role of the state in mainstreaming UNSCR 1325 through its programmes yet a non-intrusive UNMIL could negate the gains made in mainstreaming UNSCR 1325 by assuming that the state lacks capacity. In analysing this footprint dilemma one might look at the impact of the state-building role of economic development by UNMIL through a programme known as the Governance and Economic Management Assistance Programme (GEMAP).

The Liberian government and UNMIL established GEMAP as an intrusive economic oversight programme. Some partners in government feared that this programme would reduce the sovereignty of the state and the donors feared that the lack of intrusive economic oversight, especially over revenue collection within the context of the shadow economy that existed in Liberia, would forestall any economic development. They established this programme as a precondition of their continued engagement with Liberia in 2004. This imposition by UNMIL on the state through GEMAP was ill-advised according to McGovern as it further weakened the same institutions that were meant to strengthen programmes such as the implementation of UNSCR 1325.[30]

McGovern further notes that GEMAP was a form of a technocratic fix model, which was faced with four main problems. First, the duration was too short for any meaningful change in the economic sector to take place. Second, the DDRR programme initially instilled unrealistic expectations in ex-combatants, resulting in frustration when they became unfulfilled given the limited resources and time that the UN had. Third, negotiated agreements legitimize the perpetrators of the violence by engaging them as the main negotiators thereby resulting in a situation in which legitimate actors, such as the local women civil society groups involved in mainstreaming UNSCR 1325, are ignored by the system. Fourth, the GEMAP system was vulnerable to capture by criminal elements through corruption due to lack of an accountability mechanism to citizens. This could potentially erode the gains made in UNSCR 1325 by reducing the funds intended for its implementation.

Challenges

In addition to the dilemmas outlined, UNMIL faced a number of challenges that could have contributed to the lack of ownership of UNSCR 1325 at local levels. The main challenges faced by UNMIL as a peace support operation have been cited elsewhere.[31] These challenges are related to planning, leadership, organizational complexity and interagency cooperation and exit strategies. Specific challenges faced in relation to ensuring ownership of UNSCR 1325 include accountability, planning, capacity and leadership challenges. This section will explain how these challenges, coupled with the above dilemmas, have continued to impede progress in implementing UNSCR 1325 at the local and informal level.

Accountability challenges

The main challenges faced by UNMIL in ensuring accountability for UNSCR 1325 have been due to the lack of a monitoring mechanism and an enforceable compliance mechanism for governments including Liberia and other actors involved in the conflict. Equally, lack of a comprehensive impact analysis for policy frameworks and programmes related to UNSCR 1325 has made it difficult for UNMIL to be held accountable for the lack of progress.[32] This has slowed the process of ensuring local women's organizations, ownership of the resolution although there is political will from President Ellen Johnson Sirleaf. The adoption of UNSCR 1888 and 1889 in September 2009, which call for increased accountability for sexual violence and women's participation respectively, might go a long way in increasing accountability by member states.

Planning challenges

Successful planning for a UN mission is important for effective implementation for three key reasons.[33] These are to enable the UN mission to take into account unpredictability; second, to enable the mission to ensure there is room for adjustment; and, finally, to ensure planners have a deep knowledge of the actors and dynamics at national and local levels. The latter is one of the planning failures encountered by UNMIL in its attempt to mainstream UNSCR 1325. It has been argued that UNMIL failed to recognize and support the work being carried out by local women's initiatives prior to its arrival, resulting in a failure to capitalize on local women's agency in implementing the resolution. This point can be further demonstrated by the DDRR programme which almost collapsed due to lack of ownership.

> The first hard lesson learned was the 2003 November disarmament process of ex-combatants when UNMIL failed to engage the input of local peace advocates (primarily women groups and faith-based entities) that had been in the vanguard of the Liberia peace process who worked at the national, community and grassroot levels and therefore understood the culture not only of the ex-combatants but the tradition of the land. UNMIL had also not heeded the caution of the other organizations of UN and international non-governmental organizations and apparently not studied former DDR carried out by ECOMOG. To arrest a situation that was fast getting out of control, women groups and organizations, civil society groups and other local organizations had to marshal their own resources falling back on their networks used in consolidating peace and resolving conflict to lobby and persuade these former fighters to respond to the disarmament process.[34]

Additionally, Lamptey argues that UNMIL failed to capitalize on the expertise of Liberian women and other faith-based organizations that had been instrumental in advocating for peace and conflict resolution.[35] These networks had invested much effort in disseminating the Comprehensive Peace Agreement (CPA) to populations across the country, and facilitating discussions with communities around the contents of the CPA. This was an important contribution towards laying the groundwork for the work of the peacekeeping mission.

The second planning challenge that UNMIL failed to appreciate was the socioeconomic dynamics of planning a programe such as the Agricultural and Rural Resettlement Programme.[36] This programme encouraged ex-combatants to return to rural areas and practice agriculture for food security as a development and peacebuilding initiative.

In the Agricultural Programme, ex-combatants were advised to return to the rural areas to take up farming to create employment and improve food security. This caused a number of challenges since land is often owned by the older original settlers who rarely transfer ownership unless to their relatives.[37] As a result, young men and women in search of land are forced to work for the landowners for a long time to pay debts or earn cultivation rights. This dynamic is especially challenging to young men who need access to land to be able to marry in the rural areas, and it is further complicated by ethnicity since most land that is for cultivation is owned by the northerners who claim the Mandingo southerners to be outsiders. In terms of advancing UNSCR 1325, this agricultural project failed to understand the cultural dynamics surrounding land. As a result it did not plan accordingly for potential obstacles by instituting land policies guaranteeing equal opportunities for land ownership for young men and young women as a peace-building strategy through which it would have been possible to strengthen implementation of UNSCR 1325.

Capacity challenges

Like other peace support operations, UNMIL is overstretched and under-resourced, problems that could be greatly alleviated by integrating local capacities. A case in point is the role of AFELL, which has capacity at national level on legal protection. UNMIL could have benefited greatly from working with a local women's organization such as this to overcome human and logistical resource constraints. AFELL worked on legal protection for children and women, and advanced UNSCR 1325 by lobbying the government and legislature to introduce laws that prosecute rape cases. In 2005, it operated a legal clinic for victims of sexual and gender-based violence thereby advancing the protection component of UNSCR 1325.

However, despite the role played by the Association of Women Lawyers and other organizations, gross human rights violations against women such as rape have continued unabated to date.[38] This could be attributed to the fact that most of the organizations lacked capacity to ensure enforcement of protection laws for women's rights violations by security institutions and lack of relevant domestic laws to prevent violations. Also, women are now violated in the private space by people known to them such as male relatives and teachers.[39]

UNMIL has since realized the importance of local capacity and is now working more with AFELL in advancing laws that ensure protection of women such as the rape bill and gender-sensitive police reforms which have seen the deployment of the first female police force from India to patrol Monrovia and the outskirts and train women police in Liberia. A female head of police has also been appointed to head the Liberian Police Service. UNMIL also supported the Ministry of Gender and Development in mainstreaming gender in policies such as the poverty reduction strategy papers, gender budgeting, development of UNSCR 1325 Action Plan, sensitization of UNSCR 1820 and capacity-building of gender focal points on gender sensitivity.[40] In 2009, UNMIL supported the Ministry of Gender in organizing a Global Women's Colloquium on Peace and Security which developed concrete action plans for implementing UNSCR 1820.

Lessons learned from Liberia

Despite the challenges, several lessons can be learned from the Liberian case study that are relevant to making UNSCR 1325 work for women. One lesson learned is the need to build on the knowledge and experience of local actors when mainstreaming UNSCR 1325. We have learned that international organizations rarely recognize and build on local expertise and capacity. Furthermore, due to the prevailing post-conflict suspicion and need to avoid affiliation to the warring factions causing the conflict, international organizations may choose to ignore them altogether to the detriment of advancing UNSCR 1325. Striking a balance between these participation dilemmas is important.

Second, since no clear guidelines have been established for direct partnership-building between the peacekeeping missions and local organizations in mainstreaming UNSCR 1325 there is a need for effective leadership to drive the resolution. In the case of UNMIL, the Office of the Gender Advisor (OGA) undertook many initiatives and collaborated with local women's networks. Due to this drive by the OGA for the implementation of the resolution, gender issues and programmes related to UNSCR 1325 are being implemented by many organizations outside the peacekeeping mission, but the impact is yet to be felt in the rural areas and within informal women's networks at the local level.[41]

Third, the involvement of men in the implementation of UNSCR 1325 is crucial in reversing gender stereotypes and challenging flawed masculinities.[42] Research has shown that men are effective change agents, particularly against GBV, by speaking to other men and by transforming the paradigm of masculinity which allows for resolution of conflict through violence.[43] Further, sexual violence in Liberia is on the increase as a result of tacit acceptance of roles of men and women by society and it is important to combat this.[44] In 2009, during the 16 Days of Activism, the Ministry of Gender in Liberia popularized the role of men in ending violence using the theme 'Men as Agents of Change in Ending Violence Against Women' after realizing the agency that men possess in reversing the trend in sexual violence. AFELL is also pioneering the use of men in the implementation of UNSCR 1325, especially as it relates to GBV, and progress is notable though no meaningful evaluations have yet been done. UNFPA recognizes that ending GBV will mean changing cultural concepts about masculinity, and that the process must actively engage men, whether they be policy-makers, parents, spouses or young boys.[45]

Fourth, coordination of efforts is important to increase impact and avoid duplication among UN agencies and among local NGOs and local women's groups. UNIFEM should take leadership among the UN agencies and local organizations and could act as a coordination point. As in many post-conflict countries, there is a proliferation of NGOs as well as increased donor funding for peacebuilding. Without a clear action plan or roadmap for UNSCR 1325, there is a risk of ignoring or duplicating of some activities while implementing donor-driven programmes that have little or no impact on the lives of women and girls affected by the conflict, especially in the rural areas. The formation of a national secretariat to coordinate UNSCR 1325 by the Liberian government is laudable and efforts should be made to ensure local women's engagement and ownership. To achieve this in rural areas multi-sectoral committees on implementing the resolution should be formed in a partnership with local groups that have concrete monitoring mechanisms for the same.

Finally, there is some merit in advance planning prior to the arrival of a peace mission. A gender-sensitive needs assessment of potential partners at the national and local levels could be carried out early on to determine how to engage with them and what capacity-building structures are needed. Such a needs assessment for Liberia was conducted in 2003 to give a broad overview of the country with the view to secure donor funding. However, this needs assessment did not take into consideration potential partners to work with UNMIL and it lacked gender-sensitive indicators to assess the existing capacity for women's rights work. For instance, prior to UNMIL's establishment the New Africa Research Development Agency (NARDA) served as the umbrella organization for local and national organizations on children and women's research. UNMIL unfortunately did not tap into this reservoir which could have facilitated its work with the DDRR programme, among other programmes which were not as effective, as discussed earlier.

Conclusion

Did UNMIL and UNSCR 1325 make a difference in driving change nationally and regionally? Based on the foregoing discussion it can be concluded that UNMIL did use UNSCR 1325 as a tool with some impact. This is evident especially in the formal women's networks which are largely involved in technical processes such as designing and implementing the National Action Plan for UNSCR 1325. However, this change is yet to be seen in informal and rural women's networks which are largely underrepresented in technical meetings and other spaces. Efforts need to be focused on building bridges with these informal networks where most women are represented. The chapter also noted that prior to the establishment of UNMIL and UNSCR 1325 local women's organizations and peace networks were already implementing UNSCR 1325-related activities especially relating to the participation and protection components. UNMIL therefore missed an opportunity to capitalize on this local experience by failing to partner with them, particularly in relation to implementing the DDRR programme.

More importantly, the newly launched Liberian National Action Plan and National Secretariat for implementing UNSCR 1325 should increase momentum, especially among rural women's organizations and other local and informal women's organizations. The formal women's movement should continue pressuring the Security Council to institute stricter accountability mechanisms for UNSCR 1325 1820, 1888 and 1889 which should include: increased financial resources; monitoring and reporting mechanisms; answerability mechanisms for exposing perpetrators; and a compliance mechanism. Finally, the recommendations of the TRC in Liberia (2009) on gender should be implemented to change the current order while transforming the Liberian society to equality and prosperity.

Notes

1 E. Uchendu (ed.), *Masculinities in Contemporary Africa.* Dakar: CODESRIA, 2009, pp. 4–23.
2 A. Potter, 'Civil Society and Peace Negotiations; Why, Whether and How They Could be Involved'. Geneva: Centre for Humanitarian Dialogue Briefing Paper. 2006.
3 Amnesty International, *Casualties of War; Women's Bodies, Women's Lives.* London: Amnesty International Publishers, 2004, pp. 23–32.
4 UNMIL, UN FOCUS, 'At Work Together'. Monrovia: UNMIL, 2009, p. 13. Available at http://unmil.org/documents/focus/unmilfocus212009.pdf (accessed 5 January 2010).
5 See Comprehensive Peace Agreement. Available at www.iansa.org/Liberia_Comprehensive_Peace_Agreement.doc.
6 Government of Liberia, Truth and Reconciliation Commission (TRC) Report. Monrovia: Government Publishers, 2009, pp. 352–355. Available at www.trcofliberia.org/.
7 C. Call with V. Wyeth (eds), *Building States to Build Peace.* New York: International Peace Institute, 2008, pp. 337–361.
8 A. Alao, J. Mackinlay and 'F. Olonisakin (eds), *Peacekeepers, Politicians and Warlords: The Liberian Peace Process.* New York: United Nations University Press, 1999, pp. 10–17.
9 E. Cousens, S.J. Stedman and D. Rothchild (eds), *Ending Civil Wars. The Implementation of Peace Agreements.* New York: International Peace Institute, 2002, pp. 599–620.
10 See the December 2008 Report from the Gender Adviser to the UN SG on Progress Made in Mainstreaming SCR 1325 and Gender Issues in The Truth Reconciliation Commission Report at www.unmil.org.
11 See the TRC Report at www.trcofliberia.org.
12 A. Babtunde, *Towards More Informed Responses to Gender Violence and HIV/AIDS in Post-Conflict West African Setting.* Uppsala: Nordic Institute Research Papers, 2010, p. 4.
13 See United Nations Human Security Project. New York. www.humansecurityreport.info/index.php?option=content&task=view&id=24&Itemid=59.
14 A. Goetz, 'Women's Participation in Peace Negotiations: Connections Between Presence and Influence', a UNIFEM Briefing Paper, New York, 2009, p. 3.
15 Subur Consulting, External Mid-Term Evaluation of the DDRR Process in Liberia by Subur Consulting for UNDP, 2006. Available at http://erc.undp.org/evaluationadmin/downloaddocument.html?docid=1373.
16 Ibid.
17 E. Kandakai, 'An Assessment of the Status of the Implementation of the UN Security Council Resolution 1325 in Liberia: A Case Study commissioned by the Ministry of Gender and Development', Liberia, 2006.

18 UNIFEM Report, 'Who Answers to Women? Gender and Accountability'. New York, 2009, pp. 98–99.
19 Amnesty International, op. cit., pp. 23–32.
20 Kandakai, op. cit.
21 There have also been outstanding women advocates who have been pace setters for peacebuilding such as Madam Mary Brownell (the founder of the Liberia Women Initiative), Theresa Leigh Sherman (one of the founding members of the Mano River Women's Peace Network), Madam Ruth Perry (the former Head of State of the Liberia Transitional Government, 1996–1997), Chief Garmolu Walker, the first woman Paramount Chief for Bong County (a strong advocate for children and advancement of women, and community development), Counselor Elizabeth Boyenneh Nelson (President of the Association of Female Lawyers of Liberia, one of the forerunners for the passing of the "rape bill") and Dr. Esther Guluma of UNICEF-Liberia who was very instrumental in putting in place the Abused Women and Girls Centre (AWAG).
22 Subur, op. cit.
23 R. Paris and T.D. Sisk, *Managing Contradictions; The Inherent Dilemmas of Post War State Building*. International Peace Institute Briefing Papers, New York, 2007, pp. 4–7.
24 Kandakai, op. cit.
25 See www.peacewomen.org/resources/Peacekeeping/PDF/Pretoria07.pdf.
26 Ibid.
27 UNMIL, UN FOCUS, op. cit.
28 Call and Wyeth, op. cit., pp. 337–361.
29 Ibid.
30 Ibid.
31 C. Clement and A. Smith (eds) *Managing Complexities in Peace Support Operations*, International Peace Institute Briefing Papers, New York, 2009, pp. 10–15.
32 UNMIL, Office of the Gender Advisor; Update on SCR 1325 and 1820 Report, 2009. Available at www.unmil.org.
33 Clement and Smith, op. cit., pp. 10–15.
34 Kandakai, op. cit.
35 C. Lamptey, *Strengthening Strategic Partnership between United Nations Peacekeeping Missions and Local Civil Society Organizations during Post Conflict Transitions*. New York: United Nations Department of Peace Keeping Operations, 2007. Available at www.un.org/en/peacekeeping/publications/yir/yir2009.pdf.
36 Call and Wyeth, op. cit., pp. 337–361.
37 Call and Wyeth, op. cit., pp. 337–361.
38 Subur, op. cit., pp. 15–40.
39 Babtunde, op. cit., pp. 11–20.
40 See http://unmil.org/documents/today/unmiltoday50.
41 UNMIL, UN FOCUS, op. cit.
42 Uchendu (ed.) op. cit., pp. 4–23.
43 See UNMIL, UN FOCUS, op. cit.
44 See http://unmil.org/documents/today/unmiltoday50.
45 See UNFPA http://unfpa.org/gender/violence.htm.

5 Nepal and the implementation of UNSCR 1325

Lesley Abdela

Introduction

An insurgency started in Nepal in 1996 when the Communist Party of Nepal-Maoists began taking control of the countryside in the Western Terai by force. Since 2006 the small Himalayan country of Nepal has emerged from armed conflict and traditional Kingship rule to an ongoing peace and democracy-building process. Core problems include rapid population growth, insufficient infrastructure, the weak capacities of public sector institutions, social exclusion by caste and ethnicity, and discrimination against women, which is entrenched by tradition and the caste system.[1] Earthquakes, floods and mud-slides are regular occurrences. Avian flu is a new and imminent threat.[2] Historic exclusion, a rich/poor divide and political infighting were contributing causes of armed conflict. Three out of ten of Nepal's population of around 27 million people (31 per cent) live on less than US$1 a day.[3] The poorest and hardest-hit conflict regions, such as the rural midwest,[4] have a poverty incidence 20 per cent higher than that of the valley in which the capital, Kathmandu, is situated.[5]

Nepal was formerly the world's only officially declared Hindu state.[6] Following the movement for democracy in early 2006 and the breaking of King Gyanendra's power, the Nepali Parliament amended the Constitution to make Nepal a secular republican state. Nepal's Constituent Assembly (CA) elections on 10 April 2008 marked a major step forward in the peace process, paving the way for the declaration of a federal democratic republic. The Communist Party of Nepal (Maoist), (CPN-M), emerged as the largest party, winning more than one-third of CA seats.

This chapter examines how UN Security Council Resolution (UNSCR) 1325 was implemented in Nepal's peace process. The peace process in Nepal began six years after UNSCR 1325 was adopted. The UN peace mission was deployed several years after other UN agencies had been implementing UNSCR 1325-related activities in the country. The chapter examines the interaction among UN agencies, the interaction between the UN and Nepali civil society and government, and the way in which these interactions contributed to the implementation of UNSCR 1325 in the country.

The gender context in Nepal

Box 1 Milestones for women's rights in Nepal

1999 – The Local Self Governance Act – introduces mandatory representation of women in local government.

1999 – Adoption of the National Plan of Action against Trafficking in Children and their Commercial Sexual Exploitation.

2000 – Adoption of the UN Security Council Resolution 1325.

2002 – National Women's Commission.

2003 – Violence against women addressed in CEDAW Shadow Report, Nepal.

2003 – Draft Bill on Criminalisation of Domestic Violence – not yet passed.

2004 – 11th Amendment to the Country Code Bill. *Allows women: alimony rights; property rights; abortion rights; adoption rights; punishment in rape cases; age at marriage repealed.*

2006 – Ministry of Women and Social Welfare develops a Draft Bill on Violence Against Women – not yet passed.

2006 – Gender Equality Bill passed to amend Acts to increase gender equality: *Provision of Citizenship Rights under mother's name; marital rape included within definition of rape and becomes ground for divorce for women; provision depriving mother of guardianship of child after divorce is removed, and mother to have first guardianship of child, if child is a minor; increase in imprisonment term for those involved in performing abortion by force, coercion or undue influence; daughter included within definition of family under the Act Relating to Land.*

2008 – 33 per cent women elected to the Constituent Assembly. Four women Government Ministers appointed.

In Nepal the phrase 'gender and social inclusion' has a special connotation. A kaleidoscope of factors impacts on the lives and roles of women, men, boys and girls. A complicated caste system intertwined with a complex intermingling of traditions, festivals, faiths and doctrines permeates every strata of society. Within the caste hierarchies there are strict codes of conduct; these include purdah and reproductive rituals, and have an impact on gender roles. Within each caste and ethnic group, women are ranked lowest, socially, politically and economically.

Janajatis, Dalits and Badis

Janajatis have their own language and traditional culture. They are not included in the conventional Hindu hierarchical caste structure. The Janajatis are for the most part indigenous people. Some 61 communities are recognized as Janajatis. They have mostly lived lives separate from the rest of the country in isolated mountainous terrain in the north of the country and in the (until the 1960s) malaria-infested forests in the south. Janajatis are spread over nearly all Nepal, constituting 35.6 per cent of the total population. The Janajatis who are the worst off financially are those living in the Terai and the mid-hill regions. The Nepalese Government established the National Committee for Development of Janajatis (NCDJ) in 1997 to coordinate state programmes for improving the living conditions of indigenous people. NCDJ activities were mainly limited to distribution of funds to various Janajati organizations. Since 1990 there has been a substantial growth in the number of Janajati organizations officially registered with the Nepalese Government. These organizations formed the Nepal Federation of Indigenous Nationalities (NEFIN).

The Janajatis are more organized and visible than the Dalits. The Dalits face similar issues regardless of where they live, while the Janajatis comprise different groups of people at various stages of development, living in varying degrees of isolation and with a variety of agendas. This makes it difficult for the Janajati community to agree on a common set of goals. The Government has made various declarations about improving the lives of the Janajatis, and carried out various programmes, but significant results have yet to be seen.[7] The Dalit castes are at the lowest end of the social and economic scale and the Badis are at the lowest end of the Dalit hierarchy. Caste can define a person's profession over a number of generations. For example, the socially accepted profession for female Badis is prostitution, and this passed down from generation to generation.[8]

The Muluki Ain (1854) first formalized the caste system in law and also reproduced the patriarchal view of women as subordinate to men and economically dependent on them. A new provision prohibiting discrimination on the basis of caste and ethnicity was inserted into the new Country Code, but there was some ambiguity with regard to protecting 'traditional practices'.[9] Despite being a party to 16 international human rights instruments, including the Convention on the Elimination of All Forms of Discrimination Against Women (CEDAW), Nepal still has at least 118 discriminatory legal provisions spread across 54 different laws in the areas of citizenship, property, education, employment, health, sexual offences, marriage and family relations, court proceedings and identity. This is compounded by the fact that law enforcement agencies lack gender sensitivity.[10] Even when laws emphasize equal rights in the inheritance of land and property, in practice these are seldom invoked. Legal and judicial systems, as well as law enforcement mechanisms, have failed to address the high incidence of violence against women in both private and public domains.[11] Legislation protecting the physical integrity of Nepali women exists in theory, but women's rights are poorly enforced.[12] Although persons accused of murder and attempted murder may be brought to trial, physical assault is not considered a crime for which the state can be a prosecuting party. In physical assault cases, the female victim must bring a private suit through a hired attorney; this prevents the police from filing or investigating many forms of domestic violence.[13]

Nepali women's roles in the conflict

Women played a variety of roles in Nepal's conflict, and these impacted their lives in various ways. One result of the conflict was an increase in women's visibility. Women began to take on leadership roles in villages and across civil society in grassroots peacebuilding, human rights and disarmament movements. Women single-handedly led households and risked their lives negotiating with armed combatants for survival. These combatants ranged from government security forces to Maoists. Women at both communal and national levels undertook healthcare work and cared for survivors of violence, while women's NGOs provided shelter for women and children affected by the conflict. In the course of the conflict women entered the public sphere, confronted the security forces, dealt with the court system (to protect husbands and sons who had disappeared) and managed homes single-handedly, while the male members of the family fled from homes and cities. Many women crossed borders with their communities and worked in refugee camps to trace the missing and alleviate the physical and psychological effects of the violence. Women's organizations encouraged and built on the skills and confidence women acquired through becoming active in the public sphere during the period of armed conflict.

During the conflict many women and girls were subjected to abduction, displacement, trafficking, torture, rape and other forms of sexual violence perpetrated by all sides in the conflict. An analysis from NGO SAATHI indicated that 93 per cent of women were exposed to mental and emotional torture, 82 per cent were beaten, 30 per cent were raped and 28 per cent were forced into prostitution.[14] Women were deprived of healthcare, education, and health, marriage and reproductive rights. Girls were married off at increasingly younger ages for fear that rape would ruin their marriage prospects. Women living in the insurgency areas had combatants living with them, and this put pressure on their food and other resources. They were also at higher risk of violence resulting from trauma and other problems experienced by returning combatants; they also risked injury from weapons kept in their homes. In the vicinity of the Nepal Army barracks there were forced marriages with young girls aged 13–15. Many were second wives who found themselves abandoned as single mothers with no support.[15] Women and girls were also trafficked out of conflict-ridden areas to become sexual and domestic slaves in other parts of Nepal and India, exposing them to brutality and HIV/AIDS.[16] Women's household and farm-related work burdens increased dramatically because male members had left the villages. Women also took on tasks that were formerly taboo for women, such as ploughing fields.

Out of nearly 900,000 troops in the Royal Nepal Army there were only about 1,070 women, around 1.2 per cent of the total.[17] Around 40 per cent (the exact percentages are not known) of the armed wing of the CPN-M, the People's Liberation Army (PLA) were female, many of them Dalits. As part of the peace process the PLA agreed to remain in cantonments. The United Nations Mission in Nepal (UNMIN) registered personnel in the cantonments and recorded that, of the total of 19,602, 3,846 were women and 15,756 men.[18] The Nepalese media reported that, in addition to the deprivation suffered by their male colleagues, women had reproductive health concerns, and suffered from infections and a lack of basic sanitary supplies; as a result, many left the cantonments and subsequently missed Phase 1 of UNMIN registration.[19]

In Maoist strongholds the Maoists abducted or recruited as volunteers one young male or female from each family.[20] There appear to be a variety of reasons which explain why women volunteered to join the Maoist Cadres. Some women were motivated to join up because of their extremely harsh, feudal living conditions in remote areas of Nepal. The Maoists also attracted female volunteers by leading campaigns to improve women's lives. They campaigned for a 'dry law' in rural areas of Nepal in order to reduce the incidence of alcoholism among men. In the parallel justice systems established by the Maoists, men accused of abusing their wives were punished more quickly than they would have been in the ordinary Nepali courts. For some women this was the first time they had been able to access justice, thereby reducing the levels of violence within families.[21] Women had multiple roles as fighters, supporters (medics, porters, communications staff, etc), and as dependents (wives, children). The Maoist leader Hisila Yami 'Parvati' said that women were much more effective in mobilizing the masses because they facilitated the Maoists' access to other members of the family.[22] Minors were utilized by both sides in a variety of support roles as well as in paramilitary activities.[23]

The majority of Maoist female combatants were aged between 14 and 18. This age range of female recruitment was due to the Maoists' need to have a network of households available to provide supplies during the conflict; older women were not recruited so that they could maintain their households. This practice would indicate the persistence of sexist structures in the division of labour among the Maoists. However, Maoist leaders emphasized the issue of gender equality, and women's emancipation, as well as the class struggle, was central to the Maoist discourse and to their political agenda. However, they also said women's liberation would only be possible after class liberation. Equality between men and women was not achieved in the Maoist leadership structures.[24]

One positive effect of the Maoist insurgency is that marginalized groups developed a greater awareness of their rights, as well as the ability to stand up and demand equality. The girls and women who joined the Maoists wore combat dress, discarded all jewellery and cropped their hair short. They adopted liberation vocabulary and many developed a new-found confidence. Ordinary village women began to rethink traditional values concerning women. By joining the Maoists women and girls were subverting traditional Hindu symbols and ideas relating to the subordination of women; for example, they rejected the tradition that some people were 'untouchable'.[25] The strong presence of women in the Maoist ranks and the demands of women activists and women's organizations combined to give greater impetus to the call for political parties to allow greater participation by women in Nepali politics.[26]

It would not be accurate to attribute the promotion of a gender agenda only to the Maoists. Work done by women's groups in the past few decades, and particularly after the UN Fourth World Women's Conference in Beijing in 1995, laid the foundations for social transformation with regard to gender equality.[27] The conflict also had a negative impact on the health of women and girls. This was due to a number of factors, including inequitable food distribution, exposure to HIV/AIDS and limited access to health services (health posts became regular targets of destruction). Mothers who gave birth to children whose fathers were displaced, missing or dead were unable to confer citizenship on their offspring, thereby creating a generation of 'stateless children'. Discriminatory property inheritance also increased women's vulnerability. The failure of the law to protect them often resulted in women being driven from their homes, especially in cases where the husband had been killed.[28] An estimated 17 per cent of widows in Nepal are conflict widows, and most of these are between 20 and 30 years of age.[29]

Women's peacebuilding initiatives before the arrival of UNMIN

In the case of Nepal it is difficult to distinguish between progress resulting from action by local NGOs and progress resulting from interaction between civil society in Nepal and international donors,[30] international NGOs (INGOs) and academic institutions.[31] For example, an initiative may be taken by Nepal's civil society or the Nepalese Government, but it may rely on funding and technical assistance from international donors. How much progress is a result of the ongoing work of INGOs, donors and UN humanitarian agencies, some of which have been active in Nepal for 50 years? Examples of initiatives deriving from UNSCR 1325 are given in this section, along with examples of initiatives by Nepali women.

During the conflict Nepali women organized peace rallies in Kathmandu and other parts of the country. In 2004, for example, middle-aged and elderly women from Khairenitar and Dulegouda (irrespective of their religious affiliation) jointly organized a rally to exert pressure on the government and the Maoists to resume peace talks. In 2005 the United Nations Development Fund for Women (UNIFEM) held a meeting with women from 57 districts (out of Nepal's 75 districts). The women produced a ten-point declaration, which contributed to the peace process.[32]

Although women had organized protest rallies and processions demanding an end to the armed conflict, Nepalese government officials and Maoist rebel leaders failed to include women in peace talks. There was no women's participation when the 25-point Code of Conduct was issued jointly by the Government and the Maoists in May 2005. The 12-point Understanding between the Maoists and the seven other political parties was signed in New Delhi in November 2005, but women did not participate in this milestone for peace.[33] The peace negotiation teams which emerged during the transitional phase comprised only men. The Ministry of Peace and Reconstruction was led by a man and the most personnel at decision-making levels in the ministry were men.[34]

Shortly after the Comprehensive Peace Agreement (CPA) was signed in 2006, the Maoists joined an interim government. After a series of protests by women, they agreed to include two women in their 15-member committee; their task was to work on a new Constitution to replace the 1990 Constitution. Women involved in these protests said the concession was 'too little too late'. Malla Kamala Pant, a lawmaker and one of a handful of women with positions of influ-ence in the interim government, said: 'The inclusion of women took place only when the drafting of a new Constitution was almost finished.' She added, 'It's sad that despite the fact that millions of women took part in the anti-king upris-ings, their role has been undermined'.[35]

In June 2006 when the seven political parties and the Maoists signed an eight-point Understanding, there were no women signatories and no women partici-pated in decision-making roles. After strong lobbying and protests from women activists, four women were included in the 16-member committee for drafting an interim constitution.[36]

The Office of the High Commissioner for Human Rights (OHCHR) and other UN agencies also advocated the inclusion of women in the transition process. In July 2006 a UN press statement called on the Government of Nepal, the political parties and the CPN-Maoists to increase women's representation in decision-making bodies which were part of the peace process. On 3 July 2006, the UN acting Resident Coordinator, Junko Sazaki, called on the political parties and the Maoists to increase women's representation in the peace process. She said: 'Clearly the active participation of women has been crucial to the success of the recent people's movement. For the peace process also to succeed, women's par-ticipation is absolutely necessary.'[37]

In November 2006 negotiations culminated in the CPA. It laid out the path to lasting peace: there was to be an interim Constitution followed by an interim government to replace the existing parliament. It was also agreed that there would be elections to a Constituent Assembly (CA). The CA would draft a new Constitution and decide, among other things, on the future of the monarchy. This decisive peace agreement included the top leaders of the seven political parties and the Maoists, but once again women were excluded. On 30 May the recalled parliament proclaimed that one-third of seats on all state bodies would be reserved for women. Weeks later, however, the Government named a committee to draft an interim Constitution consisting only of six men, and a ceasefire moni-toring body consisting of 29 men and only two women.[38] The armed insurgency ended in December 2006, after the Nepal Government and the CPN-Maoists agreed to a detailed peace agreement. There was no direct participation of women in this process. The issue of women's and children's rights was raised in only one point (7.6) of the agreement.[39]

Nepali women continued to keep up the pressure. In December 2007 women's networks held two large national conferences bringing together women activists from the districts to strategize on how to make the peace process work better for women. The lack of progress in implementing commitments to women's repre-sentation and participation in the peace process was identified as a major obs-tacle.[40] The Interim Constitution Drafting Committee, initially made up of six men, was expanded after women's organizations led a campaign to include six women as representatives of the Dalit community.[41]

The peace process was not confined to the official process. Many initiatives from civil society, including from women's organizations, developed alongside the negotiations and contributed to the peace process. Many women's organizations demanded a greater presence and made important contributions to this process. Even during the conflict Nepali women had campaigned for legal reform to the domestic violence bill, for women's citizenship rights, for 33 per cent participation at all decision-making levels and for the strengthening of national women's access.[42] Shanti Malika's women's peace network aimed to increase women's participation in the peace negotiations, and pressurized the government, the political parties and the Maoists. Shanti Malika used UNSCR 1325 as a tool to give legitimacy to their demands. The Women's Alliance for Peace, Power, Democracy and the Constituent Assembly (WAPPDCA) is an alliance of NGOs to promote and demand the implementation of UNSCR 1325.[43]

Nepal's Interim Constitution of 2007 showed a strong commitment to dealing with gender discrimination in a number of areas including citizenship; the right to equality; the right to employment and social security; women's rights; the right to social justice; and the right to freedom from exploitation (among others).[44] The Forum for Women, Law, and Development – a Nepali NGO – ensured that reproductive rights were recognized as a fundamental right in the interim constitution. This marked the first time that a government in the region had explicitly recognized women's reproductive rights as a human right in a national constitution.[45]

Roles played by UN and local stakeholders regarding UNSCR 1325

Interaction between local civil society and UN presence in Nepal

By the time of the peace agreement, pockets of staff in UN agencies were dedicated to the implementation of UNSCR 1325. Others had not yet understood the relevance of UNSCR 1325 to their work in Nepal or felt too overloaded with existing work to take on yet another issue. Some were unaware of the existence and relevance of UNSCR 1325. Others were aware but wanted technical assistance and advice on how to integrate gender issues within their work remit. The UN Humanitarian Agency Country Directors' team requested technical assistance from the UN Gender Capacity Stand-by programme.[46] In response to the request a Senior GenCap (Gender Standby Capacity) Advisor was deployed from the UK on a six-month mission to Nepal from September 2007 to work mainly with UN agencies and their stakeholders alongside the UNMIN Gender team.[47] She was answerable directly to the Resident Coordinator and based in the Office for the Coordination of Humanitarian Affairs (OCHA).

Within Nepal some imaginative efforts were made to promote UNSCR 1325. As part of the peace process, Peace Support Working groups were formed by UN and donor agencies to deal with Constitutional Reform, Transitional Justice,

Security Reform and Disarmament, Demobilization and Reintegration. A fifth group was to look into the issues prioritized in UNSCR 1325, and to focus specifically on the inclusion of women in political activities.[49] Local NGO SAATHI, with support from UNFPA, the UN Peace Support Working Group 1325 and the Norwegian Embassy produced a simple Guide to UNSCR 1325 for the media and a comic book in Nepali explaining UNSCR 1325 for grassroots activists. When women in one local area found there were no women on the Local Peace Committee they used the comic as an advocacy tool. They went to officials waving copies of the UNSCR 1325 comic and insisted that women be included – and they were. UNMIN and the United Nations Population Fund (UNFPA) partnered with Naya Adhyaya in a pre-election street drama that was performed across Nepal by the Sarwanam theatre group. By raising awareness of the importance of women's involvement in the peace process and of the existence of UNSCR 1325, the play encouraged women's participation at all levels of decision-making.[49]

Much of the interaction between local stakeholders and the UN on UNSCR 1325-related issues consisted of campaigning and lobbying for women's participation in decision-making in peace processes; they campaigned against gender-based violence (GBV), and for the participation of women in elections. Women continued to be excluded from the top table of the peace processes, in spite of continued calls by Nepali women and members of the international community for their inclusion. There was, however, some success on the issue of inclusion in elections.[50]

In order to understand the interaction between UN agencies and local stakeholders on UNSCR 1325 in Nepal, one needs to realize, first, that there is a complicated interaction between UN humanitarian agencies such as UNFPA, the United Nations Children's Fund (UNICEF), the United Nations High Commission for Refugees (UNHCR), the World Food Programme (WFP), and the International Labour Organization (ILO). Second, there are also organizations that have been present in Nepal for many years, supporting and implementing development programmes and responding to emerging humanitarian needs. Finally, two recent arrivals which have been tasked with supporting the peace processes – UNMIN and OHCHR.[51] In 2007 all UN agencies operating in Nepal developed a joint strategy, together with UNMIN, to support the peace process.[52]

UNFPA is the lead UN Humanitarian agency on implementation of UNSCR 1325.[53] It works with UNIFEM, OHCHR and other agencies, to implement UNSCR 1325. A brief description of its role is helpful at this point. As part of the global Inter-Agency Women Peace and Security Initiative Task Force, UNFPA has spearheaded a range of activities aimed at narrowing 'the gap between the provisions of the legal instrument 1325 and the reality on the ground'.[54] One of these activities was a workshop on UNSCR 1325 held in Tunisia in October 2006. Participants included NGOs and selected UNFPA staff from conflict-affected countries, as well as the UNFPA Country Representative from Nepal, Junko Sazaki.[55]

As a follow-up to the workshop a task force worked closely with the UNFPA office in Nepal to establish an outline for a future national action plan for the implementation of UNSCR 1325. The UNFPA Representative in Nepal succeeded in rallying UN partners and stakeholders to work towards the implementation of the Resolution.[56] Later, Junko Sazaki's participation as a member of the UN Technical Assessment Mission (prior to UNMIN deployment) helped ensure that gender issues and UNSCR 1325 were included in UNMIN's final report.[57]

Notwithstanding UNFPA's attempts to ensure implementation of UNSCR 1325, other UN agencies in Nepal also undertook a range of activities in relation to UNSCR 1325. UNIFEM produced an information booklet in Nepali, which places the Resolution in the context of Nepal, and a separate rapid scan of organizations working on women and peace in Nepal. UNIFEM has also been working with government departments on UNSCR 1325, and has conducted surveys on GBV and on women's experiences on issues such as employment, migration and in the Truth and Reconciliation Commission (TRC). In partnership with Shanti Malika UNIFEM conducted a Training of Trainers workshop on UNSCR 1325 with the aim of creating a pool of experts on the Resolution. In 2008 UNIFEM produced a documentary, 'Women's Role in Democratization'. This depicted women's role in the conflict in Nepal and in the post-conflict nation-building process, and promoted the principles of UNSCR 1325 as an advocacy tool to influence policies and programmes.[58] Similarly, the OHCHR has been another leading UN entity promoting the implementation of UNSCR 1325. It was established in May 2005 with the aim of protecting human rights in the context of the armed conflict and threats to democratic rights. OHCHR is the main international respondent to human rights abuses and complaints:[59] All OHCHR training given to NGOs and the Nepali police includes one session on women's human rights – with a specific focus on UNSCR 1325.

It is interesting that in this case the UN political office on the ground was not the leading advocate for the implementation of UNSCR 1325. This is explained in part by the nature of its mandate and by the fact that it arrived on the scene long after the other agencies. The United Nations Mission in Nepal (UNMIN), a special political mission of over 2,000 personnel in support of the peace process, was established on 23 January 2007 after the Seven-Party Alliance Nepal Government and the Communist Party of Nepal (Maoist) requested United Nations assistance in creating conditions for a free and fair election to the Constituent Assembly and for the entire peace process; UN assistance was also requested in the monitoring of ceasefire arrangements.[60] UNMIN includes mine action experts,[61] Electoral Advisors,[62] Civil Affairs Officers[63] and Arms Monitors.

UNMIN's role in the implementation of UNSCR 1325 was described by its Head of Mission, Ian Martin, as follows:

> So far as gender equality is concerned, one suggestion is that we should use gender expertise of other UN organisations rather than have UNMIN staff work on that. Indeed it is the other UN agencies that have a general mandate

to promote gender equality. We have a small gender team within UNMIN in order to work with them, but also to try to ensure that UNMIN carries out its own work in a gender-sensitive way. And, we work with those other organisations in trying to promote the implementation of Resolution 1325. But again, the UN can't make your government or your political parties implement Resolution 1325. We can only continue to push for it with civil society and that we are certainly trying to do.[64]

The UNMIN Gender Team was deployed for just over six months and completed its mission shortly after the April 2008 CPA elections. It comprised 13 members, including two gender advisors, and had a presence in all five regions of Nepal. The priority for the team, according to its mandate, was to support women's political participation at all levels in the political process and to assist in the promotion of gender equality, in addition to carrying out other activities related to 1325.

UN interaction with the Government of Nepal on UNSCR 1325 National Action Plan

Three internal gender networks within the UN system in Nepal have been dealing with issues related to UNSCR 1325. The UN Gender Network is a forum solely for UN agency staff with gender focal points, but the other two networks have greater outreach. The UN Peace Support Working Group on UNSCR 1325 (PSWG 1325) is a forum established to enhance cooperation and coordination among UN agencies and donors with regard to implementation of UNSCR 1325. INGOs and NGOs are invited to present their work, to allow for discussion on local initiatives and to explain how UN and donors can assist. UNFPA and the Norwegian Embassy chair regular meetings. PSWG 1325 has assisted in the identification of gaps in the implementation of UNSCR 1325 which need to be addressed at policy and/or project levels.[65] The Sexual Exploitation and Gender Based Violence Network (SEGBVN) is chaired by OHCHR. Attendees include representatives from Nepali NGOs as well as from UN entities and other international organizations. It has been monitoring the proposed TRC to try to ensure UNSCR 1325 recommendations on impunity and women's participation/representation are included.

The UN Peace Fund was set up in March 2007 for a period of two years by the UN Country Team (UNCT), donors and the Government in support of the peace process. The United Nations Development Programme (UNDP) administers the Fund.[66] UNIFEM has been working with the Ministry for Peace and Reconstruction, the Ministry of Home Affairs and the Ministry for Women, Children and Social Welfare on implementation of UNSCR 1325. The Ministry of Peace and Reconstruction said it would start work on a National Plan of Action for the implementation of UNSCR 1325 after the April 2008 elections, utilizing three different strategies. The first is to incorporate UNSCR 1325 into the planning guidelines of the NPC. The second entails the development of separate programmes relating to UNSCR 1325, while the third focuses on reviewing existing programmes from the perspective of UNSCR 1325, including, most importantly, those of the Ministry of Peace and Reconstruction. It should, however, be noted that despite the commitment of the Government of Nepal and the allocation of a budget for this agenda, constraints with regard to human resources and capacity may impede progress.[67]

Nepal civil society and UNSCR 1325

Civil society in Nepal had been involved in 1325-related activities since long before the UNMIN presence. The Institute of Human Rights Commission Nepal (IHRICON) claims to be the first NGO to have introduced UNSCR 1325 in Nepal. In 2003, with the support of International Alert London and the Canadian Co-operation office, Nepal established Community Women Peace Volunteers in five of Nepal's 75 districts. IHRICON provided training on women's rights, human rights, UNSCR 1325 and the impact of small arms for 25 community peace groups in the five district groups. They conducted a monthly interactive programme and published a newspaper on their activities and on related women's issues in their respective villages. The IHRICON programme was introduced in mostly Maoist-affected areas. As the volunteers were from among the local population, they were able to work safely.[68]

The growing women's movement in Nepal has been building links between national and local organizations on issues related to 1325. Each NGO has its own focus of activity and priorities but they sometimes come together in alliances and coalitions such as Shanti Malika,[69] and WAPPDCA, to fight for peace or the participation of women in the Constituent Assembly. Women's civil society activities have included campaigning for peace, human rights awareness raising, voter education, legal assistance, income generation, social counselling, the provision of safe shelters, training, and campaigning against the trafficking of women and children, GBV as well as HIV/AIDS. They have also assisted in preparation for elections, and have campaigned for at least 33 per cent representation of women in decision-making posts, especially in government, parliament and the Constituent Assembly. They have also campaigned for reproductive and maternal health rights, and for the rights of single women and widows.[70]

Assessing progress

Constituent Assembly elections

Nepali women's NGOs, with the support of international organizations, have succeeded in achieving a 33 per cent quota for women in politics and public life. In 2007 the interim Government's seven-party coalition drew up an interim Constitution that required each party to include 33 per cent of female candidates in their party lists. Fifty per cent of these candidates had to be on the proportional representation lists, elected by voting for parties rather than individuals. The remainder had to be fielded for direct elections in first-past-the-post contests. A number of international donors funded training and awareness to help prepare for women's participation in elections, in partnership with local NGOs. To pre-empt any political party saying they did not know of women qualified to be election candidates, WAPPDCA, an alliance of women's organizations promoting and implementing 1325, produced a directory of over 2,000 potential female political candidates from across the political spectrum entitled, 'Who's Who: Women in Nepal'. The directory was drawn up with support from the Norwegian Embassy, UNFPA and the UN PSWG 1325.

After a couple of postponements the election for the 601-seat Constituent Assembly (CA) was held on 10 April 2008, using a mixed electoral system of first-past-the-post seats and proportional representation. Of the total number of seats, 240 were elected in first-past-the-post contests and 335 through the proportional representation system, with the remaining 26 appointed by the incoming Council of Ministers. A number of international stakeholders and donors partnered local women's NGOs for training and awareness-raising with regard to women's participation as candidates, voters and organizers in elections. thirty-three per cent of candidates elected to the CA were women, mostly through the proportional representation system. Only 29 women candidates were elected by the first-past-the-post system; 23 of these were from CPN-M.[71]

The campaigning and lobbying for representation by Nepal women's NGOs, with support from international organizations, was eventually successful. The 33 per cent of women in the Constituent Assembly were not all from high-caste backgrounds.[72] The new CA is the most inclusive body Nepal has ever elected, with much greater representation of women and castes, ethnic groups and regional communities than past parliaments. As of 2008, 191 women were CA members, including 45 widows and six wives of missing husbands.[73] Interestingly, none of the parties fielded 33 per cent women as candidates in their first-past-the-post-seats, where candidates were individually elected. This contradicted their election manifestos which promised to ensure 33 per cent participation of women in all policy and decision-making positions and governmental bodies.

Gender-based violence (GBV): overall impact on women in Nepal

GBV has been a hidden topic in Nepal. The current situation is that women and girls are afraid to report rape and other forms of violence, not only because of hostility and stigma from their community, but also due to state inaction in ensuring investigation, prosecution and punishment of perpetrators through the justice system. Women's human rights defenders face particular risks when they defend the right to a life free from sexual and other violence. Women's NGOs and student groups, with the support of the international community, including the UN Gender Network, have run a number of high-profile public awareness campaigns.

The present situation is compounded by a dearth of data on GBV. The NGO SAATHI in partnership with UNFPA has conducted a survey on violence against women in selected districts.

In some districts the Nepal police have women and children service centres at the district level to receive women and girls who have suffered from various types of abuse and domestic violence, or who have missing documents, or who have been abandoned by their husbands. These service centres also assist with property problems, alimony payments and with the filing of First Incident Reports. The UN OCHA has recently mapped these services.[74] Although police personnel have received training, further training is needed to equip them to deal with human rights issues, and especially with GBV. OHCHR has trained police in Nepal and the UNFPA is engaged in discussions to include gender and GBV as part of the police training curriculum.

In late October 2007 UNFPA chose Nepal as one of six countries to receive a special budget to roll out the Inter Agency Standing Committee (IASC) Guidelines on GBV interventions. This included a programme of orientation and training. The GENCAP Senior Gender Advisor, in partnership with UNFPA, OCHA and WFP, conducted 14 workshops across Nepal on prevention and response to sexual violence in emergencies, including a workshop for staff from a range of government ministries and stakeholders. The workshop was organized in partnership with the Ministry for Home Affairs and Ministry for Women, and was their first workshop on GBV. The UNFPA translated 4,000 copies of IASC's Gender and GBV Handbooks from English into Nepali.[75]

1325 and Internally Displaced Persons (IDPs)

In some instances UNSCR 1325 has been a useful instrument to legitimize and provide benchmarks for international technical assistance to the Nepal Government. An example was when the UN ProCap Advisor provided technical assistance to the Ministry for Peace and Reconstruction on drawing up the Procedural Directives for Internally Displaced People. The directives incorporated a number of recommendations in line with UNSCR 1325, including on the property rights of female IDPs; the right of female IDPs to be allocated their own individual documentation; and to protection from exploitation and abuse.[76]

Female IDPs have become one of the most vulnerable groups in the aftermath of the Nepal conflict. No one appears to know exactly how many people were displaced by the conflict, or how many IDPs are/were women and girls. Most women and girls who fled the countryside to seek refuge in urban areas had no skills and faced significant challenges in securing new livelihoods. Life was especially difficult for widows, single women, girls, wives of 'disappeared men' and wives of men who were unable to work.[77] Unlike other conflicts where IDPs flee to IDP camps, in the conflict in Nepal the majority of IDPs fled from the countryside to cities, where they moved in with friends or relatives or rented accommodation. In this way they became invisible to humanitarian aid organizations and NGOs like the Norwegian Refugee Council or the International Red Cross, who may want to assist but found it difficult to locate female IDPs.[78] The majority of IDPs left everything they owned in their villages. They used what remained of their assets to pay for their travel and to survive during the transitional period. IDPs from farming communities were often ill-prepared for making a living in urban areas; most IDPs who found employment were in low-paid unskilled jobs.[79]

Conclusion

As in other countries affected by conflict, the conflict and post-conflict phases in Nepal were periods when gender roles were subject to rapid change due to the fluctuating circumstances. In the aftermath of conflict there was a temporary window of opportunity in which Nepali citizens were focused on what kind of future society they wanted. It was therefore an ideal time to employ UNSCR 1325 as a tool to help bring about change in women's status and situation. At a critical time when a country is embarking on a peace process, one of the international community's roles should be to provide access to information, tools, training, funds and technical assistance to promote human rights, good governance, gender equity, economic recovery and democracy. Ultimately, however, it should be the local citizens – both female and male – who make the decisions regarding their own future.

Resolution 1325 predated the peace process in Nepal by six years. In the particular situation of Nepal, UN development and humanitarian agencies were on the ground before the arrival of the political office and the peace mission and this had an impact on the manner in which UNSCR 1325 was implemented on the ground. Much of the work of the operational agencies focused on multiple activities. Although UNFPA was the lead agency for the implementation of 1325, it had neither a coordinating nor a political role. Its role was largely operational, implementing 1325-related activities alongside other core functions. In this regard, it was no different from UNIFEM, OCHA and OHCHR. There can be no doubt that the activities of these agencies generated a multiplier effect on the ground by supporting and upscaling the work of Nepali women and assisting them to achieve the progress discussed earlier in this chapter. The main gap was perhaps the absence of a UN political presence to engage the Government of Nepal at the highest political level on UNSCR 1325. UNMIN, when it eventually arrived, took the position that the agencies on the ground were already effectively working to implement UNSCR 1325; it felt that its role was simply to support these efforts.

The UN was not the only driver of UNSCR 1325 in Nepal. It encountered an active civil society, which had begun to engage with UNSCR 1325. The collaboration between international agencies and the local civil society, particularly women's groups, was no doubt important for the implementation of UNSCR 1325. Progress on women's equality was primarily driven by Nepali women themselves, but local women's NGOs and initiatives depend for the most part on international organizations for their funding. Without foreign funding most Nepali women's NGOs would have had difficulty in conducting advocacy in support of UNSCR 1325. In addition to funding, interaction between internationals and Nepali people through meetings, conferences and workshops enabled useful two-way dissemination of information and created partnerships.

Efforts to implement UNSCR 1325 in Nepal have so far achieved mixed results. Obvious progress has been achieved with the election of women to 33 per cent of the Constituent Assembly's seats; and with the appointment of women to several key ministries. However, this was the result of a hard-fought process. Although the peace process in Nepal took place six years after UNSCR 1325 was unanimously passed by the Security Council, women were not included at the top table in the peace processes or in the interim government. This was despite the fact that during the peace process women's NGOs and UN agencies, as well as other international organizations and donors, did a great deal of work at middle and grassroot levels to help implement UNSCR 1325. And in spite of lobbying by Nepali women (with support from the UN and other members of the international community) women were also excluded from the seven-party alliance interim Government. The experience in Nepal is another example of the fact that in the aftermath of conflict men on both sides use the peace processes and the transitional government to jostle for personal power.

In Nepal the conflict has accelerated a process of change but, as with other countries, it will take decades before gender equality is achieved. UNSCR 1325 and its effective implementation is an essential tool in this process for both the Government of Nepal and the international community. A simultaneous focus on both women issues and gender equality must be sustained.

Some UN agencies, donors and international organizations working in Nepal have supported women-specific projects and programmes. Others have actively promoted UNSCR 1325 while others have been proactive in mainstreaming gender into projects or programmes they support or fund. Yet international organizations, such as the UN, often failed to lead by example. Although there was a satisfactory gender balance with regard to the UN humanitarian agency country directors, men were appointed to the three most senior UN posts in Nepal – the UN Resident and Humanitarian Coordinator, the UNMIN UNSRSG, and the Representative of the United Nations High Commissioner for Human Rights. A remaining challenge is that many UN agencies as well as other international organizations and donors claim in their written policies to mainstream gender as a cross-cutting issue, but fail to translate the policy into reality on the ground.

Notes

1 The United Nations Millennium Development Goals Report 2005.
2 The World Disasters Report 2007 states: 'Women, the elderly, minorities and people with disabilities are discriminated against in disasters. Discrimination in disasters needs to be considered in disaster preparedness programmes and in access to aid.'
3 Nepal ranks 142 out of 177 on the Human Development Index.
4 The poverty in rural areas (42 per cent) is higher than urban areas (25.2 per cent). The incidence is most pronounced in the mountain areas, followed by the Terai plains and the hills.

5 Department for International Development, Country Profiles. Available at www.dfid.
gov.uk/where-we-work/asia-south/nepal/ (accessed 23 December 2009).
6 The other main religions are Buddhism, Tantrism, Islam and Christianity.
7 'Poverty Reduction in Nepal: Issues, Findings and Approaches', a report by the Asian
Development Bank compiled for the High Level Forum on Poverty Analysis, Kathmandu, 26 February 2001. Available at www.adb.org/documents/reports/poverty_
reduction_nep/appendixes.pdf (accessed 29 January 2010). For the whole report
please see www.adb.org/Documents/Reports/Poverty_Reduction_NEP/poverty_anal-
ysis.pdf.
8 A. Waldman, 'Caste System Binds Nepalese Prostitutes', in *The New York Times*, 11
April 2004. Available at www.nytimes.com/2004/04/11/international/asia/11MUDA.
html (accessed 23 February 2010).
9 11th Amendment to the Country Code Bill.
10 Government of Nepal, 'Promotion of Gender Equality and Women Empowerment',
Kathmandu: Government of Nepal National Planning Commission, 2006, p. 27.
Available at www.undp.org.np/publication/html/mdg_NAN/Chapter_6.pdf.
11 L. Bennett, 'Unequal Citizens: Gender, Caste and Ethnic Exclusion in Nepal', Report
on Gender and Social Exclusion Assessment (GSEA), World Bank, 2006. Available
at http://siteresources.worldbank.org/INTRANETSOCIALDEVELOPMENT/Resources/
Bennett.rev.pdf (accessed 27 November 2009).
12 'Gender Equality and Social Institutions in Nepal', a report by the Social Institutions
and Gender Index for the OECD. Available at http://genderindex.org/country/nepal
(accessed January 2010).
13 M. Dunham, 'Women in Nepal Update: Interview with DS Police Chief Gita Upreti',
14 October 2008. Available at www.mikeldunham.blogs.com/mikeldunham/2008/10/
update-on-nepali-womens-issues-interview-with-ds-police-chief-gita-upreti.html?
(accessed 15 December 2010).
14 S.K. Joshi and J. Kharel, 'Violence Against Women in Nepal: An Overview',
in *Family and Marriage Community*, 22 May 2008. Available at www.thefreeli-
brary.com/Violence+Against+Women+in+Nepal+-+An+Overview-a01073875052
(accessed 17 October 2009).
15 Ibid.
16 According to a national study on 'Changing Roles of Nepali Women due to Ongoing
Conflict' conducted by Samanata-Institute for Social Change and Gender Equality
(Kathmandu) in 2005, 90 per cent of the respondents felt that due to the absence of
men, women had to bear additional responsibilities.
17 'Women in Nepalese Army', http://nepalisainik.blogspot.com/2009/09/women-in-
nepalease-army.html.
18 'UNMIN Arms Monitoring', report published online by the United Nations Mission
in Nepal. Available at www.unmin.org.np/?d=activities&p=arms (accessed 23 February 2010).
19 'Neglect Over the Issue of Female Combatants in the Arms Management Process',
United Nations Office for the Coordination of Humanitarian Affairs – Integrated
Regional Information Networks, 25 December 2006. Available at www.reliefweb.int/
rw/RWB.NSF/db900SID/KHII-6WU5HY?OpenDocument (accessed 12 November
2009).
20 United Nations Mission in Nepal, online press kit. Available at www.unmin.org.np/?d
=media&p=onlinekit&mode=nepal.
21 M. Villellas Ariño, 'Nepal: a Gender View of the Armed Conflict and the Peace
Process', in *Peacebuilding Papers*, a publication of The School for a Culture of
Peace, June 2008, p. 8. Available at http://escolapau.uab.cat/img/qcp/nepal_conflict_
peace.pdf (accessed 24 April 2010).
22 Ibid.

23 United Nations Mission in Nepal, online press kit. Available at www.unmin.org.np/?d =media&p=onlinekit&mode=nepal (accessed 15 July 2009).
24 Villellas Ariño, op. cit., p. 9.
25 L. Bennet and I. Bannon, 'Social Change in Conflict Affected Areas of Nepal', in *Development Notes, Social Conflict and Reconstruction*, No. 15, January 2004, pp. 1–4. This dissemination report was based on the findings of the report 'Social Change in Conflict Areas: Assessment Report', commissioned by DFID Nepal and authored by M.S. Lama-Tamang, S.M. Gurung, D. Swarnakar and S. R. Magar. Available at http://siteresources. worldbank.org/INTCPR/214578-1111751313696/20480283/CPRNote15legal.pdf.
26 Villellas Ariño, op. cit., p. 9.
27 Ibid.
28 United Nations Development Fund for Women, 'A Rapid Scan: Organizations Working on Women and Peace in Nepal', 2006, p. 9. Available at www.un.org.np/reports/ UNIFEM/2006/2006-9-10-UNIFEM-Final-rapid-scan.pdf (accessed 30 June 2009).
29 L. Thapa, 'Nepal's Widows', 2007. A study on the status of widows in Nepal conducted by Nepalese NGO Women for Human Rights. Available at www.opendemocracy.net/blog/nepals_widows (accessed 13 October 2009).
30 Donors in Nepal include: Canada, Norway, the US, Denmark, Finland, Germany, the Netherlands, Switzerland, United Kingdom, Japan, Korea and the European Union. A number of donors funded initiatives for women's participation in peace processes.
31 Institutions include CARE, Oxfam, International Rescue Committee, ASIA Foundation, South Asia Partnership-Nepal, IOM, Save the Children, South Asia Gender Alliance, Mercy Corps, Lutheran World Forum, etc. Association of International NGOs (AIN) – an informal group of NGOs working in Nepal, plus academic institutions namely the Joan B. Kroc Institute for Peace & Justice, University of San Diego.
32 United Nations Office for the Coordination of Humanitarian Affairs – Integrated Regional Information Networks, interview with Regional Director UNIFEM South Asia, 2006. Available at www.irinnews.org/report.aspx?reportid=34718 (accessed 23 November 2009).
33 M. Thapa, *Understanding Maoist Insurgency of Nepal: Context, Cost and Consequences*, Kathmandu: Himal Books, 2002, p. 12.
34 In addition the three most senior UN posts in Nepal were held by men: the UN Special Representative of the Secretary-General, who heads UNMIN, is the overall coordinator of the UN system's support to the peace process; the UN Resident and Humanitarian Coordinator, responsible for the UN Humanitarian Agencies and the Head of the Office of the High Commissioner for Human Rights, which was established in May 2005 with the aim of protecting human rights in the context of the armed conflict and threats to democratic rights. Country Directors of the UN Humanitarian Agencies in Nepal had an approximate gender balance of women and men.
35 United Nations Office for the Coordination of Humanitarian Affairs – Integrated Regional Information Networks, 'Nepal – Women Want a Greater Role in the Peace Process', 20 July 2006. Available. at http://irinnews.org/Report.aspx?ReportId=59819.
36 P. Bhusal, 'Women's Participation in the Constitution Making Process: Why it Matters', 2008, p. 2. Available at www.womenact.org.np/document/publication/file/P uspa_20Bhushal20English20Version1final.pdf.
37 'UN Calls for Increased Women's Participation in Peace Process', *Xinhua*, 3 July 2006. www.peacewomen.org/news/Nepal/Jul06/UNWomenParticipation.html.
38 United Nations Office for the Coordination of Humanitarian Affairs – Integrated Regional Information Networks, Interview with Regional Director UNIFEM South Asia, 2006. Available at www.irinnews.org/report.aspx?reportid=34718 (accessed 23 November 2009).
39 'Comprehensive Peace Accord Concluded between the Government of Nepal and the Communist Party of Nepal (Maoist)', 2006, p. 18. Available at www.peace.gov.np/ admin/doc/CPA_eng-ver-corrected.pdf.

40   United Nations Mission in Nepal, 'Women Speak Out for Representation', UNMIN Newspaper, no. 3, December 2007. Available at www.unmin.org.np/downloads/publications/UNMIN_Newspaper_3_ENG.pdf (accessed 24 August 2009).

41   Villellas Ariño, op. cit., p. 10.

42   Institute for Peace and Justice, 'The State of Affairs in Nepal', a Public Report, 26 May 2005. Available at www.sandiego.edu/peacestudies/documents/ipj/IPJ_Public_NepalReport_5-05.pdf (accessed 16 August 2009).

43   Villellas Ariño, op. cit., p. 11.

44   Interim Constitution of Nepal (2007) www.worldstatesmen.org/Nepal_Interim_Constitution2007.pdf.

45   Centre for Reproductive Rights, 'Prominent Reproductive Rights Advocate Named to Nepal's Constituent Assembly', 5 January 2008. Available at www.reproductiverights.org/ww_asia_nepal.html (accessed 24 November 2009).

46   Established in the last months of 2006, the project is a result of the work of the Inter-Agency Standing Committee (IASC). The GenCap focus is on strengthening a gender-sensitive and equal approach in UN humanitarian operations based on UNSCR 1325. See Norwegian Refugee Council GenCap www.nrc.no/?aid=9160724.

47   Lesley Abdela – Senior GenCap Gender Advisor to UN Humanitarian Agencies in Nepal September 2007–February 2008.

48   The Inter-Agency Questionnaire on the system-wide action plan to Implement Security Council Resolution 1325 (2000) on women, peace and security.

49   United Nations Population Fund Nepal, Naya Adhyaya – 'A New Chapter for Nepalese Women Street Drama for Women's Increased Participation in the Peace Process', 2008. Available at http://nepal.unfpa.org/en/news/news.php?ID=17 (accessed 17 July 2009).

50   After two postponements, elections to the Constituent Assembly on 10th April 2008 were a key plank in the peace process. The electoral system was a combination of single-member constituencies and proportional representation by closed lists. There were quotas for women and other marginalized groups. More than 6,000 candidates representing 73 political parties stood for election for the constituent assembly's 575 directly elected seats. Seven major parties and 50 smaller groups fielded candidates. The total number of women seeking direct election to the CA in April 2008 was 367 out of a total of 3,947 candidates.

51   Special Representative of the UN Secretary-General (UN SRSG) is the overall coordinator of the UN system's support to the peace process. UNMIN works with the UN Resident and Humanitarian Coordinator (RC/HC) to ensure all UN agencies coordinate their efforts and maximize the UN support to Nepal's peace process. www.unmin.org.np/downloads/speeches/2007-12-13-UNMIN.SRSG.Address.Human.Rights.Home.ENG.pdf.

52   United Nations Mission in Nepal, Factsheet No. 5. Available at www.unmin.org.np/downloads/publications/Factsheet_5_ENG.pdf (accessed 17 July 2009).

53   Ibid.

54   UNFPA, 'Empowering Women to Promote Peace and Security. Promoting Implementation of Security Council Resolution 1325 by Enhancing Capacity Building for National NGOs, Women's and Grass Roots Groups and Addressing Gender-based Violence in Conflict and Post-Conflict Settings', a Women Peace and Security Outcomes Briefing, 2006. Available at www.unfpa.org/women/briefing.htm.

55   Other participants were from Afghanistan, Azerbaijan, Georgia, East Timor, Indonesia, Kosovo, Liberia, Pakistan, Palestine, Sierra Leone, Sudan, Tajikistan and Uganda. One of the trainers was Lesley Abdela who subsequently became GenCap Senior Gender Advisor in Nepal.

56   UNFPA, op. cit., 2006.

57   Ibid.

58   United Nations, '2008–2009 UN System-Wide Action Plan on Security Council Resolution 1325 (2000) on Women, Peace and Security'. Available at www.un.org/

womenwatch/ianwge/taskforces/wps/actionplan20082009/pdfs/UNIFEM%20Nepal%
202008_09%201325%20Action%20Plan.pdf.

59 The parties to the CPA expressly requested OHCHR to take responsibility for monitoring the human rights situation during the peace process.

60 UNMIN was established in response to letters to the Secretary-General sent on 9
August 2006, in which the then Seven-Party Alliance Government and the Communist Party of Nepal (Maoist) requested United Nations assistance in creating a free
and fair atmosphere for the election of the Constituent Assembly and the entire peace
process. At the request of the Government of Nepal, the Security Council unanimously extended UNMIN's mandate for six months on 23 January 2008 (Resolution
1796) and for another six months on 23 July 2008 (Resolution 1825).

61 UNMIN Mine Experts advise the Maoist army on the safe storage and destruction of
improvized explosive devices, and provide advice and training to the Nepal Army in
the clearance of anti-personnel minefields to International Mine Action standards.

62 Electoral Advisors supported the Election Commission at the regional and district
level. Prior to the Constituent Assembly election small teams in all the districts
assisted in the final preparations and conduct of the election. Police advisory teams
were there to provide the Nepal police with advice on the planning and execution of
election security.

63 UNMIN Civil Affairs Officers monitor and report on the re-establishment of local
governance and public security, as part of monitoring the ceasefire arrangements.
They also encourage local dialogue to promote peacebuilding at the district level.

64 In response to a question at a talk programme organized by Human Rights Home,
Kathmandu.   www.unmin.org.np/downloads/speeches/2007-12-13-UNMIN.SRSG.
Address.Human.Rights.Home.ENG.pdf.

65 Attendees at PSWG 1325 meetings have included UNFPA, OHCHR, UNMIN,
UNICEF, GTZ, RNE, DANIDA, JICA, CIDA, OCHA, SDC, UNAIDS, UNDP,
UNESCO, EOD, EOF, EOJ, Norwegian Embassy, IDEA, CIDA, AUSAID, CCO,
EOA, ILO, Norwegian Refugee Council, IRC, WB, WFP, CMP, UK DFID.

66 United Nations Mission in Nepal, Factsheet 5, op. cit.

67 Interview conducted with Steve Askham.

68 'Women Building Peace'. Available at www.peacewomen.org/campaigns/Nepal/
Nepal.html (accessed 23 February 2010). For further reading on the Institute of
Human Rights Communication Nepal, please see www.ihricon.org.np/index.php.

69 Shanti Malika (Women Network for Peace) was formed after a consultation of about
150 women rights activists groups in March 2003 in Kathmandu after realizing that
even during the peace talks there were no women present or participating, either from
the Maoist's side or from the government side.

70 Ibid.

71 Amnesty International, 'Nepal Overturning the Legacy of War-Priorities for Effective Human Rights Protection', a press release published by Amnesty International,
12 May 2008. Available at www.amnesty.org/en/for-media/press-releases/nepal-
overturning-legacy-war-priorities-effective-human-rights-protection.

72 Ibid.

73 Thapa, op. cit, 2007.

74 Ibid.

75 UN ProCap is a small core team of Senior Protection Officers (SPOs) who provide
additional emergency capacity through permanent rotation to the field on short-term
deployments of up to six months. Their role is to strengthen the strategic and operational response of the UN Country Team and/or the Protection Cluster lead agency
through the development of protection policies, mechanisms and strategies, advocacy
and building in-country protection capacities (national as well as international).

76 With the support of UNHCR, OHCHR, OCHA and the NRC.

77 Thapa, op. cit, 2007.

78 'Nepal: Failed IDP Policy Leaves Many Unassisted', a joint report by the Internal Displacement Monitoring Centre and the Norwegian Refugee Council, 28 January 2010. Available at www.internal-displacement.org/8025708F004BE3B1/(httpInfoFiles)/FFF5958EB13C0AF8C12576B900395E1D/$file/Nepal_Overview_Jan10.pdf.
79 People fleeing the conflict travelled from rural areas to district town headquarters such as Nepalgunj, Dhangadhi or Biratnagar and from there to larger cities such as Pokhara or Kathmandu or across the border to India.

6 Nigeria and the implementation of UNSCR 1325

Eka Ikpe

Introduction

Nigeria may appear an unusual choice for an assessment of the implementation of UNSCR 1325, given that it is not formally classified as a country undergoing current or past conflict of great significance. However, the size of the country arguably masks the impact of ongoing conflicts on the population. The deaths of tens of thousands of people in countries like Liberia and Sierra Leone, which have populations of less than seven million, invariably draws more concern than a similar number of deaths would in Nigeria, which has a population of more than 150 million people. Perhaps a more important reason to focus on Nigeria in terms of implementation of UNSCR 1325 is its role as a major troop contributor to international peacekeeping efforts. Finally, since Nigeria has not served as a host nation to UN or other peacekeeping missions, it provides an interesting measure of the extent to which the implementation of UNSCR 1325 depends on the presence of international actors.

This chapter examines the extent to which UNSCR 1325 is being implemented in Nigeria. In particular, it discusses the roles of three key actors, the Federal Government, the Nigerian military and civil society, and the extent to which they have adapted UNSCR 1325 in their work. In the absence of a UN mission, there is little or no external pressure for the implementation of 1325. As a result, there is a greater role for local conceptions of security and gender equality and for strategies that have been developed to address gender inequalities, especially in conflict-affected areas. The chapter examines these issues in the following four sections. Section two distils the gendered security challenges that Nigerian women face in attempting to use the security framework. Section three highlights the reality of threats to the security of women in conflict-affected situations in Nigeria. Section four examines the status of the implementation of UNSCR 1325 in Nigeria in relation to the efforts of the Federal Executive and Legislature. It emphasises the role of the Ministry of Women's Affairs and Social Development; the Nigerian military; and the civil society initiatives of the Women in Peacebuilding Network in Nigeria. Section five concludes with a discussion of the gains that have been made and the challenges that persist, and explores emerging issues with regard to the implementation of UNSCR 1325 in Nigeria.

Setting the context: how women experience insecurity in Nigeria

The challenges to women's security in Nigeria have their roots in gender-based discrimination. Women suffer economic insecurity on account of their lack of access to property and land ownership, based on social conventions that deny women such rights. In a study of the impact of petroleum activity on the economic livelihoods of women in the Niger Delta, Omorodion[1] argues that '[lack of access to] land ownership limits their economic emancipation, autonomy and power, while continuously keeping women under the control of men'. When it comes to political security, women's reduced political participation derives from the socio-cultural characterisation of women as the repositories of decency; politics, in contrast, is seen as tainted. This can lead to disapproval of women's participation in the political sphere. For example, a Nigerian female politician reports that she is often considered to be promiscuous (and therefore of questionable moral standing) on account of the long periods she has to spend away from home with other male politicians.[2]

The social security challenges that women face can be attributed to the effect of gender discrimination on their access to education. Prevailing ideas emphasise women's reproductive functions rather than their right to receive an education. Oxfam[3] has made the point that, in Nigeria, lower literacy rates[4] for women are the result of a negative learning environment and the patriarchal belief that their reproductive functions take priority. With regard to physical security, women can and often do suffer domestic violence because they are regarded as subject to male authority within the home. In their study of women's attitudes to wife battery in Nigeria, Oyediran and Isiugo-Abanihe[5] find that 66.4 per cent of married women, 50.4 per cent of unmarried women and 60 per cent of men accept wife battery as a socio-cultural norm and a necessity for addressing the 'weaker' nature of women. They find that women who are more highly educated are less likely to accept wife battery as normal.

With regard to environmental security, women are often subject to the impact of environmental degradation resulting from decisions made for them by others. These decision-makers may have limited insight into the effect of their decisions on women's lives. Omorodion[6] has shown that in the Niger Delta, policy-makers have taken little cognisance of the impact of environmental degradation on women. This clearly undermines their ability to make a living and contribute to development.

In spite of these gender-based challenges to women's security, International Alert found that Nigerian women prioritised the following factors as having the greatest effect on their security: first was political instability, followed by lack of good governance, and then lack of institutional capacity on the part of the state, and finally gender inequality.[7] In contrast reports on the challenges to implementing UNSCR 1325 suggest that the best way to counter the effects of conflict on women will most likely be to directly confront the impact of gender on their lives.[8] There is a fundamental disconnect on the part of Nigerian women between the consideration of gendered dynamics and the realities of women's security. As Nigerian women are the most significant constituency in this debate, this conveys some sense of the challenges to the implementation of UNSCR 1325 in Nigeria.

The gendered impact of violent conflict on Nigerian women

In Nigeria, intra-state conflict has arguably been the major source of violent conflict. The roots of conflicts are complex and cannot easily be categorised as religious, ethnic, socio-economic or resource-based. These categories are often not mutually exclusive and linear causality is often of limited value in explaining the origins of particular conflicts. Although women suffer from armed conflict alongside other members of society, the resulting insecurity often affects them in particular ways, especially in so far as gender-specific rights are concerned.[9] This makes it all the more important to adopt a gendered perspective when addressing their insecurities. Conflict means reduced security for women: their existing economic, political, social and environmental exclusion and their physical insecurity is heightened in situations of violent conflict. Given that UNSCR 1325 is chiefly concerned with the security of women in situations of conflict, it is appropriate to apply this to the case of Nigeria.

In Nigeria there have been longstanding conflicts, often simplistically classified as 'ethnic' in character. These include conflicts between Ijaws and Itsekiris in the Niger Delta; Ilajes and Ijaws in the South West; Yoruba and Ijaws in the South West; Yorubas and Hausas in the South West and North; Ife and Modakeke in the South West; Tivs, Jukuns, Fulani and Kutebs in Central Nigeria; Fulani and Berom in the Riyomo district, south-west of Jos; and militant groups in the Niger Delta who are fighting against the Nigerian state, among others.

Since the passing of UNSCR 1325 in 2000, there have been escalations in violent conflict in Nigeria. Two conflicts stand out, that in the Niger Delta and that in Jos. In the Niger Delta, there has been extensive conflict as a result of face-offs between militant groups opposed to the Nigerian state. These groups are seeking to control or benefit from the oil resources in the area, which are exploited by the Nigerian state and multinational petroleum corporations. The local populations have not benefited from the oil wealth but experience the effect of environmental degradation.[10] The latest and perhaps most intense phase of conflict began in 2004, but this has tapered off with the declaration of an amnesty by the Nigerian Federal Government in October 2009.[11]

There has also been ongoing conflict between Christians and Muslims in Northern Nigeria that has been interpreted as indigene versus settler conflict. From 2001, violent outbreaks have taken place in South West Jos. A frequent commentator on the conflict, Ugar Ukandi Odey, notes that land is central to the conflict and that the Berom indigenes and the Fulani pastoralists have been in conflict over access to the land. He notes that the conflict is seen as religious because the Beroms are predominantly Christian and the Fulanis are predominantly Muslim.[12]

In 2010 a renewed bout of fighting between the Beroms and Fulanis in Jos saw the targeted killing of women, children and the elderly, with the estimated unofficial death tolls reaching over 500.[13] There is a general sense of impunity, as the perpetrators of violence (both state security actors and non-state actors) have gone largely unpunished. Several panels have been set up to review the root causes of the conflict in Jos as well as to identify perpetrators so that they can be prosecuted, but they continue to go unpunished.[14]

The conflict in the Niger Delta has seen women bear the brunt of the violence. In December 1998, when the Ijaw Youth Congress prepared for their *Operation Climate Change*, Nigerian soldiers occupied Bayelsa and Delta States and attacked protesters. In the late hours, soldiers invaded private homes, beating their inhabitants and raping women and girls.[15] Women in the Niger Delta expressed their views in the Communique of the Niger Delta Women Consultative meeting. This highlighted their increased insecurity following the 'agitation of their youth and the militarization of the region and the violation of their rights and the killing of their people, maiming of their children and raping and harassing of their girls and women'.[16] Another incident of sexual gender-based violence (SGBV) occurred in 2009, when several women, some of whom were pregnant, were kidnapped and gang-raped by Niger Delta militants in their camps.[17] Furthermore, in renewed violence between the Nigerian state and militant groups in Gbaramatu in May 2009, women constituted the majority of the internally displaced persons, following the destruction of the community.[18]

In the case of the Ife/Modakeke conflict, women were accused of having divided loyalties as a result of their natal ties (as opposed to their marriage ties); they were sometimes violently punished or economically disenfranchised. This is clearly gender-specific as men are not seen as having any ties to their wives' places of origin.[19] In Northern Nigeria, the conflict between the Christians and Muslims, which intensified with the introduction of Sharia Law, have threatened the physical security of all indigenes. Women have been particularly affected. Non-Muslim residents have been forced by vigilantes to adhere to extra-legal rules that include the mode of dress, sitting in the back of a car, the use of motorcycle taxis, keeping male company, and customs relating to sports and public recreation in Muslim societies.[20] In Nigeria's Middle Belt, there was a violent confrontation between the Tiv and Jukun in the period 1990–92. The killing of pregnant women was particularly troubling; this was, no doubt, intended as a demonstration of brutality.[21]

These conflicts highlight the vulnerability of women in these situations. The security of Nigerian women is challenged by economic, social, political, environmental and physical factors. This is not, however, to assume that the only role of women in conflict situations in Nigeria is as victims. An oft-cited example is the case of the Nigerian women of the Ugborodo and Arutan communities who took over the Chevron Texaco Escravos oil terminal and some of its flow stations in the Niger Delta in June/July 2002.[22] Another example is that of the women of the Ijaw and the Itsekiri communities who protested against their poor living conditions and demanded jobs for their youth as well as electricity, schools and medical facilities.[23] In March 2010, there was a widespread peace protest against the massacre of women and children in the Jos crisis in the capital city, Abuja.[24]

Implementing UNSCR 1325 in Nigeria: roles of the Federal Executive and Legislature, Nigerian military and WIPNET-Nigeria

The nature of these conflicts was such that most remained beneath the radar of the state and the international community; they were not regarded as examples of violent intrastate conflict. There has therefore not been official designation of Nigeria as a country in conflict; instead, it is regarded as being in a state of 'neither war nor peace'. This also means that there is no formal UN engagement with Nigeria with regard to its internal conflicts and thus no formal UN structure for the implementation of UNSCR 1325 within Nigeria (as would have been the case had a UN Peacekeeping Mission been present).

There has been some acknowledgement of the relevance of UNSCR 1325 by a former Minister for Women's Affairs and Social Development in Nigeria.[25] The general lack of consideration of the Resolution in Nigeria does not prevent one from forming an estimate of its relevance and value. Particular aspects of the Resolution stand out as speaking to the Nigerian context. These include the need for women to participate at all levels in decision-making roles relating to the prevention, management and resolution of conflict; the need for special training in the mainstreaming of gender perspectives in peace-support operations; the need to recognise the impact of conflict on women and children and to make the appropriate institutional arrangements, including peace agreements and disarmament, demobilisation and reintegration; supporting local peace initiatives; ending impunity and prosecuting the crimes of sexual gender-based violence as well as addressing challenges that displaced women and girls face from SGBV. In this section, we consider notable actions on the part of the both Nigerian state actors and of civil society actors with regard to the implementation of UNSCR 1325.

The Nigerian state's efforts to act on UNSCR 1325: examining the score card of the Executive and the Legislature

There has arguably been some show of commitment to the principles of UNSCR 1325 by the Nigerian government, which has ratified most of the regional and international treaties relating to women's peace and security.[26] These include the following, among others:

International Covenant on Civil and Political Rights (ICCPR)
International Covenant on Economic and Social and Cultural Rights (ICESCR)
Convention on the Elimination of All Forms of Discrimination against Women (CEDAW)

International Convention on the Elimination of All Forms of Racial Discrimination (ICERD)
Convention on the Rights of the Child (CRC)
Convention against Discrimination in Education (CDE)
Equal Remuneration Convention (ERC)
Supplementary Convention on the Abolition of Slavery, the Slave trade and Institutions and Practices Similar to Slavery (SCAS)
Convention against Torture (CAT)
The African Charter on Human and Peoples Rights (The Banjul Charter)

However, the Nigerian Constitution insists that only international instruments that are enacted as domestic law by the parliament shall be legally enforceable.[27] Only the African Charter on Human and Peoples Rights has been enacted as domestic law. This may indicate greater willingness to comply with the African-led instruments. It is significant that the most important precedent to UNSCR 1325, CEDAW, has yet to be domesticated, although it was ratified in 1985.[28]

Institutionally, there is little sense of actual engagement with UNSCR 1325 from the Federal Government. (Nigeria's contributions to international peace-keeping operations will be discussed below.) The Ministry of Women's Affairs and Social Development has the central statutory responsibility for addressing the situation of women, specifically within Nigerian society. It has tended to rely on the provisions of CEDAW for achieving its mandate, in spite of the fact that these have yet to be enacted in Nigerian law. However, CEDAW need not imply the irrelevance of UNSCR 1325. This point has been well made by the International Women's Tribune Centre in their Shadow CEDAW Report, in which they link CEDAW to the provisions of UNSCR 1325 and UNSCR 1820.[29] It is worth noting that, at global sessions on CEDAW, Nigerian representatives have acknowledged the Resolution in their observations.[30]

Using its CEDAW reports as a basis, it is possible to examine the efforts made by the Ministry of Women's Affairs and Social Development to at least indirectly address the provisions of UNSCR 1325. It should be noted that there was explicit encouragement of women's participation in peace and security processes at a strategic level prior to the passing of UNSCR 1325. The first CEDAW report, prepared in 1997, included a drive for the involvement of women in conflict resolution and in dialogue with the Peace Mission initiative spearheaded by the then First Lady, Maryam Abacha. This was an attempt to address the many violent conflicts in the sub-region throughout the 1990s.[31] In spite of this apparent progress, the designation of issues relating to women, peace and security to the oversight of the First Lady, who has no constitutionally defined statutory role or function, risked undermining the institutionalisation of roles for women in peace and security.

Interestingly, neither of the CEDAW reports that follow in 2003 and 2006 discuss the role of women in peace and security, even though both post-date the passing of UNSCR 1325.[32] There is an acknowledgement of gender discrimination with regard to the appointment of women in peace and security structures within government – including the police, the immigration services, the military and the strategic ministries. A number of factors may help to explain this omission reference; these include the (supposed) incapacity or inability of women, irregular work hours, the need to travel, as well as marital status.[33] There is no provision for initiatives to challenge these perceptions, which one would expect if the provisions of UNSCR 1325 were taken seriously.

In the 2003 CEDAW Report, there is mention of training for women in the Niger Delta on environmental security issues. This resulted in women's participation in compensation negotiations with oil companies in the region. This is in keeping with the provision in the Resolution for women to be better equipped to engage in conflict resolution at all decision-making levels.[34] The work of the Nigerian authorities on UNSCR 1325 has also been challenged within the CEDAW framework. The CEDAW Commission's response to the 2006 CEDAW Report from Nigeria was to request improved efforts to address the problems faced by internally displaced women (this is in line with UNSCR 1325).[35] The situation of women caught up in the hostilities in the Gbaramatu violence in 2009 (mentioned earlier) reinforces the validity of this point.

In 2007 there was a significant initiative that appears to be the only explicit reference[36] to UNSCR 1325 by the Ministry of Women's Affairs and Social Development. Unusually, this initiative also provided some evidence of the Ministry's engagement with the military on the participation of women in peace and security in Nigeria. In 2007, the Minster of Women's Affairs inaugurated an Inter-Ministerial Task Force on gender and peacekeeping. This was to enable Nigerian women to participate in 'peacekeeping processes as peace makers, peace-builders, peacekeepers and negotiators in conflict-torn countries'.[37] This addresses a vital element of the requirements of UNSCR 1325 as it relates to the participation of women in mechanisms of conflict prevention, management and resolution and the mainstreaming of gender perspectives in peace support operations. The Task Force has been an important part of a broader process that has seen Nigeria participate in a pilot programme on gender and peacekeeping.[38]

Within the Legislature there has been no reported engagement with UNSCR 1325. It is significant that (as was the case with the Ministry), the Legislature has argued for the increased participation of women within formal governance structures (including the Legislature) – sentiments which are consistent with the provisions of the Resolution.[39] However, rather notoriously, in 2008 the chair of the Senate Committee on Women and Children proposed an Indecent Dressing Bill. This attracted widespread criticism on account of its gender bias against women, who are part of an already predominantly patriarchal system and run the risk of gender-based violence.[40] This highlights the critical point that simply having more women in leadership is insufficient to achieve the objectives of UNSCR 1325. This must be accompanied by a gendered perspective as well as a commitment to reject gender-based discrimination against women in any form. This incident also demonstrated that it is imperative to challenge an elite leadership that is removed from the realities faced by the broader populace. Much of the discussion on the conflict and its impact on the Nigerian women has to do with realities that are remote from the distant, yet ruling elite (these women are often based in rural areas and have limited access to resources and power).

When one looks at the reality of the engagement of women in senior leadership positions in peace and security structures in Nigeria, one finds a troubling picture. Women are poorly represented in the political leadership, and they continue to be affected by the deep-seated gender-based discrimination against women in peace and security initiatives. Although there have been improvements within the Legislature,[41] women still constitute only 6 per cent of the Members of the House of Representatives and 6 per cent of the Senate.[42] Within the Federal Executive Council (Federal Government Ministers),[43] representation is also inadequate, although 17 per cent of Federal Ministers are women.[44]

When it comes to the representation of women in leadership positions, it should be noted that there are female senators, albeit in limited numbers, in committee leadership positions on defence and army matters, environmental and health matters and on issues to do with women and youth. On the other hand, the larger House of Representatives fares much worse, with no women in leadership positions on its committees. One could argue that the female Ministers of Petroleum Resources and of Aviation deal with security issues, given the existence of security threats to petroleum extraction and aviation in Nigeria.[45]

Exporting peace: UNSCR 1325 and Nigeria's peacekeeping responsibilities

In Nigeria, the government's greatest commitment to UNSCR 1325 is to be found within its peacekeeping responsibilities, in particular the earlier mentioned Inter-Ministerial Task Force on Gender and Peacekeeping. Nigeria's dedication to UN Peace Support Operations has been longstanding, beginning with its commitment of troops to the UN Peace Mission in Congo, only days after the granting of independence to Nigeria. Over the years this has expanded to include UNTAG Namibia, UNTAC Cambodia, UNPROVOR Yugoslavia, UNAVEM (1, 2 and 3) Angola, UNISON Somalia, UNMOZ Mozambique, UNMIR Rwanda, UNBIH Bosnia-Herzegovina, UNTAET East Timor, UNAMSIL Sierra Leone, UNMIL Liberia, MINUSTAH Haiti, UNOCI Cote d'Ivoire, UNMIK Kosovo, ONUB Burundi, UNMIS Sudan and UNAMID Darfur.

In December 2009, the number of Nigerian women that were deployed in UN Peace Support Operations within the army and the police stood at 337 out of a total of 6,807 personnel. It has been argued that this is an improvement and reflects attempts to support the implementation of UNSCR 1325 by the Nigerian authorities.[46] This is unconvincing, given that this number represents only 5 per cent of the total. However, Nigeria's contribution to UN peace missions compares well with that of other countries. As of December 2009, Nigeria was deploying the highest number of women globally; it was tied for second place (among the top ten troop-contributing countries) in respect of the proportion of military and police personnel who are women.[47] For these reasons Nigeria has received major accolades for its performance. In March 2009, a UN official,

Andrew Carpenter, cited Nigeria's impressive performance in increasing the proportion of women serving within peace support operations.[48] In February 2010, the UNMIL SRSG commended Nigeria on its deployment of women police officers in peacekeeping operations, particularly in Liberia.[49]

There are continuing efforts to increase the proportion of women among Nigeria's deployed peacekeepers. There are proposals for targeted recruitment strategies for female peacekeepers as well as for the creation of a mechanism for sharing lessons on the recruitment of female peacekeepers with troop-contributing countries.[50] Nonetheless, problems persist. The most common challenges relate to competing family commitments and a lack of relevant skills, such as driving four-wheel-drive vehicles.[51] The military response has been to adapt their operational structure to address the specific needs of female peacekeepers. This reportedly includes the provision of communication network systems as well as the institution of monthly 'welfare flights' (often at no cost). In addition, special driving, training and testing sessions with the Nigeria Federal Road Safety Corporation have been instituted for female peacekeepers.[52]

An additional issue is the extent to which those deployed function in decision-making positions. In 2010, a report by the *New York Times* suggested that the Nigerian female officers serving within UNMIL were mainly employed in traditional roles, such as cooking, nursing, clerical work and teaching.[53] The preponderance of women in these roles undermines the objective of increasing their participation in senior decision-making capacities, especially when it comes to 'hard' security matters.

The improved commitment to the role of women as peacekeepers within the Nigerian Army is no doubt necessary for the improved efficiency of the peacekeeping operation as a whole. For instance, on the basis of their peacekeeping experiences in Darfur, it became clear that societal norms provided for limited contact between women and men who were considered strangers.[54] The need for female personnel to interact with local women in Darfur was an important factor leading to the targeting of female officers within the armed forces.[55] This experience prompted the Nigerian Army Peacekeeping Centre to organise specialised training programmes on cultural sensitivities, using the expertise of Sudanese living in Nigeria.[56] As a result of their deployment of female peacekeepers, the peace force has been able to improve the perceptions of safety among Sudanese women. Female peacekeepers in many instances accompany the Darfurian women to collect firewood – an activity that previously saw them being attacked by armed men.[57]

It has also been acknowledged that female peacekeepers have an important role to play in intelligence and information gathering in particular contexts within peacekeeping operations, particularly where GBV is being investigated. Female victims are more willing to interact with other women in these cases.[58] Nigerian female peacekeepers are being trained specifically to undertake these roles and to participate in operations to gather intelligence.[59] This engagement in peacekeeping operations also led to a more general increase in training opportunities within the Nigerian security services. For instance, in 2009, the United

Nations Development Fund for Women (UNIFEM), along with the Nigerian Police Force, organised training for police officers engaged in addressing GBV against women, including human trafficking, within Nigeria.[60]

Nigeria seeks to preserve its international peacekeeping reputation, hence its willingness to introduce these progressive changes. However, its participation in peacekeeping has been marred by controversy: its troops have been variously accused of looting, of illegal trading in arms and contraband minerals and, perhaps most importantly for this chapter, of sexual exploitation, particularly of women. There was a major incident in 2005, where ten officers within the United Nations Mission DR Congo (MONUC) were accused of sexual harassment of local women. This led to the Nigerian government's withdrawal of the 120-strong police contingent with the promise 'to bring the full weight of the law to bear on those individuals found culpable'.[60] The response to accusations of sexual abuse and exploitation by police personnel has been met with the promise of severe penalties for police officers serving with MONUC who are found guilty of these offences.[62] The Nigerian Army has adopted the UN's zero-tolerance approach, and this is confirmed by its Code of Conduct for personnel on peace-support operations.[63]

In response to the drive to eliminate future risks to the reputation of the Nigerian forces, training for peacekeepers is being stepped up, specifically in relation to sexual violence which conflicts with UNSCR 1820 and 1888 (UNSCR 1325 is not explicitly mentioned).[64] It is argued that peacekeepers have limited knowledge of what constitutes sexual violence, especially in relation to war crimes.[65] The Nigerian Army has also increased the provision of recreational facilities for peacekeepers to reduce stress levels, and it provides regular travel leave for troops.[66] Unfortunately, these measures do not address the deeper challenges of structural violence against women in the Nigerian context nor the extent to which this may influence the behavior of male troops in conflict locations, and in situations where women are particularly vulnerable.

Non-state actors and UNSCR 1325: raising awareness and challenging the status quo in Nigeria

The third group of actors that has emerged in Nigeria in relation to the implementation of the UNSCR 1325 in Nigeria comprises civil society actors. We focus on the work of one of the most salient of these actors in Nigeria, the West African Network for Peacebuilding (WANEP). The aim of the Programme's Women in Peacebuilding Network (WIPNET) is to examine the efficacy of a civil society's attempts to raise awareness of UNSCR 1325. WIPNET, which was established in 2002, is essentially a regional programme, but has developed a consolidated country programme in Nigeria.[67] Its mandate is to build capacity within existing women's groups at rural and grassroots levels, utilising methods that take into account the low literacy levels that are prevalent.[68]

WIPNET's approach centred on women's peace activism, and on their participation in peace and security processes. They also address the latent culture of structural violence that dominates Nigerian society.[69] Their approach is cognisant of the challenges presented by the particular Nigerian situation. In addition to promoting the application of the Resolution in Nigeria, in June 2006 the organisation initiated the translation of UNSCR 1325 into local Nigerian languages (Ibo, Tiv and Ijaw). This supplemented existing translations in Yoruba and Hausa (WIPNET also produced the Hausa translation.[70]). These translations into major Nigerian languages gave the Resolution a wider reach and assisted in raising awareness of its provisions. In addition, the other two languages (Tiv and Ijaw) are dominant in conflict areas in the Middle Belt and in the Niger Delta and are therefore especially relevant for vulnerable populations. WIPNET has also engaged with existing initiatives, such as the 'Community Women Radio Program', in order to disseminate information on the Resolution.[71]

Although WIPNET Nigeria is a national programme, its regional origins influence its approach and help to explain its relative success, given the general lack of awareness of UNSCR 1325. The extension of conflict within the West African region necessarily means that efforts at peacebuilding have to extend to other countries in the region. This is significant given that there seems to be political will at the West African regional level (see Awa Ceesay Ebo's chapter on ECOWAS in this volume). The existence of WIPNET as a regional network means that it is able to draw on its experience in the broader sub-region in post-conflict contexts where there has been greater success at integrating the women into the peace and security agenda, as in Liberia (see the Liberian chapter by Njoki Wamai in this volume). Other countries in the region, such as Sierra Leone and Liberia, have also benefited from the presence of UN missions (see also the chapter on Sierra Leone by Barnes in this volume). WIPNET was able to bring its experience of operating in these countries to bear on the multi-faceted Nigerian context.

The significance of this regional overview is particularly apparent in WANEP's work on the Niger Delta. As the coordinator of the West African Early Warning System, it has been in a position to observe the dynamics of conflict in the sub-region, including in the Niger Delta.[72] In addition, as a partner institution with the Economic Community of West African States (ECOWAS) and its Early Warning System, it participates in addressing peace and security challenges at a strategic level. In this regard, it has highlighted the impact of the Niger Delta crisis on women, as called for by UNSCR 1325. It has led the call to address the situation of women and children as internally displaced people (as a result of the violence in May 2009). It has campaigned for the protection of women from all forms of GBV, and for the involvement of women in peace processes, including in the widely reported Niger Delta Amnesty Programme.[73]

Conclusion

Countries that are not officially recognised as being in conflict appear to be more or less excluded from the ongoing discourse regarding UNSCR 1325. This has influenced the dynamics of operationalising the Resolution in Nigeria. Government actors seem entirely unaware of the need to push the agenda of women, peace and security within Nigeria. The Resolution by the Ministry of Women's Affairs and Social Development focussed on the Inter-Ministerial Task Force and did not include the main actors on peacekeeping issues. The Ministry seems more comfortable working within the provisons of CEDAW, which does not explicitly address peace and security issues. This may explain its apparent passivity when it comes to the participation of women in peace and security structures.

The Nigerian military appears to have made great strides in addressing UNSCR 1325 and has earned accolades, chiefly as a result of its international peacekeeping duties. Although not addressed in this chapter, it would be immensely valuable to examine how this does (or does not) reflect on the way in which women are regarded within the ranks of the police and military. Recent reports of proposals by the Inspector General of the Nigerian Police present a troubling picture: female police officers with civilian spouses were to be expelled from the police barracks (along with their families), because they ought not to have the same access as men who are household heads. (This argument is of course based on the dominant socio-cultural norm which sees men as the main breadwinners.[74]

The general lack of confidence regarding the conduct of the police is also a critical source of insecurity for the citizenry, and especially women, in Nigeria. This is underscored by reports of the endemic nature of SGBV; this includes rape of women by police and security officers who usually go unpunished.[75] This disjuncture between the performance of the government and military (with regard to peacekeeping duties) on UNSCR 1325, on the one hand and the performance of police in the domestic arena on the other, suggests that there is much reliance on international oversight, notably from the UN, vis-à-vis local mechanisms, for the implementation of the various elements of UNSCR 1325 in Nigeria.

As far as the domestic implementation of UNSCR 1325 is concerned, civil society has taken the lead in a context where debate on the Resolution has been largely absent. The WIPNET approach has been very effective, with its base in local women's activism and its sub-regional structures. It is imperative that this work engages directly with statutory structures, even if this is pursued in a parallel process. Some of the proposals put forward by leaders within the legislature risk undermining the efforts that are being made with regard to the Resolution. There must be a concerted effort at all levels and by all actors to drive the objectives of UNSCR 1325, using whichever approach is most appropriate. These actors and the milieus within which they function are necessarily interdependent. The success of peacekeeping troops cannot be isolated from their performance domestically, nor can a broad-based campaign around UNSCR 1325 ignore the way in which the leadership of the Nigerian state functions.

It is strategically important to give greater prominence to Nigeria's role as a major troop-contributing country, particularly given the impact of the troops' presence in recipient countries that may be at a pivotal point in the construction of a security-related gender relations framework. This is one way in which all those who are concerned can encourage the Nigerian government to accept UNSCR 1325; this will in turn help to ensure the adequate training and preparation of the peacekeepers in the light of the principles of UNSCR 1325. This may be the most effective path to acceptance and implementation of the Resolution within Nigeria. Success here will necessarily influence Nigeria's approach to the relationship between women, peace and security within Nigeria.

WIPNET[76] rightly argues that the onus for implementation must lie with the women themselves, 'in order to ensure that the instruments remain relevant and are applied appropriately'. This implies that women need to be included in the necessary local, national and regional processes. Because gender relations involve both men and women; every effort must be made to engage men in this discourse. Although there are valid grounds for criticising the lack of awareness of UNSCR 1325, this does not preclude ongoing work to protect the peace and security interests of women. Every effort must be made to tap into those structures that are grounded in valid local perceptions of how best to preserve women's security. This remains the strongest avenue to gaining acceptance of the relevance of UNSCR 1325 for Nigeria.

Notes

1 F. Omorodion, 'The Impact of Petroleum Refinery on the Economic Livelihoods of Women in the Niger Delta Region of Nigeria', *JENDA: A Journal of Culture and African Women Studies*, 2004, Issue 6.

2 M. Muhammad, *Nigeria: In the Shadows of Men – Women's Political Marginalisation*, Inter Press News Service, 12 March 2010, http://allafrica.com/stories/201003130001.html (accessed 17 March 2010).

3 Oxfam, *Women and Poverty in Nigeria in Measuring Poverty in Nigeria*, 2003, www.oxfam.org.uk/what_we_do/resources/downloads/wp_nigeria/wp_nigeria_womenpov.pdf (accessed 3 May 2006).

4 According to UNFPA, the illiteracy rate for women in Nigeria is 36 per cent, as against 22 per cent for men. UNFPA, *United Nations Population Fund Profile: Nigeria*, 2005, www.unfpa.org/profile/nigeria.cfm (accessed 12 May 2007).

5 K. Oyediran and U. Isiugo-Abanihe, 'Perceptions of Nigerian Women on Domestic Violence: Evidence from 2003 Nigeria Demographic and Health Survey', *African Journal of Reproductive Health*, 2005 Vol. 9, No. 2.

6 F. Omorodion, op. cit.

7 International Alert, *Report of the National Consultation: Implementing UN SCR 1325 in Nigeria*, 2005, www.international-alert.org/pdfs/niger_cns.pdf (accessed 18 June 2006).

8 Wilton Park, *Peace and Security: Implementing Peace and Security Resolution 1325*, 2006 www.wiltonpark.org.uk/documents/conferences/WP816/pdfs/WP816.pdf (accessed 21 January 2007).

9 International Alert, op. cit.

10 I. Uwafiokun, 'The Changing Phases of the Niger Delta Conflict: Implications for Conflict Escalation and the Return of Peace', *Conflict, Security & Development*, 2009, Vol. 9, Issue 3, pp. 307–331; F. Iyayi, 'Niger Delta Crisis: Development and socio cultural implications', Paper presented at the Forum organised by Petroleum and Natural Gas Senior Staff Association of Nigeria (PENGASSAN) at Gateway Hotel Ijebu Ode, 17 June 2008; UNDP, *Niger Delta Human Development Report*, 2006, Abuja: UN House.

11 Vanguard Newspapers, *Post Amnesty – Govs, Clark, Mitee, Others Task FG As Talks Kick Off Today*, 15 March 2010, http://allafrica.com/stories/201003150004.html (accessed 15 March 2010).

12 Christian Science Monitor, *Nigeria Violence: Muslim-Christian Clashes Kill Hundreds*, 8 March 2010, www.csmonitor.com/World/Africa/2010/0308/Nigeria-violence-Muslim-Christian-clashes-kill-hundreds (accessed 17 March 2010).

13 BBC News, *Nigeria Ethnic Violence Leaves Hundreds Dead*, 8 March 2010, http://news.bbc.co.uk/1/hi/8555018.stm (accessed 14 March 2010); Daily Champion, *Jos Crisis Re-Echoes The Vulnerability of Women, Children*, 14 March 2010, http://allafrica.com/stories/201003150500.html (accessed 14 March 2010).

14 IRIN Humanitarian News and Analysis, *Investigations of Mass Killings in Nigeria*, 13 April 2010, http://m.irinnews.org/88797.htm (accessed 15 April 2010).

15 Human Rights Watch, *The Niger Delta: No Democratic Dividend*, 2002, www.hrw.org/reports/2002/nigeria3/ (accessed 12 April 2006).

16 Banjul Accord, *Communique of the Niger Delta Women Consultative Meeting, Banjul, Gambia*, 7–12 August 2000, www.peacewomen.org/resources/Nigeria/Niger-DeltaWomen2000.html (accessed 1 March 2007).

17 BBC News, *Nigerian Militants Rape Women*, 16 March 2009, http://news.bbc.co.uk/1/hi/world/africa/7945820.stm (accessed 6 April 2009).

18 West Africa Network for Peacebuilding, 'Ending Niger Delta Crisis: Exploring Women's Participation in the Peace Process', *West Africa Early Warning Policy Brief*, August 2009, www.wanep.org/image/pb_nigeria_aug09.pdf (accessed 29 October 2009).

19 International Alert, op. cit.

20 A. Imam, 'Women, Muslim Laws and Human Rights in Nigeria Africa Program', *Occasional Scholar Series*, 2004, Woodrow Wilson International Center for Scholars.

21 J. Asuni, 'Nigeria: The Tiv-Jukun Conflict in Wukari, Taraba State', in *Searching for Peace in Africa: An Overview of Conflict Prevention and Management Activities*, 2000, International Books, Christian Science Church Center, Boston, Massachusetts.

22 IRIN Humanitarian News and Analysis, *Women's Stand-Off With Chevron-Texaco in Day Four*, 11 July 2002, http://allafrica.com/stories/200207110485.html (accessed 26 September 2006).

23 Vanguard Newspapers *Itsekiri, Ijaw Women Seize Shell, Chevron Delta Facilities*, 10 August 2002, http://allafrica.com/stories/200208100100.html (accessed 27 September 2006).

24 Daily Champion, *Jos Crisis Re-Echoes The Vulnerability of Women, Children*, 14 March 2010.

25 At the 2004 Sub-Regional Meeting on the Decade Review of the Implementation of Beijing Platform of Action chaired by the former Minister for Women's Affairs (and Youth Development, at the time), Mrs Rita Akpan, it was noted that 'Women should be systematically included in conflict prevention and resolution mechanisms; states should be enjoined to comply with convention 1325 relating to peace from UN Economic Commission for Africa', *Sub-Regional Meeting on the Decade Review of the Implementation of Beijing Platform of Action Synthesis Report*, 13–15 April 2004, Abuja, Nigeria, http://66.102.9.104/search?q=cache:9DpsAGE00DMJ:www.uneca.org/acgd/Publications/West%2520Africa%2520ReportBeijing%2B10.doc+ministry+of+women%27s+affairs%2BNigeria%2B1325&hl=en&gl=uk&ct=clnk&cd=3 (accessed 12 April 2006).

26 International Alert, op. cit.

27 International Alert, op. cit.

28 This Day Newspapers, *CEDAW Bill to be Re-presented to the National Assembly*, 3 March 2010, http://allafrica.com/stories/201002040684.html (accessed 5 March 2010).

29 IWTC, *The Intersections between CEDAW and UN Resolutions 1325 and 1820*, Geneva, January 2009, www.wilpf.int.ch/PDF/humanrights/HR%20Update%2009/CEDAW%20on%201325%20and%201820.pdf (accessed 18 May 2009).

30 Ibid.

31 UN, *Consideration of Reports Submitted by States Parties under Article 18 of CEDAW Second and Third Periodic Reports of States Parties: Nigeria*, 1997, http://daccess-dds-ny.un.org/doc/UNDOC/GEN/N97/267/73/IMG/N9726773.pdf?OpenElement (accessed 26 September 2007).

32 UN, *Consideration of Reports Submitted by States Parties under Article 18 of CEDAW Sixth Periodic Report of States Parties: Nigeria*, 2006, http://daccess-dds-ny.un.org/doc/UNDOC/GEN/N06/687/84/PDF/N0668784.pdf?OpenElement (accessed 26 September 2007); UN, *Consideration of Reports Submitted by States Parties under Article 18 of CEDAW Combined Fourth and Fifth Periodic Reports of States Parties: Nigeria*, 2003, http://daccess-dds-ny.un.org/doc/UNDOC/GEN/N03/345/65/PDF/N0334565.pdf?OpenElement (accessed 26 September 2007).

33 UN, *Consideration of Reports Submitted by States Parties under Article 18 of CEDAW Combined Fourth and Fifth Periodic Reports of States parties: Nigeria*, 2003, op. cit.

34 Ibid.

35 UN, *Response from CEDAW Committee to Nigeria's Sixth Periodic Report on CEDAW*, July 2008 http://www2.ohchr.org/english/bodies/cedaw/docs/CEDAW.C.NGA.CO.6.pdf (accessed 26 September 2009).

36 When the former Minister of Women's Affairs and Social Development, Mrs Saudatu Usman Bungudu, responded to a Committee on CEDAW in response to a query on the implementation of UNSCR 1325, the only reference made on this was to the Inter-Ministerial Task Force on Gender and Peacekeeping. UN *Notes from CEDAW Committee Hearings*, 3 July 2008, www.un.org/News/Press/docs/2008/wom1691.doc.htm (accessed 25 June 2009).

37 S.U. Bungudu, *Statement by Her Excellency, Mrs Saudatu Usman Bungudu, Honourable Minster of Women's Affairs and Social Development, Federal Republic of Nigeria at the 52nd Session of the Commission on the Status of Women*, New York, 27 February 2008, www.un.org/womenwatch/daw/csw/csw52/statements_missions/nigeria.pdf (accessed 10 April 2009); Daily Trust Newspapers, *Ministry Wants Women in Peace-Keeping*, 1 October 2007.

38 UN DPKO, *Notes from Strategy Workshop on the Implementation of UNSCR 1325 on Women Peace and Security in Peacekeeping Contexts with Women's Constituencies from Troop and Police Contributing Countries*, 7–9 February 2007, Pretoria, www.peacekeepingbestpractices.unlb.org/PBPS/Library/Recommendations%20and%20Conclusions.pdf (accessed 28 July 2009).

39 Daily Independent, *Women Lawmakers Want More Slots in Parliament*, 16 July 2009, http://allafrica.com/stories/200907160377.html (accessed 11 December 2009).

40 Alliances for Africa, *Unconstitutional and Indecent: A Legal Opinion on the Indecent Dressing Bill*, 2008, www.imow.org/dynamic/user_files/file_name_183.pdf (accessed 12 April 2010).

41 As of March 2010.

42 Website of the National Assembly of Nigeria, www.nassnig.org/ (accessed 23 March 2010).

43 As of April 2010.

44 The Nigeria Exchange website www.ngex.com/nigeria/govt/officials/ministers.htm (accessed 14 April 2010).

45 As has been discussed, the petroleum extraction in Nigeria has given rise to militant activity targeting the Nigerian state on the basis of perceived injustices on the part of the state in a failure to include people of the Niger Delta in oil wealth distribution and the environmental degradation of the region. In addition, in December 2009, there was an attempted terrorist attack by a British-trained Nigerian, Umar Farouk Abdul

Muttalab, on a North Western US aeroplane, en route from Lagos, Nigeria, which led to Nigeria being placed on the US terror watchlist in February 2010. Next Newspapers, *Muttalab is a Stranger, Dora Akunyili Says*, 24 December 2009, http://234next.com/csp/cms/sites/Next/News/5503108147/Mutallab_is_a_stranger,_ Dora_Akunyili.csp (accessed 9 January 2010).

46 Interview with Colonel Koko Essien of the Nigerian Army, 16 February 2010.

47 UN DPKO, *Report of Rankings of Military and Police Contributions to UN Operations*, December 2009, www.un.org/en/peacekeeping/contributors/2009/dec09_2.pdf (accessed 26 February 2010).

48 Women's eNews, *UN Official Calls for More Female Peacekeepers*, 10 March 2009, www.womensenews.org/story/international-policyunited-nations/090310/un-official-calls-more-female-peacekeepers (accessed 10 March 2010).

49 UNMIL Press Release, *UN Envoy Lauds Nigeria for Enhancing Women's Role in Peacekeeping Missions*, 9 February 2010, http://unmil.org/1article. asp?id=3707&zdoc=1 (accessed 10 March 2010).

50 M. Cabrera-Balleza, S. Cook, R. Johal, N. Johnston, M. Kihunah, H. Leneveu, V. Nadjibulla, K. Picirrilli, V. Semler, S. Shteir, *From Local to Global: Making Peace Work for Women. The NGO Working Group on Women, Peace and Security, Security Council Resolution 1325 on Women Peace and Security – 5 Years On Report*, October 2005, www.womenpeacesecurity.org/media/pdf-fiveyearson.pdf (accessed 28 September 2006).

51 Interview with Colonel Koko Essien of the Nigerian Army, 16 February 2010.

52 Ibid.

53 New York, *The Female Factor: A Female Approach to Peacekeeping*, 5 March 2010, www.nytimes.com/2010/03/06/world/africa/06iht-ffpeace.html?pagewanted=all (accessed 10 March 2010).

54 Interview with Colonel Koko Essien of the Nigerian Army, 16 February 2010.

55 Ibid.

56 Ibid.

57 Ibid.

58 Ibid.

59 Ibid.

60 UNIFEM News, *Nigerian Police Officers Trained in Responses to Violence Against Women and Human Trafficking*, 26 November 2009, www.unifem.org/news_events/ story_detail.php?StoryID=994 (accessed 26 February 2010).

61 ISN Security Watch, *Nigeria Recalls UN Peacekeepers Over Sex Abuse Scandal*, 19 September 2005, www.peacewomen.org/SP/un/pkwatch/pkindex.html (accessed 17 June 2006).

62 Ibid.

63 Interview with Colonel Koko Essien of the Nigerian Army, 16 February 2010.

64 Ibid.

65 Ibid.

66 Ibid.

67 WIPNET-WANEP Nigeria website, www.wanepnigeria.org/program.php?pr=193 (accessed 12 April 2010).

68 WIPNET *Report of 4th Annual Women in Peacebuilding Regional Conference – Revisiting the UN SCR 1325 on Women, Peace and Security; Opportunities and Challenges for the Future*, 2005, WIPNET-WANEP.

69 WIPNET–Nigeria: *The Importance of Translating UN SCR 1325*, www.peacewomen. org/1325inTranslation/using_1325_translations/WIPNET_Nigeria.html.

70 Ibid.

71 Peace Women E-News, *Peace Women Interview with Bridget Osakwe of WIPNET – Nigeria: The Importance of Translating UN SCR 1325*, Issue 100, April 2008, www. peacewomen.org/news/1325News/Issue100.html (accessed 10 June 2009).

72 WANEP 'Ending Niger Delta Crisis: exploring Women's participation in the Peace Process', *West Africa Early Warning Policy Brief* August 2009 www.wanep.org/ image/pb_nigeria_aug09.pdf (accessed 29 October 2009).
73 Ibid.
74 This Day Newspapers, *Onovo versus Police Officers*, 18 February 2010, http:// allafrica.com/stories/201002180549.html (accessed 20 March 2010).
75 Amnesty International, op. cit.
76 WIPNET, 2005, op. cit.

7 Rwanda and the implementation of UNSCR 1325

Kiri-Ann E. Richardson Olney

Introduction

The targeting of women during the Rwandan genocide and the critical role that they played in the immediate aftermath both justify and validate the intended purpose of UN Security Council Resolution 1325 (UNSCR 1325). The 1990–1994 civil war, which left the population of Rwanda with a 70 per cent female majority,[1] catapulted women and girls into new roles during the process of rebuilding the country and effecting a lasting peace. While UNSCR 1325 was not created until October 2000, six years after the Rwandan genocide, the way in which women's roles had been radically transformed during that time is crucial for understanding why it is needed and how best to implement it.

The Rwandan genocide was highly gender focused in that women, both Hutu and Tutsi, were targeted as a group of their own. Ostensibly the conflict stemmed from ethnic tensions between Hutus and Tutsis, but in actuality it was a societal power struggle in which influential women were targeted by Hutu extremists who perceived them as a threat. The consequent infringement of women's security was extreme and manifested itself in gender-based violence (GBV), particularly rape.

With men conspicuously absent in the aftermath of the genocide, women in Rwanda have gained higher status in both the formal and informal spheres in society. They have become peacebuilders, government officials, 'heads of households, community leaders and financial providers', all of which were previously considered masculine roles.[2] While this development is consistent with the objectives of UNSCR 1325, it actually arose from necessity, rather than in response to progressive peacebuilding processes under an UNSCR 1325 framework. Instead, the inefficacy of the peacekeeping efforts in Rwanda to manage the violent conflict unleashed on its population led to a process of negotiating gender roles. This contributed to changes in women's socially understood responsibilities as they were forced to rebuild their lives and communities with very little support.

The experiences of Rwandan women during and after the conflict demonstrate the relevance of UNSCR 1325 and illustrate its functionality, respectively. The emphasis of brutality on women during the conflict could arguably have been ameliorated by the gender-sensitive conflict management processes as recommended by the Resolution, if it had been in place. In fact, the inadequacy of the efforts of the international community to support the Rwandan population, and especially women, during the genocide is a critical justification for the need for UNSCR 1325. Moreover, the success of Rwanda's post-conflict reconstruction, which was driven by women (albeit by necessity), demonstrates the importance of their involvement in the process. Understanding how Rwanda's reconstruction developed 'naturally' can provide a model for implementing UNSCR 1325 in other countries. Furthermore, in spite of being six years too late for Rwanda, UNSCR 1325 still has much to offer the country's continuing process of reconstruction and recovery.

This chapter examines the Rwandan case study by considering the idea of security as a gendered concept and by applying this idea to women's roles and security in Rwanda before and after the genocide. The chapter also explores the involvement of the international community in the Rwandan genocide of 1994 and its aftermath and, within this context, compares the development of post-conflict reconstruction and peacebuilding in Rwanda with the prescriptions of UNSCR 1325 by focusing specifically on the articles that refer to peacekeeping, peacebuilding and the protection and care of women and girls during and after armed conflict.

Security as a gendered concept

The way in which women were targeted during the Rwandan conflict highlights the importance of considering human security as a gendered concept. Rwanda's national security was compromised during the conflict, and UNSCR 1325 focuses on international peace and security, but in addition it was the human security of women in Rwanda that was violated and subsequently re-established. The infringement of individual security during the conflict, whether economic, food, health, environmental, personal, community or political security, demands that security be considered in human terms.[3] The particular ways in which Rwandan women suffered the violation of their security in all of these categories before and during the genocide, as well as the progress in their improved circumstances afterwards further emphasise the need to consider human security as a gendered concept.

Women's security is affected differently from that of men because of their 'physical, emotional and material differences and due to the important social, economic, and political inequalities existing between women and men'.[4] This was precisely the case in Rwanda, but women's security was breached most profoundly on a personal, physical and emotional level by extreme sexual violence. They were also politically marginalised in the lead-up to the genocide, and particularly economically marginalised in the aftermath.

Regardless of their ethnicity, it is estimated that over 250,000 women were raped during the genocide.[5] Women's bodies were treated as 'the figurative and literal sites of combat'.[6] Rape and other forms of sexual violence in Rwanda were 'a way of inverting all social norms and destroying society'.[7] This highlights the complexity of the conflict, and the depth of a power struggle that was not just between ethnic groups, but also between men and women. All Tutsi women were targets of sexual attack; Hutu men employed rape as a weapon of war 'to destabilize Tutsi society and to break its resistance', which is clearly a breach of community security.[8] Educated, elite women of both ethnicities were attacked, and some Hutu women were specifically targeted in retribution for the violence that Tutsi women had suffered.[9]

Sexual violence was a violation not only of women's personal security, but also of their security in social terms as a result of risks presented to their health. Gender-specific healthcare for the injuries that they suffered, and for the pregnancies that were a consequence of the sexual violence that they endured, was practically non-existent during the conflict, and quite limited in the aftermath. Individual testimonies suggest that women looked after themselves and each other as peacekeeping forces were not trained or resourced to provide such care.[10]

The under-representation of Rwandan women in parliament before the conflict, where they held 18 per cent of the seats,[11] undermined women's engagement within the political sphere, thus limiting their representation within the governance system and possibly challenging their political security. The conflict intensified this poor participation of women in the political system, with representation falling to an abysmal 4 per cent in the immediate aftermath.[12] Within the economic sphere, the broad prohibition in Rwandan law and culture of women owning or inheriting land or property challenged their economic security until the law was changed after the conflict.[13] The severity of this marginalisation shows the constraints on women's security until reconstruction was well under way. For instance, in the aftermath of the conflict, many women who had relied on male relatives were destitute and unable to access resources as a result of inheritance norms that were not codified, discriminatory against women and ethnically motivated, as Hutu wives of Tutsi husbands were sometimes threatened by Tutsi in-laws with regards to inheritance claims in the post-conflict period.[14]

Rwandan women are not unique in their suffering, yet UNSCR 1325 was necessary to force gender-specific security issues onto the international stage and to give gender-sensitive responses a more prominent place in the mandates of peacekeeping operations and in security policy. The hope of recognising gender as a critical issue in security policy formulation and implementation has been realised in UNSCR 1325, which 'not only focuses on violence experienced by women, but also recognizes the important role a gender perspective has with regard to peacebuilding and conflict resolution'.[15] The resolution recognises that the unique impact conflict has on women also has a consequent impact on lasting peace, and therefore stresses the importance of their role in conflict prevention and management, peacebuilding and post-conflict reconstruction.

Women's roles and security before the genocide

The later 1980s and the early 1990s saw urban Rwandan women challenge the more subordinate roles to which they had been traditionally assigned. This was as a result of their increasing and widespread acquisition of formal higher education as well as high-level jobs in the formal sector.[16] As such, women who had been expected to work in the home, for example, began to secure powerful jobs in business and government.[17]

Although educated urban women were beginning to enjoy political and economic gains in the decade before the genocide, the result was that their insecurity increased exponentially. Women's rights were repressed immediately before the genocide to an even greater extent as the Habyarimana regime tightened its grip on the country. Well-educated, single women were among the first to be targeted. Extreme persecution and acts of sexual violence increased dramatically in the name of public morality, as progressive women were a symbol of development feared by Hutu extremists.[18] In 1983, for example, the government attempted to repress young urban women who 'either dressed too stylishly or had European boyfriends'.[19] Taylor reports that they were intimidated by authority figures such as policemen and soldiers, and that some 'literally had their clothes cut off their bodies with bayonets' before being carried off to detention centres.[20] Most of these women were employed, financially self-sufficient and highly educated.[21] With an ethnically motivated dimension to these developments, Tutsi women suffered disproportionately as the main target of Hutu extremist propaganda. They were portrayed as conniving 'temptresses' and regarded as 'pivotal enemies' in the struggle to regain patriarchal control and the Hutu domination.[22]

The apogee of the targeting of well-educated and powerful women was the assassination of Prime Minister Agathe Uwiringiyimana. This woman, a well-educated and successful Hutu, who had criticised Habyarimana's regime for failing to implement the Arusha Accords, was a threat as an anti-ethnicist, and as an educated, articulate woman.[23] She was killed within hours of the start of the genocide. Her death can also be interpreted as a tragic manifestation of the societal power struggle within the apparently ethnic conflict.

Women's security was greatly challenged within the social sphere as a result of marriage relationships. They were seen as a source of tension because they represented a 'permeable boundary between the two ethnic groups'.[24] This was based on the reality of intermarriage across ethnic boundaries, a prevalent practice that spanned centuries.[25] However, notably in times of heightened tensions, especially on an ethnic basis, married women's identities were called into question. According to Mamdani, people always identified themselves as either Hutu or Tutsi: there were no 'hybrids', no one was 'Hutsi'.[26] A wife adopted her husband's ethnicity, which was passed on patrilineally.[27] In fact many high-level Hutu extremists had Tutsi wives or mistresses, which also placed them in the unfortunate predicament of having relationships and children with enemy women.[28]

The origin of women's insecurity in Rwanda was a deeply embedded social power struggle, as well as being entwined in the ethno-political issues of the genocide. Women were perceived to be taking the societal positions that Hutu extremists felt were rightfully theirs. This compounded the gendered dimension of the atrocities committed during the genocide, which had repercussions not just for progressive urban women, but for all Rwandan women.

... after the genocide

The state of total devastation in which Rwanda was left following the genocide, and the radically changed demographic, with women now a 70 per cent majority of the population,[29] necessitated a change in their roles. Women were left with the responsibility of rebuilding their country, which, in spite of their continued gender-specific suffering in the immediate aftermath, became an opportunity for their security to be improved. This improvement in their security stance was also largely the result of their sound engagement in decision-making processes regarding all spheres of security.

Economic security was a significant challenge to women following the geno-cide. Women whose husbands had been killed or put in prison were left with no property and no financial resources to support their families,[30] due to the pre-existing laws preventing them from inheriting. In addition, although the law stated that returning exiles could not reclaim their property if they had been away for more than ten years, Tutsi returnees and their descendants who fled between 1990 and 1994 were illegally occupying the properties of Hutus.[31] This implied that Hutu women arguably found themselves in precarious positions given the already challenging realities that they faced on inheritance.

In addition to problems with economic security, there were continued challenges to the physical and emotional security of women. The abject poverty that women were left in as a manifestation of their severe economic insecurity, combined with the devastating effect of rape and sexual violence, was accompanied by an increase in prostitution.[32] Victims of rape continued to experience violations of their personal security, being frequently pressured into sex on the basis that they were already social outcasts.[33] In addition, achieving justice for the sexual violence they have suffered continues to be a problem for Rwandan women. Rape is a crime under Rwandan law and it is an obligation under the Geneva Conventions, signed by Rwanda, to prosecute rapists.[34] However, in practice the implementation of this legislation is left wanting. Unfortunately there is a lack of investigation of rape and sexual violence, and frequently both the women themselves and the judicial investigators are 'unaware that rape is prosecutable'.[35] Women are frequently too frightened to report it due to 'lack of faith in the system and fear of reprisal'.[36] It is possible to expect that had UNSCR 1325 existed during this period the UN peacekeeping force, the United Nations Assistance Mission for Rwanda (UNAMIR), and other international actors may have been better prepared to protect women, and to help them achieve justice.

It was the women survivors of the Rwandan conflict who made a difference to their own compromised security. Powley reports that Rwandans perceive that women 'really initiated the change at a grassroots level'.[37] Left with nothing, women had to reconstruct their lives and their society in all spheres. This included to start producing food again, to rebuild their homes and broader society and to wrestle back some semblance of security. This was an inversion of the gender roles being contested before the genocide: traditionally women would not have engaged in manual labour. In this initial period of reconstruction women would reportedly go out at night to mend the roofs on their houses and address other traditionally masculine jobs.[38] The fear of being seen to usurp previously masculine roles disintegrated, and women simply got on with ensuring their own, and their families' survival. In the immediate aftermath, women 'buried the dead, found homes for nearly 500,000 orphans, and built shelters'.[39] The change in gender roles has continued in Rwanda, such that it is now common to see female security and police officers, road crews and bus drivers, a radical transformation from the 'behind-the-scenes' role that women had played previously. Female education has also been on the increase: whereas female university admissions were very low before the genocide, the government now claim that they are about equal.[40] There is still clearly some way to go, given that women constitute 70 per cent of the total population.

Women's organisations began to take a leading role in rebuilding the country, as women took on the responsibility of finding ways of cooperating to solve common issues of security through a familiar and traditional medium. Before the genocide, every prefecture in Rwanda had a *foyer social*, a formal women's organisation responsible for collective child care, firewood collection, health issues and care of the aged.[41] After the genocide the reformation of these groups was not only one of the country's 'few enduring social continuities', but also provided support networks for women with shared experiences.[42] They offered various services that were designed to help women rebuild their lives, encompassing 'emergency material assistance, counselling, vocational training, and assistance with income-earning activities'.[43]

While most of the women's groups were organised around ethnicity, a few areas created multi-ethnic associations, an important step in healing the ethnic divide that had precipitated the conflict. In order to re-establish their security, women in these areas identified the need for cooperation and collaboration, which led them to 'overcome the mistrust spawned by the war and genocide'.[44] A basket-weaving initiative, for example, was started by one woman who wanted to provide other women with an activity that would heal the social wounds of the war, and allow them to earn money. Both Hutu and Tutsi women became involved in this project, which has since become an internationally lucrative business. Women come together every week to socialise and weave 'peace baskets',[45] demonstrating how they have improved their own economic and personal security. Other examples of women working together to improve their economic security include the founding of coffee cooperatives, an industry for which Rwanda was not previously known, and coaxing tourists back to the country with gorilla-tracking expeditions.[46]

Women's organisations were not only active at the grassroot level. The Campaign for Peace, for example, drafted in late 1994, was a policy-level innovation by the Pro-Femmes/Twese Hamwe, a pre-existing umbrella organisation of women's groups. The programme aimed to address Rwanda's post-genocide social and economic problems by focusing on the 'critical needs' of Rwandan women and children, and by 'involving women in efforts to promote overall reconstruction and reduce social tensions'.[47] The work of women's organisations at various levels was a major factor in the success of post-conflict reconstruction in Rwanda.

The significant increase in women's political security is most obviously illustrated by their improved representation in parliament. Rwandan women have the highest representation in parliament in the world, occupying 56.3 per cent of the seats.[48] Indeed, women's involvement in government was enshrined in the new constitution adopted in 2003, which called for 30 per cent of the decision-making positions to be taken up by women.[49] There are two theories on why this rather progressive gender quota was instated. The first claims that it was due to pressure from women's organisations and other civil society groups, the second is more sceptical and hypothesises that 'the government could be using the inclusion of women and youth as a means of diverting attention from the absence of ethnic pluralism'.[50] Regardless of the motive, however, the Rwandan government had the 'political will to constitutionalize the inclusion of women in parliament'.[51]

The examples of women's social and political progression in Rwanda, in addition to their creative initiatives to rebuild the country, correspond to the recommendations and strategies in UNSCR 1325, making a strong case for its implementation in other similarly affected areas.

The international community and Rwanda

The inadequacy of the efforts of the international community to assist the Rwandan population during the genocide significantly justified the need for UNSCR 1325. The efforts that they made were too little, too late, were certainly not gender-sensitive, and did not offer any way of addressing the specific needs of women and girls. As part of the international community, UN peacekeepers already in Rwanda were hamstrung by their mandate, which was never altered sufficiently to empower the force to efficiently manage the conflict outcome and 'keep the peace'. One could then argue that on the basis of the performance of the UN in the Rwanda experience, UNSCR 1325 came about in order to prevent, or at least mitigate, the impact of any such atrocities that might occur in the future on women and girls.

During the early stages of the Rwandan civil war in 1990, French troops and subsequently the United Nations Uganda–Rwanda Observation Mission were deployed to assist the national government in quelling the unrest that had been attributed to the return of Tutsis who had been exiled in previous ethnic conflicts.[52] These forces were subsequently replaced by UNAMIR, deployed to assist the implementation of the Arusha Peace Accords (a series of negotiations and demands by all parties involved in the initial stages of the conflict).[53] Unfortunately, the UNAMIR force was unable to do anything except watch the horror unfold with the genocide, given the fact that their numbers were few and their mandate was for a different task altogether.

UNAMIR was established by UNSCR 872 with a mandate

> to assist in ensuring the security of the capital city of Kigali; monitor the ceasefire agreement, including establishment of an expanded demilitarized zone and demobilization procedures; monitor the security situation during the final period of the transitional Government's mandate leading up to elections; assist with mine-clearance; and assist in the coordination of humanitarian assistance activities in conjunction with relief operations.[54]

Peacekeepers operating under this mandate would clearly not have the power to successfully abate the violent conflict that characterised the genocide. Aware that UNAMIR were unable to protect civilians or even themselves (as evidenced by the deaths of ten Belgian peacekeepers who were trying to protect the Prime Minister, Agathe Uwiringiyimana)[55] the Security Council amended the mandate with UNSCR 912. The renewed mandate, however, still did not give UNAMIR the authority or resources to actively enforce peace. It merely allowed the peacekeepers to

> act as an intermediary between the parties in an attempt to secure their agreement to a cease-fire; to assist in the resumption of humanitarian relief operations to the extent feasible; and to monitor and report on developments in Rwanda, including the safety and security of the civilians who sought refuge with UNAMIR.[56]

While UNAMIR's mandate was amended on five occasions, it was never enough to authorise the use of adequate force, nor did it include any mention of the specific needs of women during and post-conflict, or in peacebuilding.

In spite of these limitations, the clear need for the mandate to be strengthened, and the troops to be reinforced and better equipped, was met with universal reluctance. Two major international actors, Belgium and the US, were especially reluctant to engage in the crisis. The Belgian government had had their fingers burnt by the deaths of the Prime Minister's bodyguards,[57] and the US was recovering from the losses suffered in Somalia when 19 US soldiers were killed in a battle in Mogadishu.[58] Desperate not to get involved, the US State Department attempted to avoid its obligations under the 1948 Genocide Convention[59] by declaring on 10 June, 1994: 'Although there have been acts of genocide in Rwanda, all the murders cannot be put into that category.'[60] Worse still, the UN initially voted to reduce the size of UNAMIR's force to only 270 men, demonstrating that the militia had nothing to fear from the international community.[61] One can expect that if the international community had universally condemned the atrocities, the genocide would have not spiralled so far out of control. In fact, evidence suggests that militia leaders halted the public killings when it was made clear that the 'interim government could not succeed in the international arena'.[62]

Although UNAMIR continued to be active in Rwanda until March of 1996,[63] the Rwandan government, and many of the women's organisations leading the reconstruction efforts, agree that the international community, UNAMIR in particular, did not respond to their priority needs.[64] The UN force was widely disregarded due to its inadequacy and due to the perceived neglect of Rwanda by the international community during the genocide.[65] Consequently the people of Rwanda, and in particular Rwandan women, were left to help themselves by coordinating reconstruction and providing relief services, by reforming their pre-existing *foyer sociales*, as explained in the previous section. While many women were in need of specific care as a result of sexual violence suffered, UNAMIR was not mandated or even trained to provide any gender-specific services. Once the genocide had ceased, UNAMIR was mandated to continue 'its efforts to ensure security and stability, support humanitarian assistance, clear landmines and help refugees to resettle'.[66] Although the humanitarian assistance included medical care, it is unlikely that there were enough appropriately trained personnel to take care of the vast numbers of women who needed special medical attention. This is evidenced by the fact that post-conflict reconstruction was designed by those who needed it, and that Rwanda actually requested the end of UNAMIR mission, stating that it had not met their 'priority needs'.[67] The result made for unique development and progression of women's rights, as has been discussed earlier.

The Rwandan genocide was a grave failure of the international community's collective security responsibility. The extensive sexual violence that was perpetrated against women, among other heinous acts, was allowed to rage with impunity, along with the massacre of hundreds of thousands of civilians. Moreover, the special needs of women in the post-conflict stage were not properly addressed, even though thousands of women were suffering from horrific injuries and disease, including HIV/AIDS, as a result of rape and sexual mutilation.

Even twenty years on, this catastrophic stain has not been removed from the international conscience; it was a key impetus to create UNSCR 1325, and unquestionably justifies its existence. Had UNSCR 1325 been in existence during the Rwandan genocide, purely as a result of article 5 which states that it, 'Expresses its willingness to incorporate a gender perspective into peacekeeping operations, and urges the Secretary-General to ensure that, where appropriate, field operations include a gender component', a gender perspective might have been incorporated into UNAMIR's mandate, so that women and girls should have experienced better protection and care. Consequently, the entire mandate might have been better able to protect civilians in general, as peacekeeping forces would have needed a considerably stronger force and mandate in order to protect and care for women and girls. Peacekeeping forces not only have the responsibility to support the conflict management process with gender-sensitive approaches, but also the responsibility to support the post-conflict process as changes occur within these societies. UNSCR 1325 has crystallised these responsibilities into international legislation and the Rwandan case study has starkly underscored the urgent requirement for such legislation.

It is important, however, to call attention to the eternal problem the UN faces with member states with their own agendas and priorities. This challenge is seen clearly in the Rwanda case by the extreme unwillingness of the international community to contribute troops to UNAMIR or even speak out against the mass killings. This issue will not be changed by UNSCR 1325. Yet, even if nothing about the Rwanda case were different, except for the existence of UNSCR 1325, gender sensitivity might have been written into the mandate (article 5), UN personnel would have been trained on the protection, rights and the particular needs of women (article 6), and they might have been able to take special measures to protect women and girls from GBV (article 10).[68] These changes would have significantly strengthened UNAMIR. UNSCR 1325 cannot solve the limitations of the UN's structure but it can make the existing structure more effective.

UNSCR 1325 in Rwanda: a natural development

UNSCR 1325 in itself has influenced Rwanda very little during the time that it has been in existence. Yet the approach to peacebuilding and post-conflict reconstruction that developed in Rwanda, including the enhancement of women's status and rights in the country, bears a strong similarity to the prescriptions of UNSCR 1325. Article 1 of the Resolution calls for increased representation of women at decision-making levels, which is evident in the current situation in Rwanda, with vast amounts of the post-conflict reconstruction driven by women. The social and political progression experienced by women is also in line with this. Women's organisations took a leading role in advancing the position of local women and provided a platform through which to address their security concerns as these were not being met by the international peacekeeping force.

This UNSCR 1325-like development in Rwanda is due to a malleable setting for change that was created by a combination of factors, including the political origins of the conflict, civil war, a supportive and progressive post-conflict government, and active women's organisations. As Powley explains, the 'unique' status of the situation in Rwanda was due to the 'magical coalescing of top-down and bottom-up support and involvement of women, the returnees, the magnitude of the conflict, and gender sensitive men in key political positions'.[69] The situation in Rwanda was unique; the interaction of these factors can be understood in their particular context and inform how this successful outcome emerged. Yet, this example can arguably present a guide to the UNSCR 1325 implementation process in other conflict-affected areas with similar characteristics, but more broadly on the basis of delicately understanding the particular interaction of factors.

The political origins of the conflict in Rwanda played a considerable role in the development of the unique approach to peacebuilding, and the targeting of women undoubtedly contributed to the way that reconstruction developed. The targeting of women, both before and during the conflict, is likely to have fed feelings of resentment and a desire to break through the socially constructed barrier between women and leadership. It led to a fostering of a united bond between women, which often overcame ethnic differences, such as in the basket-weaving initiative, which was mentioned earlier, in hope of rebuilding their lives, and repositioning themselves in the broken society.

The physical targeting of women necessitated female-specific recovery programmes that, as mentioned earlier, were led by the Pro-Femmes/Twese Hamwe, an umbrella organisation of women's groups. The development of these programmes was influenced by a distinctly bottom-up approach to post-conflict reconstruction in that 'Rwandan women's groups and leaders, by the post-genocide government, and by expatriates convinced of the importance of gender' lobbied members of the international community to provide 'special attention to the needs and roles of women' in the aftermath of the genocide.[70] This was despite the fact that the international community abandoned Rwanda during the genocide, and it was necessary for women's groups to appeal for the expert help that they needed from groups such as Medecins Sans Frontieres in the aftermath.[71]

The radically altered demographic in Rwanda's population, with large numbers of men dead or in jail, contributed to the development of Rwanda's UNSCR 1325-like approach to post-conflict recovery, as women had little choice but to involve themselves in reconstruction. Accordingly, this had positive implications on all aspects of their previously jeopardised security.

The policies of the Rwandan Patriotic Front (RPF) government, which came to power immediately after the genocide, played a part in the development of an UNSCR 1325-like approach by encouraging the involvement of women in post-conflict reconstruction.[72] This was demonstrated by the establishment of representatives of the Ministry of Gender and Promotion of Women's Development (Migeprofe) in each prefecture and commune to support women's groups.[73] These representatives 'worked alongside and placed pressure on local government authorities to bring attention to women's concerns'.[74] It is important to acknowledge that the UNSCR 1325 is all-inclusive as it addresses the specific involvement of women in post-conflict reconstruction, going beyond just the need for gender-specific care, as is stated in articles 1, 2 and 8.[75]

The strength of women's organisations themselves was a major factor in the evolution of an UNSCR 1325-like approach. Their capacity for action meant that crucially, change was not just top-down: it was also bottom-up. Change was not effected solely by the edicts of higher-level organisations, but largely by local women working in their own communities to address their own and shared needs. This type of bottom-up change is unusual in many post-conflict societies. The women's organisations were successful in part because of their focus on and remarkable affinity for reconciliation. Rwandan women are regarded within their communities as being better at reconciliation than men, as the testimony of a male taxi-driver in Kigali suggests: 'My [Tutsi] sister is a nurse. She treats Hutu patients. Some of them are genocidaires. Maybe they killed my father. I could never do it. Women are better at it than men.'[76]

The reasons for this include suggestions that women involved in conflict, especially widows, have 'nobody to turn to' and therefore of necessity require relatively 'more cooperation in the community'.[77] This therefore boils down to women being left as the major constituency to deal with the negative consequences of war, which gives them a deeper interest in its prevention. Former UN Secretary-General Kofi Annan extends this observation to women in general, explaining that women have acted as 'peace educators' in both family and society, building 'bridges rather than walls', as they recognise the necessity for working across ethnic lines to move forward with daily life.[78]

Rwanda's post-conflict model has shown itself to be a natural progression of responses to the post-conflict situation, evolving well before UNSCR 1325. Finding the right synergy of factors at play in particular contexts to promote post-conflict reconstruction, has been put forward by the Rwanda case as being crucial to effecting lasting peace and security. This is arguably often one of the most difficult steps to implementing change in post-conflict societies. The difficulty is usually that solutions are often not accepted by all parties because they are imposed from the top down, with little reference to the interplay of factors, and are therefore not necessarily appropriate. Rather, it is more useful for the way forward to arise directly out of the needs of the parties involved.

The Rwanda case is unique in that it produced intended outcomes of UNSCR 1325 even before its formulation. However, the success in Rwanda reinforces its necessity in the many instances where such widespread and devastating violent conflict has not had a similar effect of challenging social norms and allowing the negotiation of gendered roles, especially to feature women in strategic decision-making capacities. The natural evolution of the peacebuilding process in the Rwanda case provides three clear elements that are essential to other post-conflict societies to aid in a natural implementation of an UNSCR 1325 approach. These elements are: the need for the provision of support to women's organisations at the grassroots level; the need for the provision of support to post-conflict governments to enable greater representation of women at all decision-making levels; and the need for awareness of the necessity that all members of society including women play a critical role in ensuring their human security that could be provided by increased education about the resources and documents, such as UNSCR 1325, applicable to women in post-conflict situations. In other post-conflict settings the peacebuilding journey should be driven by the post-conflict government and supported by a variety of actors including regional, sub-regional and international institutions, including the UN.

The systems for care and reconstruction that developed in Rwanda through women's organisations worked more effectively than many programmes set up by the UN and other NGOs, because they were created by the people who needed them. Rwandan women had the most accurate understanding of their immediate needs, and how change would be effectively implemented. They knew, for example, that women would be reluctant to come forward to report rape, because of the stigma involved, an issue that needed to be addressed in both caring for victims and prosecuting perpetrators. UNSCR 1325 refers to working with women's organisations only twice, in articles 8 and 15.[79] Moreover, it only acknowledges the need to 'consult' women's organisations (as, for example, in article 15).[80] This is not enough: the UN and the international community must learn to work in conjunction with existing women's organisations, rather than simply consulting them. It must encourage the formation of suitable grassroots organisations where there is a void, and must support these organisations in other post-conflict countries. Although it will be difficult to eliminate top-down approaches to peacebuilding entirely, external groups can minimise the negative effects of a top-down-heavy approach by encouraging the maximum involvement from local women, and devising creative ways to make this comfortable and easy for them. This involvement of women will facilitate more successful peacebuilding, as has been shown in Rwanda.

The Rwanda case highlights the need for more awareness and education about UNSCR 1325. The massive surge in the election of female parliamentarians in 2003 seems, on the surface, to be directly related to the passing of UNSCR 1325 in 2000. In fact, the most frequently cited motivational documents were the Convention on the Elimination of All Forms of Discrimination against Women (CEDAW) and the Beijing Platform for Action, not UNSCR 1325. Studies suggest that Rwandan women have almost no knowledge of UNSCR 1325, but, when informed about it, are extremely receptive to the idea.[81] It is crucial, therefore, that there is more education on UNSCR 1325 (and previous provisions including CEDAW) and how its implementation can improve human security in post-conflict societies. Some NGOs spend considerable time and money in this exact occupation, but there is still more to be done to synchronise the design of international efforts and peacekeeping programmes with ensuring the awareness of post-conflict governments of their own obligations. By making women aware of the support to which they are entitled under UNSCR 1325 they might be encouraged to take the initiative both at the grassroots level and in seeking participation in higher-level government. In addition, by gleaning from the Rwanda experience the international community may learn more effective means of communicating these provisions to the broadest constituencies.

UNSCR 1325 prescribes a number of very useful and valid steps to increase women's representation, and to provide for their specific needs during and after conflict. By using some of the lessons learned from the Rwanda case study, UNSCR 1325 can be implemented more successfully in future situations.

Rwanda and UNSCR 1325: the future

The Rwanda case, and the performance of UNAMIR, demonstrate the requirement for UNSCR 1325 which places considerable emphasis on gender-sensitive peacekeeping forces, and high-level decision-making positions, yet UNSCR 1325 pays insufficient attention to grassroots-level change. This is unsurprising, considering it was drafted by the UN, an intergovernmental body, concerned with overarching national and international security, which would in any case struggle with implementing grassroots-level change. It is important, however, that in implementing UNSCR 1325, UN organisations work *with* rather than *for* communities, and that they encourage bottom-up initiatives, and co-ordinate policy-level top-down approaches with them. It would be helpful in achieving this goal if the international community were to place greater emphasis on individual and human security, and if Resolutions and their supporting programmes could move in line with the local nature of human security. This would essentially support individuals at the grassroots level, enabling them to play a greater and necessary role in effecting change. Most countries in a fragile post-conflict state are not automatically ready to receive, or cope with, a powerful top-down approach imposed from outside their society. The Rwandan case has proved that with a more creative bottom-up approach to peacebuilding and reconstruction, change within society can be achieved with a lasting peaceful impact.

Rwanda's future is uncertain. At this stage in the post-conflict process, it is still too early to tell how lasting the peace will be and whether it will continue to be peaceful and productive, or whether this is a temporary state. The reality is likely to involve both situations. While Rwanda has experienced positive development over the last fourteen years, the nature of the 1990–1994 conflict means that it has the potential to re-ignite.

The international community will benefit from assisting in increased implementation of UNSCR 1325 in Rwanda and learning from the examples that it has set. The UN and the international community at large need to see positive examples of a Resolution's impact in order to maintain an interest in its sustained promotion. The Rwandan experience so far and the consolidation of these gains with the use of UNSCR 1325 in Rwanda could easily provide the much needed, positive success story confirming that the Resolution's prescriptions are worth pursuing globally.

The Rwandan case study has not only provided an innovative model for improved implementation of UNSCR 1325 in other post-conflict situations, it has also validated the Resolution and highlighted its relevance even if inadvertently. It has demonstrated both the advantage of involving women in critical roles in peacebuilding, and how a society like Rwanda can benefit from UNSCR 1325 for consolidating its peacebuilding process. Rwanda has also shown how the failure of the UN to engage with the conflict management and peacekeeping with a gendered perspective can jeopardise the process and the immediate post-conflict recovery period. Perhaps most critically, Rwanda has emphasised the essential need to engage local processes as the foundational element of any UNSCR 1325 implementation process. This prioritisation of a home-grown and-driven process is arguably what is at the greatest risk in the implementation of UNSCR 1325 as an international mechanism first and foremost. The Rwanda experience has highlighted that it cannot be optional for UNSCR 1325 to support a working home-grown process and not risk undermining it. This resolution is a groundbreaking piece of international legislation. With appropriate and forward-thinking implementation, it has the potential to play a major role in assuring people-centred sustainable peace and development. As the experiences of Rwandan women show, UNSCR 1325 can, and should, have a phenomenal, positive effect on women, peace and security worldwide.

Notes

1 Human Rights Watch, *Shattered Lives: Sexual Violence during the Rwandan Genocide and its Aftermath*, p. 7.
2 E. Powley, *Strengthening Governance: The Role of Women in Rwanda's Transition*, Washington DC: Hunt Alternatives Fund, 2003, p. 5.
3 *Human Development Report – New Dimensions of Human Security*, United Nations Development Programme, 1994, pp. 22–23. Available at http://hdr.undp.org/reports/global/1994/en/ (accessed 8 March 2007).
4 Kristofferson quoted in S. McKay, 'Women, Human Security, and Peacebuilding: A Feminist Analysis', in H. Shinoda and H.W. Jeong (eds), *Conflict and Human Security: A Search for New Approaches of Peace-building*, IPSHU English Research Report Series No. 19, pp. 152–175, http://home.hiroshima-u.ac.jp/heiwa/Pub/E19/Contents.htm (accessed 3 July 2007).
5 C. Twagiramariya and M. Turshen, '"Favours" to Give and "Consenting" Victims: The Sexual Politics of Survival in Rwanda' in M. Turshen and C. Twagiramariya (eds), *What Women Do in Wartime: Gender and Conflict in Africa*, London: Zed Books Ltd, 1998, p. 102.
6 C. Bunch and N. Reilly in Turshen and Twagiramariya, op. cit. p. 103.
7 L. Hilsum in Turshen and Twagiramariya, op. cit., p. 105.
8 Ibid.
9 C. Newbury and H. Baldwin, 'Profile: Rwanda', in K. Kumar (ed.), *Women and Civil War: Impact, Organizations, and Action*, London: Lynne Rienner Publishers, 2001a, pp. 27–38.
10 Human Rights Watch, *Shattered Lives: Sexual Violence during the Rwandan Genocide and its Aftermath*, New York: Human Rights Watch, 1996, p. 84.
11 E. Powley, 'Rwanda: Women Hold up Half the Parliament', in A. Karam and J. Ballington (eds) *Women in Parliament: Beyond Numbers*, Sweden: International Institute for Democracy and Electoral Assistance, 2009, p. 154.
12 Inter-parliamentary Union, *Women in Parliaments 1945–1995*, Geneva: Inter-parliamentary Union, 1995, p. 214.
13 Human Rights Watch, op. cit., p. 84.
14 Ibid.
15 G. Hoogensen and S. Rottem, 'Gender Identity and the Subject of Security', *Security Dialogue*, Vol. 35, 2004, p. 167.
16 E. Powley, op. cit., p. 11.
17 C.C. Taylor, *Sacrifice as Terror: The Rwandan Genocide of 1994*, Oxford: Berg, 1999, pp. 154–161.
18 Ibid., p. 154.
19 Ibid., p. 161.
20 Ibid., p. 161.
21 Ibid., p. 161.
22 Ibid., p. 155.
23 Ibid., p. 164.
24 Ibid., p. 155.
25 M. Mamdani, *When Victims Become Killers: Colonialism, Nativism, and the Genocide in Rwanda*, Princeton: Princeton University Press, 2001, p. 53.
26 Ibid.
27 Ibid.
28 Taylor, op. cit., p. 166.
29 Powley, op. cit., p. 13.
30 Twagiramariya and Turshen, op. cit., p. 112.
31 Ibid.
32 Newbury and Baldwin, op. cit., p. 31.

33 Ibid.
34 Human Rights Watch, op. cit., p. 36.
35 Ibid. p. 89.
36 Ibid. pp. 90–91.
37 Powley, discussion.
38 Powley, discussion.
39 Powley, op. cit., p. 13.
40 Ibid.
41 Twagiramariya and Turshen, op. cit., pp. 114–115.
42 C. Newbury and H. Baldwin, 'Confronting the Aftermath of the Conflict: Women's Organizations in Postgenocide Rwanda', in K. Kumar (ed.), *Women and Civil War: Impact, Organizations, and Action*, London: Lynne Rienner Publishers, 2001b, pp. 97–128.
43 Ibid., p. 97.
44 Ibid., p. 98.
45 A. Young, 'Rwanda Rising', directed by CB Hackworth, GoodWorks Productions, Washington DC, 2007.
46 Ibid.
47 Newbury and Baldwin, op. cit., 2001b, p. 98.
48 Inter-Parliamentary Union, Women in Parliaments – World Classification, 2008. Available at www.ipu.org/wmn-e/classif.htm (accessed 23 February 2009).
49 H. Schwartz, 'Women's Representation in the Rwandan Parliament – An Analysis of Variations in the Representation of Women's Interests Caused by Gender and Quota', Department of Political Science, Gothenburg University, Sweden, 2005, p. 11. Available at www.quotaproject.org/other/Schwartz_2005.pdf (accessed 1 July 2007).
50 Ibid.
51 Ibid.
52 G. Prunier, *The Rwanda Crisis*, London: Hurst & Company, 1995, p. 194; United Nations Department of Information, *Basic Facts About the United Nations*, New York: United Nations, 2000, pp. 84–85.
53 The Arusha Peace Accords were a series of negotiations and demands on all parties involved in the Rwandan civil war which began in 1990, and were conducted on neutral territory in Arusha, Tanzania. The Arusha Accords included a ceasefire agreement in 1992, and a peace accord between the government and the RPF in 1993 that 'called for a multi-party government with RPF participation' (Taylor, *Sacrifice as Terror: The Rwandan Genocide of 1994*, 49–50). The final piece of the Arusha Accords was a military integration agreement, and to facilitate its implementation, the UN Secretary General, in late September of 1993, agreed to the creation of the United Nations Assistance Mission to Rwanda (Prunier, 1995, *The Rwanda Crisis*, p. 194).
54 Rwanda UNAMIR Mandate www.un.org/Depts/dpko/dpko/co_mission/unamirM.htm (accessed 1 July 2009) & S/RES/872 United Nations Security Council http://daccess-dds.un.org/doc/UNDOC/GEN/N93/540/63/PDF/N9354063.pdf?OpenElement(accessed 1 July 2009).
55 Prunier, op. cit., p. 274; Taylor, op. cit., p. 14.
56 The UNAMIR mandate was amended for the first time on 21 April 1994 by Security Council Resolution 912 (1994). The resolution mentions the word 'women' in the following article:

> Appalled at the ensuing large-scale violence in Rwanda, which has resulted in the death of thousands of innocent civilians, including women and children, the displacement of a significant number of the Rwandese population, including those who sought refuge with UNAMIR, and the significant increase in refugees to neighbouring countries.
> (S/RES/912 (1994) United Nations Security Council http://daccessdds.un.org/doc/UNDOC/GEN/N94/190/85/PDF/N9419085.pdf?OpenElement, 1 July 2009)

The mandate was then further revised by UNSCR 918 on 17 May 1994, where women are referred to once, 'Deeply concerned that the situation in Rwanda, which has resulted in the death of many thousands of innocent civilians, including women and children, the internal displacement of a significant percentage of the Rwandan popula- tion' (S/RES/918 (1994) United Nations Security Council http://daccessdds.un.org/ doc/UNDOC/GEN/N94/218/36/PDF/N9421836.pdf?OpenElement 27 August 2007). The three subsequent resolutions (S/RES/965 1994, S/RES/997 1995 and S/RES/1029 1995) do not make any references to women at all. It is important to note, however, that UNAMIR's changing mandate, which is detailed within the resolutions, did not ever refer specifically to women or girls.

57 Prunier, op. cit., p. 274.
58 *Guardian* (14 September 2009) 'US Military Action in Somalia: Black Hawk Down to Today's Attack'. www.guardian.co.uk/world/2009/sep/14/black-hawk-down-us-somalia.
59 Prunier, op. cit., p. 274.
60 *International Herald Tribune* (13 June 1994) quoted Prunier, *The Rwanda Crisis*, p. 274.
61 UNAMIR, www.un.org/Depts/dpko/dpko/co_mission/unamirS.htm (accessed 21 August 2007).
62 Human Rights Watch, *Leave None to Tell the Story: Genocide in Rwanda*, 1999. Available at www.hrw.org/legacy/reports/1999/rwanda/Geno1-3-05.htm (accessed 19 February 2009).
63 UNAMIR, www.un.org/Depts/dpko/dpko/co_mission/unamirS.htm (accessed 21 August 2007).
64 Ibid.
65 Ibid.; and S.N. Anderlini, Former Director of Women Waging Peace Policy Commis- sion, Independent Consultant, in discussion with the author, 11 July 2007.
66 UNAMIR, www.un.org/Depts/dpko/dpko/co_mission/unamirS.htm (accessed 21 August 2007).
67 Ibid.
68 S/RES/1325 United Nations Security Council, http://daccessdds.un.org/doc/UNDOC/ GEN/N00/720/18/PDF/N0072018.pdf?OpenElement (accessed 22 February 2007).
69 Powley, discussion.
70 Newbury and Baldwin, op. cit., 2001b, p. 99.
71 MSF in Rwanda, www.msf.org/msfinternational/countries/africa/rwanda/index.cfm (accessed 15 July 2009).
72 Powley, discussion.
73 Newbury and Baldwin, op. cit., 2001b, pp. 99–100.
74 Ibid.
75 S/RES/1325 United Nations Security Council, op. cit.
76 Name withheld, personal interview, July 2002, in Powley, op. cit., p. 16.
77 Name withheld, female Rwandan employee of an international NGO, personal inter- view, June 2002, in Powley, op. cit., p. 16.
78 Press Release SG/SM/7598, www.peacewomen.org/un/sc/countrystatements/annan. pdf (accessed 20 June 2007).
79 S/RES/1325 United Nations Security Council, http://daccessdds.un.org/doc/UNDOC/ GEN/N00/720/18/PDF/N0072018.pdf?OpenElement (accessed 22 February 2007).
80 Ibid.
81 Powley, discussion.

8 Lost in translation?

UNAMSIL, UNSCR 1325 and women building peace in Sierra Leone

Karen Barnes

Introduction

This chapter examines the peacebuilding process in Sierra Leone, exploring the implementation of UN Security Council Resolution (UNSCR) 1325 by the United Nations Mission in Sierra Leone (UNAMSIL). The chapter argues that women were not perceived as legitimate actors in the formal peacebuilding process, and that UNAMSIL failed to take gender mainstreaming and UNSCR 1325 on board as anything more than an 'add women and stir' strategy. Women's organisations, on the other hand, approached gender and peacebuilding in a more holistic way, and although few organisations used the Resolution itself during UNAMSIL's presence, many of their activities echoed the actions that it calls for.

The conflict in Sierra Leone broke out in March 1991 when the Revolutionary United Front (RUF), backed by Charles Taylor's National Patriotic Front of Liberia (NPFL), launched a rebel invasion in the eastern border region of the country. During the 1990s, there was a series of coups, periods of military rule and failed negotiations as control of the country passed between government and rebel hands. During this time, the civilian population bore the brunt of the violence, and hardship and displacement, the abduction of children and the destruction of social networks became characteristics of everyday life. The causes of conflict in Sierra Leone were rooted in complex internal and external factors, yet for many years the war remained underneath the radar of the international community.[1] Following the signing of the Lomé Peace Agreement (LPA) in July 1999, the international community finally committed to the creation of UNAMSIL with the adoption of Security Council Resolution 1270 on 22 October 1999.[2]

This marked the beginning of UNAMSIL's extensive engagement in the country, where it undertook a range of peacebuilding activities in the social, economic and political spheres until its eventual drawdown on 31 December 2005. UNAMSIL's original mandate from 1999 was adopted prior to UNSCR 1325 and, as such, gender issues were not initially accorded priority by the UN peacekeeping mission, which was at the time the largest in the world. However, the case of Sierra Leone is particularly interesting for examining the impact of UNSCR 1325, since the peacebuilding process in the country has evolved largely at the same time as the international community has articulated its commitments in relation to women, peace and security issues. At the same time, women's organisations in Sierra Leone were active in civil society efforts to build peace at the community level, but were largely excluded from the 'formal' UN-led peace-building process. For these reasons, it is a useful case in which to explore the assumption that gender became an increasingly important priority within peace-keeping missions following the adoption of the resolution.

UNAMSIL's efforts to mainstream UNSCR 1325

The establishment of UNAMSIL in late 1999 was a belated attempt by the UN to provide the peacekeeping force that had been promised, but never delivered, since the Abidjan Accords of 1996. Originally limited in size, it was given a broad mandate that ranged from facilitating the delivery of humanitarian assistance to assisting the government with implementing the DDR process.[3] However, the original mandate of UNAMSIL did not extend to gender issues, and in fact the only mention of these issues was limited to the need for gender-related training for UNAMSIL personnel.[4] It is telling that few of the subsequent reports of the Secretary-General on the peacekeeping mission in Sierra Leone mainstream a gender perspective, and the scant references to women that were made tended to be in the context of the sexual violence that they suffered during the war.

Although UNSCR 1325 had not yet been adopted in 1999, other instruments relating to women's rights and gender equality could have been referred to in UNAMSIL's mandate. For example, in East Timor, the mandate of the UN-established Transitional Administration (UNTAET) was explicitly linked to the Convention on the Elimination of All Forms of Discrimination Against Women (CEDAW), which provided an important tool to guide the work of the gender affairs office.[5] Subsequent resolutions on UNAMSIL demonstrated little improvement, with only a few mentions of the 'special needs of women' mentioned from 2002 onwards. In 2004, UNSCR 1562 provided UNAMSIL with a revised mandate to guide its work as the mission drew down, but again an opportunity to link the work of the peacekeeping mission with UNSCR 1325 and to recognise the needs, interests and contributions of women's organisations was overlooked.

UNAMSIL also reflected a structural marginalisation of gender issues. During the early years of the mission, UNAMSIL's human rights section had a 'gender specialist', although the section was under-staffed and the position was not always filled.[6] In an evaluation of gender mainstreaming within UNAMSIL conducted for the UN Department of Peacekeeping Operations (DPKO), it is noted that the attention given to gender mainstreaming within the mission's different divisions varied significantly, and that it tended to receive low priority.[7] As a result of the adoption of UNSCR 1325 and the continued lobbying of civil society groups for a dedicated gender advisory capacity within peacekeeping missions, such a position was eventually established within UNAMSIL in 2003.[8]

The gender advisor (GA) was placed within the human rights section, and this, coupled with the fact that no independent budget and only limited authority was attached to the position, was a serious limitation. This resulted in a reactive rather than proactive response to gender issues within the mission.[9]

At the beginning of 2005, the position was moved to the office of the Special Representative of the UN Secretary-General (SRSG), making the GA a member of senior staff and giving her access to the higher decision-making levels within the organisation. Previously, the GA had had to report to the head of the human rights section who would then feed back to the SRSG, resulting in a circuitous line of reporting and accountability for gender issues. However, at one year prior to the drawdown of the mission, this move came too late to have any real sustainable impact on the ability of UNAMSIL to mainstream gender throughout its activities.[10]

The severe operational limitations that faced UNAMSIL's GA are a clear example of how UNSCR 1325 and the gender equality policy of DPKO failed to translate into practice on the ground. At its peak, UNAMSIL was the biggest ever peacekeeping mission, and to expect a single person to be able to effectively fulfil a gender mainstreaming mandate was simply unrealistic, particularly given the lack of resources allocated to this job.[11] The fact that gender issues were not included in the mandate of UNAMSIL from the outset also served to restrict the potential for successful mainstreaming, given that the decisions about funding and authority are frequently made at the earliest stages of a mission's life-cycle.[12] The experience of UNAMSIL illustrates how critical the mention of gender issues and UNSCR 1325 in the mandate of peacekeeping missions can be in terms of lending legitimacy, articulating and sharing responsibility, and providing the potential for the allocation of resources that all help to ensure that the job is done.

Nevertheless, UNAMSIL did make some progress in addressing gender issues, especially during the latter half of the operation. For example, a programme on gender issues and women's human rights was a regular weekly fixture of Radio UNAMSIL and this seems to have been an effective way of reaching the population and discussing potentially controversial issues such as rape and domestic violence. Representatives from the UN agencies as well as local women participated in these broadcasts, which are credited with having played a role in raising awareness about women's rights, particularly related to sexual violence.[13]

UNAMSIL's GA also actively supported the Truth and Reconciliation Commission (TRC) and was involved in setting up a Women's Task Force in 2001 to ensure that the Commission upheld its responsibility to pay special attention to the issue of sexual violence. In 2002, UNAMSIL collaborated with an NGO, Physicians for Human Rights, to undertake extensive research into the war-related sexual violence that women and girls had been subject to.[14] This report became a useful advocacy tool for both the UN and other members of the international community and drew attention to the critical need for documentation of women's human rights abuses in post-conflict contexts.

The GA also played an important role in introducing a range of UN, government and civil society actors in Freetown to UNSCR 1325 through training and sensitisation workshops throughout 2004 and 2005. Several government officials indicated that these trainings were the first time that they had been made aware of UNSCR 1325.[15] The GA also contributed to gender training for senior UN staff members, including those at the peacekeeping mission. However, despite the trainings that new military personnel and some civilian personnel within UNAMSIL received on UNSCR 1325 and human rights, significant resistance to gender issues remained within the mission and awareness of the content of the resolution appears to have been relatively low. Gender issues continued to be perceived as unimportant by some UNAMSIL officials, and the GA believed that she was able to have more impact through training outside of the mission than within it.[16]

The advisory and consultative role that the GA played in relation to women's organisations was a particular contribution of note, and the importance of consultation is also highlighted in UNSCR 1325. Although UNAMSIL did not have any regular and institutionalised meetings between mission staff and local women's organisations, the GA herself did play a key role in this regard. She acted as an advocate inside the UN system for women's organisations and was a point of contact within the bureaucracy of UNAMSIL, even if this collaboration was largely ad hoc.[17] This was repeatedly mentioned by women's organisations as critical to their ability to access the formal corridors of the UN and provide them with the needed support for their peacebuilding work, and the GA was unanimously praised for having been accessible and supportive.[18] Given that women's organisations are often active in the informal sphere and can face obstacles to accessing key decision-makers and international representatives, such a channel is vital to making the work of these groups more visible.

From this brief overview of the experience of implementing UNSCR 1325 within UNAMSIL, two structural issues relevant to the implementation of gender-related policies should be highlighted. These are the location of the GA in relation to the SRSG's office, and the commitment of the mission's senior leadership, in particular the SRSG. If these two factors are favourable, then this can have a multiplier effect on efforts to mainstream UNSCR 1325. Although the leadership of UNAMSIL was generally considered to have been receptive to gender issues at the discursive level, these issues were frequently deprioritised within its planning and programming.[19] According to a senior UN official in UNAMSIL, efforts to promote women's empowerment by the mission were nominal, in part due to the lack of capacity and manpower.

> I can say this was a major weakness on our part [...] we did not give it the attention that it requires. But you know as in everything, there is a time for things. Sometimes it is a question of demand and supply also.[20]

For example, one of the most important elements of UNSCR 1325 is women's participation, but the UN too frequently falls into the trap of confusing quantitative increase with the qualitative impact of greater women's participation, although clearly the former is easier to both bring about and to measure. In Sierra Leone, where women do have more equal roles in decision-making it is within the ward development committees, where it is voluntary and non-renumerative. As soon as you move up to the local district levels and beyond, then fewer than 20 per cent of women tend to stand for election because they don't have the skills or the money to get there.[21] As one UN official pointed out,

> [UNSCR] 1325 is useful in the Sierra Leonean context because it provides the legal framework for greater involvement of women, the greater *recognition* and involvement of women. But what is needed is to pour the resources into making that greater involvement a reality. If you want women to be involved you have to empower them. It takes resources to empower them.[22]

From 2004 and onwards, delegations from New York, including the UN DPKO senior gender advisor, periodically made trips to Sierra Leone and this high-level support was helpful vis-à-vis the implementation of UNSCR 1325 within the mission. Nevertheless, at the time the mission drew down, little had been done to support a more gender-sensitive peacebuilding process. A review of UNAMSIL's activities reinforces the notion that most of the programmes designed to support women focused on their roles as victims or emphasised the fact that they were marginalised and vulnerable, rather than reinforcing their ability to be empowered as actors in the peacebuilding process.

As part of the drawdown of UNAMSIL, donors were keen for Sierra Leone to make the transition from a country receiving peacebuilding assistance to a strategy of long-term development assistance. In preparation for the handover from UNAMSIL to the new UN Integrated Office in Sierra Leone (UNIOSIL), a detailed strategy was developed, outlining the priority areas for the transition and the roles of the different UN Country Team (UNCT) actors in carrying out these tasks. In the preamble to the activities chart of this UNAMSIL/UNCT document, emphasis is placed on the continued need to consolidate and support a durable peace in Sierra Leone.[23] However, no mention is made of the role of women in this process, or of the relationship between peace and gender equality. Gender is only mentioned specifically in four of the 27 issue areas of the transition strategy (public information, women, education and gender mainstreaming) despite the many opportunities to integrate a gender perspective throughout the entire document.

The departure of UNAMSIL and the creation of UNIOSIL resulted in a smaller UN presence than the previous UNAMSIL mission. There was an opportunity to consolidate the limited advances towards gender equality that had been made by UNAMSIL by ensuring that the new integrated office accord sufficient attention and resources to the issue, however, the GA position was terminated.[24] According to a former UNAMSIL officer in charge of Disarmament, Demobilisation and Reinterpretation (DDR), 'the overarching fact is that in failing to formalise the gender perspective in peace negotiations as well as in the implementation, the process has failed to capitalise on the significant strengths of women.'[25] The chapter will now turn to the activities that many women were undertaking to build peace in Sierra Leone in parallel with UNAMSIL's efforts.

Women, conflict and peacebuilding in Sierra Leone

Despite entrenched discrimination, poverty and a lack of access to resources and opportunities, women in Sierra Leone have a history of agency within their communities and households. The shift in the traditional gendered division of labour and patterns of gender relations during wartime blurred the lines between formal and informal, public and private, and often increased women's roles in the community.[26] For example, many women assumed new responsibilities such as being the sole family breadwinner, and had to develop mechanisms to cope without traditional networks and support structures as the conflict destabilised civilian life throughout the country. At the same time as it changed their daily lives, often in negative ways, the war also offered opportunities for women to organise around shared issues, in particular to foster peace within their communities.

It can therefore be argued that women were affected by the conflict in both empowering and in disempowering ways.[27] Although the experience of women and girls as victims of sexual violence is the most documented of their war experiences, to see women only as victims is to ignore their role as agents in processes of violent conflict and peacebuilding. In addition to, or perhaps in spite of, their vulnerability and insecurity, women played a key role in mobilising civil society to demand peace. While women's organisations have a long history in Sierra Leone, the conflict provided a unifying purpose and became a focal point for activism during the 1990s, enabling many women's groups to work collaboratively for the common goal of restoring peace to their communities. Given the continuing conflict in the country, they found a common thread in their activities based on the need for peace and security and they began to mobilize collectively.

In the 1990s many women became actively involved in peacemaking efforts within their communities and at the national level. According to Thorpe, "at the onset of war, women were indeed not prepared. At organizational level they were nominally weak, and many organizations figuratively speaking, were dormant. However the organizational potential was there awaiting the catalytic effect of the war."[28] Although this activism in large part emerged due to the socioeconomic and security threats facing women at the time, it was also influenced by the growing momentum of the international women's movement.

The Sierra Leone Women's Movement for Peace (SLWMP) was established in January 1995 as a member organization of the Sierra Leone Women's Forum (SLWF), and was founded on the basis that women as 'natural peacemakers' could make a vital contribution to the peace process. The SLWMP sought to influence the parties to the conflict through non-confrontational strategies including protests, marches and demonstrations, such as those held in January 1995 in Freetown, Bo, Kenema, Makeni and Kabala involving women from throughout the country.[29] The movement was non-partisan and initially shied away from direct involvement in politics, but in order for the women's peace campaign to have an impact it became clear that engagement with the political establishment in Sierra Leone would be necessary.

Women activists played key roles during Bintumani I and II, as the public consultations that took place in 1995 and 1996 on elections came to be known, and are largely considered to have been leaders of the civil society movement calling for 'elections before peace'.[30] These conferences represented the beginning of women's participation in national politics through organised groups, and as well as leading the public campaigning on the issue they also advocated in their communities for women to participate in the elections of March 1996.[31] These actions had important knock-on effects that may not have been planned at the time, but that contributed to the strengthening of women's peacebuilding roles at the national and local level, as well as bringing about an end to the conflict.[32]

A clear impact of these achievements was that for the first time, women were invited to be present during the discussions and negotiations leading up to the signing of the Lomé Peace Agreement (LPA).[33] It has been suggested that their presence resulted in some attention to women's issues reflected in Article 28 of the LPA, which proposed that women should play 'a central role in the moral, social and physical reconstruction of Sierra Leone'.[34] However, this commitment was never really fulfilled, and more crucially the Agreement failed to mention the potential of women to play political and economic roles in post-conflict Sierra Leone. Despite the signing of the LPA, fighting in Sierra Leone continued, and in May 2000, women's organisations led and mobilised other civil society organisations to participate in two major protests in Freetown that were important factors contributing to tipping the balance towards eventual peace in the country.[35]

The case of women's organisations in Sierra Leone illustrates how women in conflict-affected regions actively build peace at the community level outside of 'formal' peacebuilding or conflict resolution structures.[36] Notably, in Sierra Leone, women were also doing this long before the UN began to develop its women, peace and security agenda, and with little support from outside actors. The conflict was a catalytic experience in many ways, exposing women to new responsibilities and requiring them to acquire new skills that changed their perceptions of themselves and their role as women in society. As Thorpe puts it,

> the survival skills and sense of responsibility consequently developed during the process provided these women with basic developmental tools, a sense of independence, and the desire for social advancement on their return to their areas of origin after the war.[37]

In addition to their important efforts during the war, since 2002, women's organizations in Sierra Leone have developed innovative coping strategies in the aftermath of conflict. These activities are not necessarily framed as 'empowerment of women' or 'promoting gender equality', which is common language at the UN. However, an inevitable off-shoot of the training, support and capacity-building that women gain through these activities means that they are better placed to negotiate their rights, needs such as protection from violence or economic independence, and roles within society. The fact that many women's organizations operate at the grassroots level and have extensive reach throughout the country means that they have the potential to play an important collective role in influencing conflict dynamics and fostering efforts to consolidate peace.

There are several women's organizations that have a high profile in Freetown such as the Fifty-Fifty group (50/50), the Forum for African Women Educationalists (FAWE), SLWF and the Mano River Women's Peace Network (MAR-WOPNET). To different degrees, these organizations and networks also have branches or members throughout the country, and claim to be representative of women's needs and interests. Although MARWOPNET, and to a lesser extent the Sierra Leone branch of the Women in Peacebuilding Network (WIPNET-SL), are the only two women's organizations working explicitly on peacebuilding issues, other organizations also address issues related to overall peacebuilding efforts. In post-conflict contexts, the focus is sometimes not on equality as such, but other issues:

> Instead of working to *promote and advance* the rights of women and girls, they now directed their resources and energies towards *resisting conflict* and *protecting basic rights*, including, for example, the right to life and freedom of movement [...] Crucially, their responses were grounded in the real and complex priorities of women and girls affected by the conflicts. Hence, their new interventions were often multidisciplinary and flexible, shifting rapidly to respond to the mounting and varied impacts of the violence.[38]

The aftermath of conflict constitutes an opportunity to rebuild or transform old, discriminatory structures and practices into ones that offer new possibilities for women's empowerment and participation in the post-conflict phase.[39] As one woman activist put it,

> in Sierra Leone, even up until now, the concept is still very new to so many people, this concept of gender or women's emancipation. People just think it's supposed to be like this [...] For me personally, I saw the war as an option to kind of change the situation.[40]

However, as was pointed out by a group of women's NGOs in their submission to the TRC, many challenges remain: 'since the end of the war, women continue to face pressing problems. Men continue to be dominant players in decision-making, even though women shoulder most reproductive, productive and community management responsibilities, many of which are not re-numerated.'[41]

Some women's organizations such as WIPNET and MARWOPNET were involved in trainings on UNSCR 1325 and actively used the resolution in their work. Others implicitly addressed women, peace and security issues without explicitly drawing on the discourse. For example, the Sierra Leone chapter of the Forum for African Women Educationalists (FAWE) was established in 1995 during the height of the war, and focused its efforts on establishing coping mechanisms in conflict for women and girls.[42] FAWE focuses on education as its starting point, but uses it as an entry-point to support work in other areas such as addressing the culture of violence among youth, issues of reconciliation and reintegration, and gender-based violence (GBV). Similarly, women's political participation is a priority area within UNSCR 1325, and this is something that has a long history of support in Sierra Leone, but the resolution itself was not necessarily always linked into the activities of local NGOs working in this area.[43]

Despite the efforts of civil society, the weakness of the government in addressing and supporting gender equality in Sierra Leone has been a significant obstacle to the advancement of the UNSCR 1325 agenda at the national level. With the support of the international community, the Ministry of Social Welfare, Gender and Children's Affairs (MSWGCA) was able to prepare the country's first CEDAW report, lobby for legal reforms, raise awareness of gender issues throughout the government through a system of gender focal points, and provide some expert input into the PRSP process. However, capacity and resources are so limited, and progress so slow that the donor community became increasingly frustrated with the failure of the MSWGCA to move forward. As a result, many donors looked for opportunities to bypass the MSWGCA by channelling their support through civil society organizations instead, which has in some cases benefitted women's organisations in Freetown.[44]

Overall, this research found that awareness of UNSCR 1325 was low among the peacebuilding community in Sierra Leone during the time of UNAMSIL's involvement. However, the activities of these women's organisations reflect the spirit, if not the letter, of the Resolution. This is evident even when reviewing the statements made by some of the women's organisations present at Bintumani I and II, years before the Resolution itself was adopted.[45] Although UNSCR 1325 itself may not have been used by the women of Sierra Leone in the years following the conflict, the ideas contained within it were firmly entrenched within the women's movement long before the donor community was prepared to recognise women's roles in peacebuilding.

Interviews with Sierra Leonean women activists demonstrate that an understanding of gender roles and relations is critical to their understanding of how women's position within society can be changed.[46] The founder of the Sierra Leone chapter of FAWE makes the important point that

> as we live in a traditionally male dominated society, it would be like preparing for a stillbirth of the organization if provision for male participation were left out especially the participation of the Paramount Chiefs who are the traditional rulers.[47]

Indeed, the approach of women's peacebuilding organisations appears to be more 'gender-focused' than that of the donor agencies operating in the country. In articulating their objectives and the role of gender in peacebuilding, local women accorded greater recognition to the crucial role that men play in buying into the empowerment of women, and in leading the attitude shift necessary for gender equality to become accepted. This could be explained by the fact that women's organisations are more familiar than donors are with the particular gender dynamics of the country and therefore more aware of the limitations that the patriarchal culture and attitude place on women's efforts, making engagement with men a critical aspect of success.

It is important to recognise that lessons can be learned from alternative local mechanisms for advancing gender equality. However, the work of women's organisations often exists at the community level, or in the informal sphere, and as such is not always acknowledged or capitalised on by the international community. This means that women's organisations do not receive the necessary support for their activities, and the marginalisation of their valuable insights, expertise and resources constitute a missed opportunity for the formal peacebuilding process. Furthermore, these local mechanisms or traditional channels of conflict resolution and reconciliation can be weakened through lack of support or diversion of attention and resources to the more formal processes supported by the international community. Research done by de la Rey and McKay confirms that 'women's peacebuilding actions and areas of focus are often unrecognized by the broader national and international community because women have little power within these structures.'[48] The question remains, then, of how, if at all, UNSCR 1325 can be used as a tool by women peacebuilders and donors alike to bridge the gap between formal and non-formal peacebuilding activities, and as an entry-point for mainstreaming gender into these processes.

The impact of UNSCR 1325 in Sierra Leone

Although many women remain optimistic that UNSCR 1325 is a useful and relevant advocacy tool for Sierra Leone, and UN officials are well-versed in the key messages of the Resolution, an analysis of both women's organisations and UNAMSIL reveals that UNSCR 1325 itself has had limited impact in terms of directly supporting their work. Indeed, the evidence would seem to indicate that UNSCR 1325 and the mechanisms to apply it are ill-matched for the objectives and structural changes that it was adopted to bring about.

The case of Sierra Leone has shown that local initiatives for building peace and promoting gender equality have usually been in place for a long time, often prior to the conflict itself, and that women's organisations may use different discourses and strategies to achieve these goals. An important shortcoming of UNAMSIL's engagement was the failure to capitalise on women's deep involvement in peacebuilding in informal, local spheres to strengthen their attempts to build peace and contribute to the attitudinal shift required to end the violence.

Again, their victimhood was emphasised over the agency that many women displayed during the conflict.

To some extent, UNAMSIL did succeed in raising the awareness of UNSCR 1325, particularly among government officials and other key decision-makers. Since the end of the conflict, there have been legal reforms to address the ongoing discrimination against women, Family Support Units have been established within the police to address GBV, and gender issues are more frequently discussed. However, these changes were still too often only at the policy level and the reality was that most women, particularly in rural areas, continued to face significant obstacles that prevented their effective participation in formal peacebuilding processes. Thus, turning raised awareness into empowerment remains a serious challenge.

Raising awareness around women's rights and UNSCR 1325 should not be seen as an end in itself, but rather should be targeted towards supporting the development of a more inclusive and sustainable peace.

> Actors in the 'international peace industry' have no common agenda of what post-conflict societies should be transformed *to*, and many have no agenda to support transformation *at all* [...] In this context, different discourses and values, shaped locally and internationally, tend to collide, rather than interact; to co-exist, rather than transform. For the moment at least, it is unclear what major policy shifts might be possible in this area in the foreseeable future, even if we regard the ultimate transformation of gender relations as inevitable.[49]

Making UNSCR 1325 relevant at the national and local levels is an important challenge for those who seek to promote women, peace and security issues. Innovative strategies should be developed to link the resolution to already existing laws, frameworks and national priorities. For example, CEDAW, is well known among women activists in Sierra Leone and therefore could have constituted an important entry point. Change needs to be driven from the inside and it is here that UNSCR 1325 and other tools, such as CEDAW could be potentially powerful tools for local activists to use.

As noted earlier, the gender advisor did have some limited successes, however, much of the gender work of UNAMSIL was ad hoc. It tended to focus on a 'tick-box' approach to involving women, and not enough efforts were made to incorporate a gender dimension across the full range of peacebuilding activities, particularly in security-related issues such as the DDR process.[50] Although UNAMSIL was mandated to mainstream gender and increase the participation of women following the adoption of UNSCR 1325, this was rarely followed through in practice and the perception that gender issues were expendable, at least in the short-term, prevailed.

It is not just in Sierra Leone where the vital contribution of local initiatives is overlooked. According to Corrin, the failure to involve 'local, experienced and motivated community leaders' in the implementation of international-led work aimed at empowering women and women's organisations in Kosovo was a missed opportunity.[51] One of the biggest problems facing women peacebuilders and those who seek to support the engendering of peacebuilding is how to consolidate the gains that women make during wartime to ensure they are not lost. 'The historical record confirms that societies neither defend the spaces women create during struggle nor acknowledge the ingenious ways in which women bear new and additional responsibilities.'[52]

While raising awareness around UNSCR 1325 is important and policymakers play a critical role in taking it into account in their decision-making processes, tokenistic approaches need to be resisted. 'The UN needs to make it [gender mainstreaming] mandatory. The perception is that you can live without it [...] people see gender as a choice and this is a problem.'[53] The international community, including UNAMSIL, displayed a reluctance to place women at the front and centre of peacebuilding initiatives, instead preferring to ghettoise them in 'women's projects', if at all. UNSCR 1325 is an incredibly useful advocacy tool for women in post-conflict contexts throughout the world, as well as for gender focal points within the UN and other organisations. However, in terms of being a relevant, practical tool, it has been less effective.

UNSCR 1325 appears to encourage a certain degree of tokenism due to its broad prescriptions. For example, while ensuring that a certain minimum percentage of decision-making roles or beneficiaries of a project are women is a laudable goal, it can be counter-productive. This encourages UN staff to 'tick boxes' in terms of conceiving the idea of mainstreaming as a measurable action rather than a process of structural change. Perhaps to some extent, the failure to build on local initiatives and to contextualise assistance to the needs of the country can be explained by the short-term, time- and resource-pressed nature of post-conflict environments. As an official of Medecins sans Frontieres in Sierra Leone said, 'often the responses are bureaucratic, not effective and concrete answers to people's needs'.[54] This was evident in the activities of UNAMSIL where a reductionist interpretation of UNSCR 1325 is made, and projects that target women were often confused with achieving gender equality. In contrast, the local initiatives being undertaken by women's organizations often reflect a more holistic approach to gender and peacebuilding, but they do not receive the support or recognition of the international community.

Conclusion

In conclusion, it must be remembered that UNSCR 1325, as a UN Security Council document, can only achieve so much. As Meyer and Prügl point out,

> the significance of international documents is not that governments will automatically implement them but that national and local groups can use them to hold their governments accountable. In this sense, what appears as universal standards can be adapted and used in local contexts to further specific emancipatory agendas.[55]

The experience of Sierra Leone would seem to indicate that the potential for UNSCR 1325 to assist women in pushing for gender equality in peacebuilding exists, but the international community is falling short of its obligation to support these organisations in adapting the tool for their own purposes. As the case of Sierra Leone shows, UNSCR 1325 is in danger of being lost in translation and could become a convenient loophole enabling an 'add women and stir' approach to gender and peacebuilding. However, women's organisations at the community level offer an important counter to the dominant discourse and practice of peacebuilding thereby bringing about more engendered peace and security processes. Bridging this gap between the formal and informal, the international and the local, may represent the real challenge in the implementation of UNSCR 1325.

Postscript

While this chapter only covers the duration of UNAMSIL's deployment in Sierra Leone, it is important to note that since then, much progress has been made in terms of implementing UNSCR 1325 in the country. Most notably, in March 2010, the government launched its National Action Plan on UNSCR 1325.[56] This plan was realised through several years of advocacy and consultation, driven largely by coalitions of civil society organisations working at the national level, supported by UNIFEM and INGOs such as International Alert. Through linking up together, these actors were able to use UNSCR 1325 to gain visibility, call the Sierra Leonean government and donor community to account, and garner resources to support the development of a plan to address women, peace and security issues. Regional networks such as MARWOPNET and WIPNET also facilitated the process, and cross-learning between Sierra Leoneans and other countries enabled national NGOs to identify strategies to advance UNSCR 1325 that had worked elsewhere.[57]

From 2007 to 2009, UNSCR 1325 was also used as an instrument to mobilise civil society and government representatives to identify, articulate and act on women's priorities in relation to the peace process. As one of the first countries on the agenda of the Peacebuilding Commission (PBC) and Peacebuilding Fund (PBF), Sierra Leone has also benefitted from this entry point to integrate gender issues into the peacebuilding process, given the PBC's mandate to implement UNSCR 1325. While UNAMSIL's successor, UNIOSIL, did not prioritise gender issues, the mandate of the UN Integrated Peacebuilding Office in Sierra Leone (UNIPSIL), established in August 2008, emphasises UNSCR 1325, making it more likely that it will be prioritised as Sierra Leone continues on the path to long-term peace and development.

While UNSCR 1325 may have only had limited impact during UNAMSIL's deployment in the country, it is possible that during this time the UN, INGOs and women's civil society networks began laying the groundwork and raising awareness around the potential of the Resolution to be used as an advocacy tool. There is undoubtedly a long way to go before the lives of women and gender relations in Sierra Leone are transformed, but UNSCR 1325 has resulted in some gains at the policy level, and with global efforts to ensure better monitoring and accountability for its implementation it is possible that it could also continue to be an entry point for changing practices on the ground.

Notes

1 For detailed analyses of the conflict in Sierra Leone see David Keen, *Conflict and Collusion in Sierra Leone*, New York: International Peace Academy, 2005 and Lansana Gberie, *A Dirty War in West Africa: The RUF and the Destruction of Sierra Leone*, London: C. Hurst & Co, 2005.

2 Although the UN established an observation mission (UNOMSIL) in July 1998, it was limited in resources and scope and ultimately withdrawn in early January 1999 as the rebel forces advanced on Freetown.

3 See Security Council Resolution 1270, S/Res/1270, 1999. http://daccessdds.un.org/doc/UNDOC/GEN/N99/315/02/PDF/N9931502.pdf?OpenElement (accessed on 6 December 2005).

4 See Resolution 1270, op. cit.

5 Sherrill Whittington, *United Nations Goals for 'Gender Mainstreaming' in Post War Peace and Democracy Building ... Theory behind Security Council Resolution 1325: Its Implementation in Afghanistan and Iraq*, Conference on Women and Post-War Reconstruction: Strategies for Implementation of Democracy Building Policies, Florida International University, 12–14 March 2004, p. 5. http://hon.fiu.edu/~conference/transcripts_5.doc. See also East Timor chapter in this volume.

6 See Human Rights Watch, '*We'll Kill You if You Cry' Sexual Violence in the Sierra Leone Conflict*, New York: Human Rights Watch, 2003. In addition to a gender specialist, there was also a focal point for women to assist with gender balance within the mission. However, according to a mid-mission report, this position was ineffective and the focal point did not have enough information or access to senior management to effectively carry out her job. See UN DPKO, *Lessons Learned from United Nations Peacekeeping Experiences in Sierra Leone*, Peacekeeping Best Practices Unit, New York: UN, 2003, p. 79.

7 Eugenia Date-Bah, *Evaluation of Gender Mainstreaming Work and Impact of United Nations Assistance Mission in Sierra Leone (UNAMSIL)*, New York: UN DPKO, 2006, pp. 22–3.

8 The first gender position created within a UN peacekeeping missions was in Kosovo in June 1999. A gender unit was planned for East Timor at the outset of UNTAET, but it was cut due to budgetary reasons and instead two focal points were assigned in October 1999. By mid-2000, a full-scale gender unit had been established in UNTAET and was the first of its kind in a peacekeeping mission.

9 Personal interview with Theresa Kambobe, UNAMSIL gender advisor, Freetown, 25 May 2005.

10 Ibid; Multi-donor Review of Implementation of Security Council Resolution 1325 on Women, Peace and Security by the United Nations Missions in Liberia (UNMIL) and Sierra Leone (UNIOSIL), 2–10 April 2006, unpublished report.

11 Date-Bah, op. cit., p. 17.

12 Ibid.

13 Personal Interview with Theresa Kambobe, UNAMSIL gender advisor, Freetown, 25 May 2005; Date-Bah, op. cit., p. 23.

14 Physicians for Human Rights, *War-related Sexual Violence in Sierra Leone: A Population-based Assessment*, Boston: Physicians for Human Rights, 2002.

15 Interviews with two programme officers from the Ministry of Social Welfare, Gender and Children's Affairs, Freetown, 22 June 2006.

16 Personal interview with Theresa Kambobe, UNAMSIL gender advisor, Freetown, 25 May 2005.
17 Personal interview with Gebremehdin Hagoss, Chief, Peace and Governance Section UNIOSIL (previously with UNAMSIL), 29 June 2006.
18 This was mentioned during various interviews between the author and representatives of women's organisations in Freetown, June and July 2006.
19 For example, the key policy frameworks guiding the UN's peacebuilding activities fail to incorporate gender fully in their respective analyses, budgets or activity matrices. For example, see UN Country Team, *Peace, Recovery and Development: UN Development Assistance Framework for Sierra Leone*, UN: Freetown, 2003; and UN, *From Peacekeeping to Peacebuilding: UN Strategy to Support National Recovery and Peacebuilding in Sierra Leone*. New York: UN, 2002.
20 Personal interview with a member of UNAMSIL senior management, Freetown, 29 June 2006.
21 Personal interview with an Oxfam governance advisor, 25 February 2005.
22 Personal interview with Jebbeh Forster, UNIFEM, 13 June 2006.
23 UNCT, *UNAMSIL/UNCT Transition Strategy: Laying a foundation for durable peace and sustainable development*, Unpublished draft, 1 March 2005.
24 A gender advisor from the UN mission in Burundi was seconded to UNIOSIL for one month in June 2006 to support the office in engaging women in the run-up to the elections in August 2007, and then finally in June 2007 a gender advisor was recruited for a six-month contract, which was subsequently renewed.
25 Desmond Molloy, 'The Gender Perspective as a Deterrent to Spoilers: The Sierra Leone Experience', *Conflict Trends* 2, 2004.
26 Campaign for Good Governance, *The Situation of Women and Girls in the Pre-conflict, Conflict and Post Conflict Sierra Leone, Presentation to the TRC Thematic Hearing*, no date.
27 While this chapter frequently refers to 'women in Sierra Leone', it is important to note that this is not assumed to be a homogenous category, and each individual's experience of their gender varies. Women are also differentiated by whether or not they remain behind or flee conflict, or are actively involved in combat, community-based peacebuilding, or any other activities. Other factors such as religion or their access to income also influence the hardship experienced by women during conflict, as well as their position in society and the opportunities available to them since the end of the war.
28 Christiana Thorpe, 'The Rebel War Years Were Catalytic to Development in the Social Advancement of Women in Post-war Sierra Leone', Masters Dissertation, St. Clements University. Unpublished manuscript, 2006, p. 21. Thorpe reports (p. 77) that prior to 1990 there were only ten NGOs headed by women throughout the entire country, but that after the war more than a hundred organisations run by women have been established.
29 Yasmin Jusu-Sherrif, 'Sierra Leonean Women and the Peace Process', *Accord: An International Review of Peace Initiatives*, 2000. www.c-r.org/our-work/accord/sierra-leone/women-peace.php and Filomina Chioma Steady, *Women and Collective Action in Africa: Development, Democratization, and Empowerment, with Special Focus on Sierra Leone*, Basingstoke: Palgrave MacMillan, 2006, p. 43.
30 John L. Hirsch, *Sierra Leone: Diamonds and the Struggle for Democracy*, International Peace Academy Occasional Paper series, London: Lynne Rienner Publishers, 2001, pp. 40–1.
31 Thorpe, op. cit., p. 40.
32 In addition to their role in publicly campaigning for elections, delegations of women also sought to meet with the rebels to convince them to lay down their arms. These efforts were not always successful: in one particularly bad incident, a group of women were gunned down in Kenema when they tried to approach rebel bases,

killing several activists. Personal interview with Gladys Gbappy-Brima, Freetown, 26 June 2006.

33 There is some discrepancy in accounts of the Lomé negotiations regarding the number of women present. According to a report by Femmes Africa Solidarité, four of the nine key negotiatiors at Lomé were women (see Femmes Africa Solidarité, *Engendering the Peace Process in West Africa: The Mano River Women's Peace Network*, Geneva: FAS, 2000, pp. 23–4). However, the TRC reports that only two women were involved in Lomé, and one was an OAU representative and not Sierra Leonean (TRC Report: 194, para 424), whereas Mazurana and Carlson indicate that two women were present, one as part of the government delegation and another as an RUF representative (Dyan Mazurana and Khristopher Carlson, *From Combat to Community*, Washington, DC: Hunt Alternatives Fund, 2004, p. 16).

34 Lomé Peace agreement. Please see the full text at www.sierra-leone.org/lomeaccord. html.

35 See Mazurana and Carlson op. cit. for an account of the 6 May incident where the actions of elder women resulted in a curse being placed on Foday Sankoh, leader of the rebel Revolutionary United Front (RUF).

36 For example, see Sheila Meintjes, Anu Pillay and Meredeth Turshen (eds), *The Aftermath: Women in Post-conflict Transformation*, London: Zed Books, 2002.

37 Thorpe, op. cit, p. 36.

38 Jane Barry, *Rising Up in Response: Women's Rights Activism in Conflict*. Boulder: Urgent Action Fund for Women's Human Rights, 2005, pp. 28–9.

39 Meredeth Turshen, 'Engendering Relations of State to Society in the Aftermath', in Meintjes, Pillay and Turshen (eds), p. 94.

40 Personal interview with a Sierra Leonean women's activist, Freetown, 22 June 2006.

41 *Submission by the Women NGOs Collaboration to the Truth and Reconciliation Commission*, May 2003 and TRC Report, op. cit., p. 257.

42 FAWE, *The Situation of Women and Girls in the Pre-Conflict, Conflict and Post Conflict Sierra Leone, Presentation to the Thematic Hearing*, no date.

43 For example, see the work of the Fifty-Fifty Group, http://fiftyfiftysl.com/.

44 Personal interview with a DFID official, Freetown, 25 May 2005.

45 Several of these statements are reprinted in Thorpe, op. cit.

46 This is based on more than 30 interviews with civil society activists carried out by the author in Sierra Leone during 2005 and 2006.

47 Thorpe, op. cit., p. 64.

48 Cheryl De la Ray and Susan McKay, 'Peacebuilding as a Gendered Process', *Journal of Social Issues*, Vol. 62, No. 1, 2006, p. 150.

49 Donna Pankhurst, 'Making a Difference? The Inclusion of Gender into Institutional Conflict Management Policies', in Marianne Braig and Sonja Wölte (eds), *Common Ground or Mutual Exclusion? Women's Movements and International Relations*, London: Zed Books, 2002, p. 134.

50 For more information on the gender dimensions of the DDR process in Sierra Leone, see Mazurana and Carlson, op. cit.; Anita Schroven, *Women After War: Gender Mainstreaming and the Social Construction of Identity in Contemporary Sierra Leone*, Spektrum 94, Berlin: Lit Verlag, 2006.

51 Chris Corrin, 'Developing Policy on Integration and Re/construction in Kosova', *Development in Practice*, 13 (2 and 3), 2003, p. 195.

52 Sheila Meintjes, Anu Pillay and Meredeth Turshen, 'There is no Aftermath for Women', in Meintjes, Pillay and Turshen (eds), p. 8.

53 Personal interview with Theresa Kambobe, UNAMSIL gender advisor, Freetown, 25 May 2005.

54 Quoted in Jon Henley, 'Sierra Leone – Did we Make it Better?', *Guardian*, 20 May 2003. www.guardian.co.uk/westafrica/story/0,,1008080,00.html (accessed on 17 December 2006).

55 Mary K. Meyer and Elisabeth Prügl (eds), *Gender Politics in Global Governance*, Oxford: Rowman & Littlefield Publishers, 1999, p. 13.
56 For a summary of the National Action Plan please see NAP Sierra Leone 1325/1820. Available at www.cordaidpartners.com/rooms/women-and-violence/documents/964-nap-sierra-leone-1325-1820.
57 For example, in February 2009, International Alert organised a three-day workshop in Brussels involving 16 women from eight different conflict-affected regions around the world, including Sierra Leone, to engage, share lessons learned and discuss ways to achieve progress in implementing UNSCR 1325.

9 The impact of UNSCR 1325 and peacekeeping operations in Sudan

Gihan Eltahir-Eltom

Introduction

This chapter examines key issues in the implementation of the UN Security Council Resolution 1325 (UNSCR 1325) on Women, Peace and Security in Sudan and assesses the various mechanisms that are being used to create a desirable change. The chapter discusses the local perceptions of gender equality and security, the relevance of UNSCR 1325 to Sudanese women and Sudanese women's involvement in the peace processes. It also considers the United Nation Mission in Sudan (UNMIS), and other United Nations agencies' mechanisms in mainstreaming the Resolution.

There are currently no national action plans that mainstream women's issues, especially ones that focus on UNSCR 1325. Some of the main reasons for this include lack of knowledge and awareness of the Resolution itself; ineffectiveness of the Resolution as an advocacy tool with national/local perceptions of it being associated with Western models of thought; and a lack of coordination and communication between the different actors involved in the implementation of the Resolution.

This chapter relies heavily on interviews conducted in Sudan with a broad range of participants including human rights and civil society activists, political actors, gender advocates and specialists, women who are/were involved in the peace process, International Non-Governmental Organisations (INGOs) staff, UN agencies staff, UNMIS staff and members of the government of National Unity (GoNU). There was particular emphasis on the engagement with UNMIS and United Nations Population Fund (UNFPA) because of their direct relation to UNSCR 1325, as discussed later in this chapter. The interviews focused on local perceptions of UNSCR 1325 in the national context, and of peacekeeping missions; as well as identifying good and/or bad practices of addressing gender issues in the peacekeeping mission in Sudan. This approach was particularly useful given the dearth of literature on this subject particularly as it relates to Sudan. Additionally, the understanding of gender equality and security is largely linked to perceptions both individual and those rooted in social structures, which made the use of interviews the most suitable approach to ensure a full and credible engagement with these very dynamic issues and involving a fairly diverse range of relevant actors.

The next section provides a contextual background. Section three addresses the relevance of UNSCR 1325 to the reality of Sudanese women's lives and whether or not it is being used effectively as an advocacy tool. It also discusses Sudanese women's perceptions of gender, peace and security. It highlights the historical background of the Sudanese women's movement in order to give the reader an idea of the extent of women's role in civil society. Section four looks at the Sudanese women's interactions with the peace processes, both before and after the arrival of the UN mission and the lessons carried from Naivasha to Abuja. Section five discusses the role of the international community in supporting the Resolution, specifically with regard to how it is being mainstreamed into existing programmes. The roles of UNMIS and UNFPA are discussed for their direct relevance and also because UNFPA is explicitly tailoring UNSCR 1325 into its programme. It also investigates whether the arrival of UNMIS has changed local approaches to and understanding of gender equality, and if it has succeeded in giving gender issues a higher profile than before.

Sudanese contextual background

Sudan is the largest country in Africa, and the most ethnically, culturally and geographically diverse. It was also one of the first countries in the continent to gain its independence (1956). It continues to be characterised by disasters and humanitarian crises,[1] which have hindered the development of the country and resulted in ongoing political instability and violent conflicts. The wars and violent conflicts in Sudan erupted at different levels and times for many different reasons among which is the 'multiple marginalisation' across the country with gender inequality as one of its central elements, despite the fact that Sudan has a history of women's movement, which will be discussed later in this chapter.

By signing the Comprehensive Peace Agreement (CPA) in 2005, the two signatory parties – The Government of Sudan (GoS) and Sudan People's Liberation Movement/Army (SPLM/A) – ended decades of civil wars which had first erupted in 1955 before the country's independence. The CPA is composed of six protocols including division of wealth and power, self-determination, and peace and security arrangements, among others.[2] However, the CPA was not comprehensive for several reasons. Besides the CPA's exclusion of many parties and factions of the country, it also does not take into account gender issues as they related to the conflict, in addition to which Sudanese women's participation at the negotiation table was non-existent.

In order to address some of the challenges of the CPA and to monitor its progress, the UN Mission in Sudan (UNMIS) was established to support the parties in the implementation of the CPA. Mandated by UN Security Council Resolution 1590/2005, UNMIS was also assigned to provide political and logistical support to the African Union Mission in Sudan (AMIS), which has since ended following the creation of the hybrid mission, the United Nations–African Union Mission in Dafur (UNAMID).

The country has also undergone other peace processes and more than one agreement was signed. The Darfur Peace Agreement (DPA)[3] was stillborn for many reasons, one of which is its mandate for monitoring without a workable ceasefire agreement.[4] Thus, the DPA has had limited effectiveness on the ground. However, gendered realities as well as women's issues were given higher consideration in this peace process in comparison to the considerations in the CPA, as will be shown later in this chapter.[5] The Eastern Sudan Peace Agreement (ESPA), on the other hand, was signed between the GoS and the Eastern Sudan Front,[6] in Asmara, Eritrea, in October 2006.

In Sudan, civil war lasted from 1955 to 2005 except for the 11 years of the Addis Ababa agreement which preceded UNSCR 1325 by many decades. The conflict affected women drastically and increased their vulnerability substantially. The conflict also put women in a situation where they had to take over new roles not least as heads of households.[7] With local dynamics in women's adaptation to the conflict situation and arguably engagement with security processes, Sudan provides the ideal context in which to explore how local initiatives have been either strengthened or weakened by the arrival of the peacekeeping mission in 2005.[8] The Mission was at that time well placed to benefit from the five years of experience that the international community had in implementing UNSCR 1325, in terms of global lobbying and advocacy. In addition UNSCR 1325 was considered in the formulation of its mandate and structure.

Sudanese women and UNSCR 1325

UNSCR 1325 and its relevance to Sudanese women: a note from history

Sudanese women's involvement in the political sphere started as early as political rights were recognised in the Sudanese modern state. Since the 1950s, women took significant steps toward addressing their issues and entered the Parliament for the first time in 1965, and their presence increased gradually in the education sector as well as other fields that were previously male-dominated.[9]

The recognition of rights in a democratic setting began even before Sudanese women gained the right to vote in the multi-party election of 1965. On this occasion, women voted in the graduate constituencies of the 1953 elections,[10] and were actively involved in the political struggle for independence.[11] However, the institutional foundation for women's political engagement was set by the establishment of the Sudanese Women's Union (SWU) in 1952, which was also preceded by a number of women's groupings and societies. Although these organisations at the time were limited to the 'enlightened' educated women and were not addressing wider political objectives,[12] they formed the foundation of an institutionalised women's movement in the country. The publication of the *Women's Voice* monthly magazine in 1955, as the first magazine in Sudan and the Horn of Africa that precisely tackled issues of women's equal rights and liberty, contributed substantially to awareness raising and advocacy in this matter.[13]

Following this, women took active roles in the resistance to British Administration; they participated in and led demonstrations, distributed political pamphlets and attended political nights.[14] However, it is worth noting here that this movement did not proliferate throughout all communities and components of society. For instance, historically, rural women in the agricultural sector were largely excluded from these activities. The reality of the Sudanese context is its diversity, which sees different communities, with particular perceptions of gender roles and therefore the way that the role of women is understood and reinforced.[15] As such, the low level of women's representation in the decision-making levels and senior managerial, administrative and political positions does not reflect the reality, where the proportion of women with higher education degrees is much higher.[16]

Sudanese women's perceptions

The Sudanese experience underscores the reality of women in conflict situations in terms of gender gaps that are rooted in the broader manifestation of power structures which, in turn, are reflected in the socio-economic situation, resource allocation, access to justice and exclusion from formal systems. Based on the responses of interviewees from the Sudan study, gender security and women's security are completely different issues. The former necessarily addresses the situation of both men and women. It was noted that the security and livelihood of men has tended to be ignored with the continued increasing focus on women. A gender specialist interviewed elaborated on this issue by noting that 'money is being invested in women, while in a devastated community both men and women are disempowered. Gender security should be about providing security to men and women and catering for the definition of men and women'.[17]

On the other hand, it is arguable that women's security issues are unique and hence need to be addressed separately and in many cases in a different manner from those of men. Despite the fact that both men and women are victims of war, in most violent conflicts, the form of violence can often differ. Violence against women is not random. Women and girls are subjected to rape and other sexual-related violence[18] because of their gender. However, women are also veterans and combatants of war, but usually they (both victims and warriors) have no room on the negotiation table. They are expected to resume domestic roles after the end of the war while positions of leadership are usually given to their male counterparts. Additionally, this Resolution is primarily concerned with women and as such addresses their level of participation in decision-making, peacekeeping and peace talks.

Understanding of UNSCR 1325

There was a strong emphasis among the interviewees on the low awareness of UNSCR 1325, which presents an obstacle and deters people from relating to it. As was stated by a civil society (Darfurian) activist: 'There is a very low awareness of SCR 1325, it's been only known among the activists and elites who go to New York and attend forums. But women at the grassroots' level remain far away from these things.'[19] One of the problems facing the implementation of UNSCR 1325 is the absence of mechanisms of engagement and ownership, and according to all interviewed actors there is no existing action plan to implement it at all levels. Within these levels, the government, civil society (CS) and local communities, people are not fully aware of UNSCR 1325 and feel that they do not have any means of influence on its implementation. Surprisingly, this is a particular challenge in countries such as Sudan where a peacekeeping mission is incorporating the Resolution in its mandate, and had the advantage upon its establishment to benefit from the five years of experience the international community has had in implementing it. According to a Sudanese INGO employee,

> We don't know if it is relevant to Sudanese women, because not all Sudanese women know about the Resolution, only those who are exposed to NGOs. Gender is a societal and behavioural issue; if we want an article to be reinforced we have to expose people to it to be more effective.[20]

Overall, many interviewees, from civil society, INGOs, the government SPLM wing and UN agreed on the importance of this document for women in general, and acknowledged women's vulnerability and welcomed this extra protection. However, some of the interviewees within these various groups opposed what they think is the classical approach of treating women largely as victims, and wanted to address how women can be part of the process and how they can take an active role. They understood UNSCR 1325 to be a mechanism that activates the positive role that women can play but greater focus tends to be placed on the protective role, seeing women as victims. Implementation of the Resolution should see women transform their role as recipients to become active players. The challenges in Sudan are to do with how UNSCR 1325 is applied, how effective it is and how it fits with the process on the ground with regards to enhancing women's rights. According to a senior SPLM official and a member of parliament:

> It is a good document. Before I became a member of the People's House, we used it extensively during the negotiations, to do the workshops and rally women's opinions and put pressure on the negotiating parties, it is being also used extensively during the Abuja talks. It didn't come out openly, now we have problems and we don't see it as relevant to Sudanese women but it is a real tool that women can use to engage with the government, and the UN.[21]

Why has UNSCR 1325 not been used effectively as an advocacy tool?

There was near unanimous agreement among the interviewees that the Resolution has not been fully utilised yet. Assessing the Resolution's relevance and effectiveness within the Sudanese context, is an important part of the essence of its implementation and that has not been done yet. Other reasons noted among the interviewees – mainly civil society and some UN staff – for the inadequate use of UNSCR 1325 include the gap between policy and practice, and more importantly the lack of awareness among policy makers of the Resolution itself. This was apparent in the absence of experience sharing with other countries and therefore no obvious empirical basis for global good practices. Some interviewees argued that the Resolution is associated with Western models of thought and that Sudanese women's groups should engage more with initiatives such as those led by African women's groups to develop the protocol on the rights of women in Africa. This was seen as being more context relevant and a stronger basis for advocacy, in having a clearer African origin. Additionally, it was argued that it is difficult to assess the efficacy of the Resolution because not enough time has passed to be able to fully evaluate and measure its performance.

Furthermore there are social, economic, legal and political factors that hinder women's activism in Sudan. Women's groups tend to encounter challenges such as limited access to resources, media, limited cooperation from authorities, lack of social recognition and limited access to the grassroots. Additionally several Sudanese human rights activists indicated that the narrow engagement on UNSCR 1325 means it continues to be known among only a few women activists. This limits its effectiveness in advocating for basic and essential issues of gender equity and equality.

Based on interviews, the assessment of UNSCR 1325 by various groups reveals confusing messages, variant interpretations and weak support for the Resolution. The complexity of relations between various stakeholders and the different ideological bases of the two major parties comprising the Government of National Unity (GoNU) and the Government of South Sudan (GoSS), is a deterrent to the implementation of the Resolution. The CS groups, on the other hand, encounter different forms of challenges to their work, which undermine their capacity for advocacy. This is in addition to the low level of awareness and comprehension of the Resolution.

Engendering peace: Sudanese women and the peace process

From the mid to late 1990s, women's organisations grew in large numbers in Sudan. The Women's Civil Society Network for Peace (WCSNP), for example, has 65 member organisations registered. This expansion happened in a parallel process to developments within the wider CS movement with the beginning of the peace talks in the south. Women Civil Society Organizations (CSOs) have focussed on addressing the issues and problems of the Sudanese women as the prime victims of war and crises in Sudan. The challenges are wide-ranging and include poverty, illiteracy, disease, threats to their children and neglect at all decision-making levels, as exemplified by their exclusion from previous peace talks. The lack of participation of, and exclusion of, women is due to deep-rooted gender inequalities and the continuous ignorance of UNSCR 1325 by the broader governance system. This is despite occasional political and intellectual rhetoric on how the inclusion of women, who represent half of the population in Sudan,[22] will help in consolidating the peace and its sustainability.

In early 1993, CSOs began to incorporate peacebuilding in their activities.[23] The issue of peace was highly politicised and was considered a national security issue. The Sudanese Women's Empowerment Network (SuWEP) was founded in 1997 and formatted an umbrella for five women's groups: Women's Civil Society for Peace Network; the National Democratic Alliance (NDA);[24] Southern Women's Group;[25] the Nuba Mountains' Women's Group; and the National Committee for Peace Network (GoS initiated). The network worked closely with its sister organisation SuWEP-South, which was established by the SPLM's women secretariat and southern CSOs based in Southern Sudan and Nairobi and received great support from the Dutch Embassy.[26] Within the women's movement, the establishment of SuWEP has institutionalised their participation as civil society groups as it sets the framework for lobbying and advocacy for women's participation in the peace process, but it did not reach the negotiation table as will be shown later in this section.

The network has been most successful in initiating a North–South dialogue and has managed to bring together women activists, from both the North and the South, around their common concerns. Additionally, women activists managed to voice their concerns and develop strategies and approaches to peacebuilding, stating their right to gain entrance into formal mechanisms and commissions that were set up to establish the framework and policies that govern Sudanese domestic arrangements for the interim period.[27] As stated by Dr. Pricilla Josef, Chairperson of the Human Rights Committee in the Parliament and Secretary-General for the Parliamentary Focus of the SPLM, 'we have benefited as a group – SWEP/the Dutch initiative, the Netherlands Embassy. It worked well. That money was well spent.'

Sudanese women and the Comprehensive Peace Agreement (CPA)

Although UNSCR 1325 has obliged member states to ensure the inclusion of women in peace talks, this was not the case in the CPA. Women's groups were excluded from the peace process and little effort has been made to include them in the decision-making and negotiations reached by the parties.[28] Furthermore, neither have the monitors nor the International Partner Forum included a fair representation of women.[29] In addition, the literature of UNSCR 1325 was not used while advocating for women's concerns and the working environment for women's groups at the time of the negotiations, due to the prevalence of restrictive laws and regulations around the ability of women's groups to register and operate. According to a Sudanese youth activist,

Women's representation in the peace talks can be seen, but the question is do they have an input? Do they have influence? It is very few who managed to give a real input. Those who were given a chance to participate were present as individual women, but they did not push hard for the issues of gender sensitivities and other women's issues, at the same time they were not part of the decision-making.

A civil society activist also had this to say about women's participation in the CPA:

[I]t is very disappointing in terms of women's participation in the CPA itself. Women's representation needs to be improved, even now as the CPA is being implemented the women are not very visible. There is a long way to go in terms of gender equality.

None of the items of the 'Agenda for Peace'[30] that were presented by those women activists was formed in the six protocols that constitute the CPA.[31] These protocols included guidance on power sharing, wealth sharing and security arrangement, among others. Furthermore, the memorandum that was raised by these groups and sent to the secretary of Inter-Governmental Authority on Development (IGAD) and all the participants in the negotiations, pointed out that women's and children's rights were not embodied in the protocol and that they were not reflected in the results of the negotiations.[32] The CPA lacks provisions for accountability to war crimes and violence against women, and it did not result in the endorsement of the Convention to Eliminate All Forms of Discrimination Against Women (CEDAW),[33] which was a major demand of the Agenda for Peace. The reality of gender sensitivity was not addressed or recognised with regard to power and wealth sharing. In addition, there were no provisions for women members of the Joint National Transition Team (JNTT), which is assigned to prepare and allocate budgets for the reconstruction of the post-conflict interim period. The only reference was made in paragraphs one to four of the general principles of a just division of wealth.[34]

Women's presence within the commissions that were formed upon signing of the CPA is very weak, with almost no representation in security and joint military commissions at least in the early stages of CPA implementation. The percentages guaranteed by the interim constitution for women representation by the decision-making bodies were not fulfilled.[35] For instance, the first cabinet of the first National Unity Government formed after the signing of the CPA included only four women ministers: Dr. Tabita Sokaya, Minister of Health; Ms Samia Ahmed Mohamed, Minister of Social Welfare; Ms Teresa Eyru, Minister of State for Environment; and Ms Ann Eto, Minister of State for Agriculture and Forestry. Moreover, out of the 12 special advisors of the president, only one was female, Ms Farida Ibrahim. Although many argue that there are not enough qualified women to fill those positions, it is not only a question of women's capacities, it is also about obstacles to gender equality in the institutions that shape the ways decisions are made, allocation of resources and policy implementation.[36]

The Darfur peace process

Women's priorities in the peace process were given higher consideration compared to what was given in the CPA. This was due to the strong advocacy for the implementation of UNSCR 1325 provided by the African Union (AU) and the international partners, namely, Canada, Norway, Sweden and UNIFEM who have pushed hard for women's inclusion in the delegates. As a result, a Gender Expert Support Team (GEST) was formed to represent women with different backgrounds and ethnicities; the team managed to present women's priorities and address their issues in the seventh round of the negotiations.[37]

Security, power and wealth sharing were the main issues that were brought up by GEST. Sudanese women were able to raise their concerns and recommendations with reference to the local, regional and international treaties, protocols and mechanisms that supported the increase in women's participation in the peace process and to reaffirm the importance of the roles women can play in peacebuilding, conflict prevention and transformation.[38] Unlike the Naivasha's Agenda for Peace, women in Abuja talks were able to voice their needs and concerns. They had learned from the previous lessons in Naivasha and Machakos, as shown by their demands for reconstruction, reconciliation and building peace in Darfur. Their recommendations included percentages for representations at the decision-making levels at both the regional and the state level, and vague words and phrases were avoided.[39] The 55 main recommendations presented in 'Woman Priorities in Peace and Reconstruction in Darfur' in the seventh round of the negotiations argue for women's rights and equal representation and participation at all decision-making levels. These include the commissions, committees and unions according to the Sudanese Interim Constitution and the international and regional mechanisms. It also addressed issues of education, positive discrimination, training and capacity building, poverty and protection.[40]

UNSCR 1325 and international community in Sudan

Role of the UNMIS Gender Unit

UNMIS is the first UN mission to have an explicit gender mandate in its Resolution,[41] where the agenda is set to assist the parties to the CPA, in addressing the need for a national inclusive approach, including the role of women, towards reconciliation and peacebuilding. Interestingly, not much hope was held within Sudanese society that the UN will be able to make a real difference in addressing issues of gender inequality. As stated by a civil society activist, 'I don't want to sound pessimistic, but gender equality is very much an internal social process, and the UN peacekeeping mission is very much an external actor. They would have an effect, but it would not be drastic.'

UNMIS Gender Unit's staff stated that the presence of the Gender Unit within the mission is tasked to promote, provide technical support, to facilitate and to guide the mission on its gender mainstreaming and to ensure that the issues of men and women are being addressed and incorporated in each unit.[42] The unit contributes to the efforts to combat all forms of gender-based violence (GBV) enhancing women's contribution to peacebuilding, and improving the effective discharge of the mandate of UNMIS in accordance with international standards on gender equality,[43] peace and security.

In terms of disseminating information on UNSCR 1325; the Gender Unit aims to create massive awareness not only for UN staff but also for the local community, through sensitization workshops, gender awareness training at various levels in each sector, bimonthly workshops for all the stakeholders at the field level, and by translation of UNSCR 1325 into local languages. The Gender Unit has been in the process of pursuing the establishment of young women peace clubs in the universities in Khartoum first, with possible future replications in other states, as peace models to carry on the message of UNSCR 1325.[44]

On advocacy, UNMIS Gender Unit staff stated that the section had addressed itself to issues of GBV.[45] This is centred on the provision of strategies for dealing with GBV including training and research, dissemination of information, monitoring assessment to enhance women's political leadership in the future election and to increase women's economic capacity. The interviewed staff also stated that there remains much work to be done on GBV. Challenges to physical security are on the increase, as is poverty. Much needs to be done to enhance women's access to security, including increasing awareness of UNSCR 1325 and contextualising it with the situation in Sudan. On the other hand, some UNMIS staff expressed some dissatisfaction as regards advocacy for gender issues and gender mainstreaming in UNMIS in particular and indicated the need to oblige the GoNU to show commitment and translate it into action.

However, there is a contradiction between the role articulated by the Gender Unit and the views of the CS groups as well as the members of the GoNU institutions, in which there appears to be a clear absence of coordination. Interviews with different UNMIS units indicated that gender-related issues are part of their work; however, they are not coordinated with the Gender Unit.[46] Moreover a Strategy Session organised by the Gender Unit in December 2005 showed a more limited role:

> To-date, the Gender Unit has focused its initiatives on raising awareness about the Resolution. We have delivered a number of presentations, held discussions with civil society groups, UN and governmental actors in order to identify the entry points for implementation efforts here in Sudan.[47]

The Gender Unit's vision of the implementation of UNSCR 1325 is very ambitious and looks very good on paper. It aims at translation and contextualisation of the Resolution in the revision of the Sudanese laws, advocacy and influencing local actors as well as providing support to the CS and extensively raising awareness. However, the reality is different, as the basic elements required to turn this vision into a plan of action are missing. For instance, the unit lacks the essential communication capacity to reach out to CS as indicated by the CS actors.[48] As such, those elements relating to advocacy and influencing local actors are not possible in reality. In addition, the translation of UNSCR 1325 has not been adequate to enable local comprehension. This is because it is necessary to go beyond mere language translations to contextualising its understanding and engaging community leaders in these activities. For instance, the revision of laws cannot be pursued without local leadership on these issues. Therefore any action on this must be undertaken in cooperation with the GoNU, especially to avoid the perception of UNSCR 1325 as a foreign imposition.[49]

The extensive awareness that was cited as an underlying goal of the Gender Unit was yet to be achieved at least as of the time of revising this chapter for publication, in addition to which the coordination between the Gender Unit and other sections within the mission seemed to be problematic with no clear action on the way ahead.[50]

United Nations Population Fund (UNFPA) supporting implementation of UNSCR 1325 in Sudan

Other UN agencies have been active in pursing the implementation of UNSCR 1325 in Sudan. In particular, UNFPA seems to be moving forward on the implementation of UNSCR 1325 in Darfur. This has been done in its advocacy for reproductive health and human rights of women and girls in emergency situations.[51] This includes ensuring adequate protection for girls and women in the conflict zone, Internally Displaced Persons (IDP) camps and urban settings as well as coordinating activities addressing reproductive health (RH) and GBV especially with regards to humanitarian responses, post-conflict reconstruction and rehabilitation and prevention of GBV.[52] It has especially supported emergency RH projects, providing RH supplies which are essential for the rehabilitation and the recovery of the health system in the area. It also anticipates continuing response to emergency needs and comprehensive RH services, and has finalised a comprehensive RH strategy. It has also led inter-agency efforts to design GBV prevention and response strategies in Darfur.[53]

At a particularly strategic level, UNFPA has worked on promoting women's empowerment and human rights, by supporting women's active participation in personal and community decision-making. The programme also considered the provision of support to peacekeeping and peacebuilding in Darfur, and had plans to extend work on implementation of UNSCR 1325 in the Nuba Mountains and eastern and southern Sudan.[54] UNFPA has also been actively advocating the support of a conducive policy environment, which resulted in drafting the policy for Post Exposure Prophylaxis (PEP) for survivors of rape.[55]

Although it is the only UN body in Sudan apart from UNMIS with a clear programme incorporating UNSCR 1325, the UNFPA programme activities show a focus on only two elements of the Resolution; protection of women and girls in armed conflicts and women's active participation in that area. The approach to this first element was very much needs-based and focused on provision of health services rather than long-term environment changing.[56]

A note on the African Mission in Sudan (AMIS)

In April 2004, a Humanitarian Ceasefire Agreement was reached, whereby parties agreed – among others things – 'to create a team of military observers for the ceasefire protected by an armed force jointly called the African Union Mission in Sudan (AMIS)'. Deployment of the African troops in Darfur was set with a mandate to monitor the ceasefire agreement between signatory parties.[57] However, the AU reports to the AU Peace and Security Council did not provide data disaggregated by sex,[58] nevertheless, a noticeable change was observed with the number of women rapidly increasing, from a zero representation, to seven women monitors and one observer at its height[59] before the mission was drawn as part of the transition into UNAMID. In addition, a woman, Ms Monique Mukaruliza,[60] was the acting head of mission. This was an important development especially with regard to UNSCR 1325's call for more women in senior decision-making roles on issues around security, but it was not a strong enough indicator of a systematic implementation of UNSCR 1325 within AMIS.

Conclusion

Despite the efforts to implement UNSCR 1325 in Sudan, the gap between policy and practice remains huge. The awareness of the Resolution is largely among the elites and gender activists whose understanding, utilisation and sense of ownership of UNSCR 1325 remains far from adequate. This could be attributed to a lack of awareness and comprehension. However, awareness-raising in itself does not guarantee successful implementation. It is important to note that appreciation of the Resolution alone will not lead to proper application, and as such, training and printing the Resolution in local languages will not create the 'massive awareness' that UN employees are seeking to achieve. The Resolution is not being domesticated or localised for effective understanding by the stakeholders. Subsequently, there is an urgent need to break it down into practical, achievable goals and put it into a Sudanese perspective.

Women are usually given honorary roles to fulfil the 'inclusion requirement'. The phrase *Khalas aha gibna niswan*, which could be translated as 'OK, here are the women', reflects an attitude that restricts women's roles to the lower rungs of the ladder of participation. They are not given as much representation as their male counterparts at the decision-making levels. There is also a lack of adequate consultation by the UN with the civil society/women's groups. This undermines the inclusion efforts and makes it difficult to successfully respond to their needs. This is compounded by a lack of equal partnership.

Perhaps most importantly, there has been an absence of a 'national action plan' at the state level, which is crucial for the implementation of UNSCR 1325. Furthermore, there is widespread confusion with other controversial UN Resolutions on Sudan, and there are contradictory messages in terms of the level of understanding of the Resolution among members of the GoNU. This is rooted in the different perceptions of the two partners and leads to conflict regarding what the Resolution is about, whether or not to take it forward, and if so, how. There is no unified method for the implementation of UNSCR 1325 between the civil society, the GoNU and the UN. There is also lack of coordination between the UN agencies driving change at the national and regional level. But notwithstanding all of this, the presence of international actors makes a difference in terms of giving visibility to efforts to advance gender equality.

Overall, however, there is a tendency to focus efforts on one aspect of the Resolution – protection and prevention – at the expense of equal gender representation within peacebuilding and reconstruction initiatives. Additionally, there are different responsibilities to be taken by the different stakeholders. The government is supposed to be the main driver and it ought to take the necessary steps in adopting a national plan and civil society should be receptive to the message the Resolution is trying to convey. The UN peacekeeping mission is very much an external factor and its role should be to support the main actors in implementation and to take on a monitoring role. This has not been the case in reality.

UNMIS did not build on the women's peacebuilding activities that existed before its arrival because of its focus on the formal peace process and the two main parties to the CPA. UNMIS priorities were set by the worsening conflict in Darfur and the relationship between the two parties involved in the conflict rather than by the aspirations of the local population. The impact of UNMIS was minimal because of the limited interaction it had with local communities and organisations with regard to women and gender issues. UNMIS' contribution looks better on paper than in reality where the implementation level has been considered inadequate by various stakeholders. UNMIS officials interviewed regarding UNSCR 1325 pointed out the gap between theory and practice when it comes to implementation and awareness of UNSCR 1325.

The impact on international support for local initiatives appears to have been marginal in terms of the capacity to upscale these local efforts. Local women's peacebuilding initiatives such as the engendering peace process initiative, which had been previously supported by the international community, lost this support after the signing of the CPA.

For UNSCR 1325 to bring about transformation in women's lives in Sudan, a number of changes are necessary. These include the following, for example: first, the GoNU must fully adopt UNSCR 1325, and ensure women's inclusion in post-conflict reconstruction and governance. Second, breaking down the articles of UNSCR 1325 is as important as its translation. More effort must be made to train women to use the Resolution effectively as an advocacy tool and develop new and creative ways to make it understandable and applicable to women in different regions of Sudan. Third, CSOs should build bridges with parliament e.g. gender issues can be addressed in open forum between CSOs and members of the parliament. Fourth, there should be better coordination between the UN mission and the different stakeholders in terms of advancement of women and security issues; CSOs should become involved in the process of developing the UNMIS action plan.

Fifth and last, UNMIS represents great potential for building peace. It has access to all parties, finances and expertise and these elements of success should be utilised to the maximum. Women's presence in the mission should be more visible in its structure and key positions. UNMIS should also support women's engagement in building the new legal frameworks and should work together with women's groups and activists to ensure women's inclusion in the law reform committees to ensure gender-sensitive judicial and law enforcement agencies.

Notes

1 Decades of civil wars, drought and desertification had drastic effects on Sudan's economy and social fabric. See (in Arabic) Suliman Mohamed [*Al Sudan Horoob Al Mawarid wal Hawya*], Institute for African Alternatives, 2000.
2 A summary and the full text of the six protocols are available at www.unmis.org/English/cpa.htm.
3 The DPA signed on 5 May 2006 between the faction of the Sudan Liberation Army – Minni Minawi (SLA/MM) and the GoS. However, two other rebel movements, the Justice and Equality Movement (JEM) and the SLA faction – Abdulwahid Mohamed Nour – refused to sign, putting the DPA on an uncertain footing from the start.
4 The DPA has a lot of shortcomings which include the peace process itself, where parties were not given enough time and were constrained by the deadline diplomacy.
5 Sudanese women participated in the seventh round of the negotiations in Abuja, Nigeria, on 30 December 2005, and addressed their priorities in the peace process and reconstruction in Darfur.
6 The Eastern Front – an alliance between two rebel movements, the Beja Congress and a smaller insurgent group, the Rashaida Free Lions – has been active in the eastern region near the Eritrean border and demands greater autonomy.
7 For more information on the impact of war on Sudanese women and the 'forced empowerment', see the Child Labour study produced by Save the Children UK in South Darfur and Northern Bahr Al Ghazal states in 2005.
8 Karen Barnes Concept Note, 'Engendering security? The impact of Security Council Resolution 1325 and peacekeeping operations on conflict-affected regions', 25 May 2006.
9 Angel Izaac was the first Sudanese woman to enrol in the university in 1945 and who graduated from the Faculty of Arts in 1948.
10 There was a strong campaign in the 1950s, calling for women's political rights upon the independence of Sudan. The campaign was led by the Sudanese Women's Union. As a result, Sudanese women gained the right to vote but it was predominantly university and high school graduates who took the initiative to join in the graduate's constituencies. However, the 1957 electoral law cancelled the graduate's constituencies and, hence, women's right to vote. After the 1964 uprising, the law was amended giving women the right to vote in the graduate's constituencies and the geographical constituencies as well. This was also a result of women's activism and participation in the political movement at the time. See http://sudanray.com/Forums/showthread.php?t=378 (in Arabic).
11 F. Mahmoud, 'African Women: Between Tradition and Modernity' [*Al Mar'aa AL Afrigheea bain Al Irth wal Hadatha*], Cambridge: Cambridge University Press (in Arabic), 2002.
12 Ibid.
13 Ibid.
14 Ibid.

15 Education and economic opportunities contributed to major transformations for women in rural and urban areas of Sudan. This can be attributed to the colonial legacy, for example, the Sudanese modern state, which was created by the British Administration in 1898, was focusing on the Nilotic northern and central Sudan, for economic reasons mainly the Al Jazeera Scheme (which was producing, at the time, cotton for Lancashire factories). The political and economic output of the scheme contributed to creating a political and educated new middle class within Sudanese class structure. The political movement in that region was more advanced in fighting for the rights of women for education and political participation in comparison with the rest of Sudan which was less developed economically. For instance, South Sudan was a 'closed area' because it was not contributing to the British economic and political interests. So women's political participation and education levels developed differently and progressively compared to other regions. Additionally, although the division of work in the Sudanese rural economy depends highly on women's contribution (in terms of agricultural and nomadic sectors), tribal structures shape gender roles, and limit women's participation in decision-making. For instance, women cannot be part of the Mediation Council *Juddyya*, or become tribal leaders *Umdda, Nazir or Shiekh.*

16 Women represented 48 per cent of students in the higher education institutions in 1998.

17 Interview, Khartoum, on 5 October 2006.

18 Examples of sexual-related violence such as trafficking, forced prostitution, genital mutilation, purposeful infections with Sexually Transmitted Infections (STI), forced impregnation, forced abortion. For more information see www.womenwarandpeace.org.

19 Interview, Khartoum, on 15 September 2006.

20 Interview with a Gender Officer in an INGO, Khartoum, on 1 October 2006.

21 Interview, Khartoum, 3 October 2006.

22 1993 census.

23 Interview with Ms Tamadour A. Khaleel, formal coordinator of Engendering Peace Initiative, 26 September 2005.

24 A coalition of women activists and members of established political parties.

25 Southern women organisations in the North.

26 Interview with the former network coordinator Tamadour A. Khaleel on 26 September 2005. Also see A. El Kahrib, 'Gender Profile in Sudan: Challenges into the 3rd Millennium', Khartoum: The Civil Society Network for Peace, 2000.

27 Interview with Ms Tamadour A. Khaleel, the formal coordinator of this initiative, on 26 September 2005.

28 See Gender Centre for Training and Research 'Women in the Machakos Protocol', Khartoum, 2005.

29 Ibid.

30 Agenda for peace was presented in September 2000 by women activists in civil society organisations in North, South, East and Western Sudan in a meeting in Nairobi under the auspices of the Netherlands Government. The agenda spoke of women's participation in peace initiatives, and peace negotiations, gender-based violence, respect of cultural and religious diversity and freedom of movement in Sudan, among others.

31 This was based on interviews with women who took an active part in the initiative, also see A. El Karib, op. cit.

32 Ibid.

33 Convention to Eliminate All Forms of Discrimination Against Women (United Nations); an international women's rights treaty that spells out women's rights and obliges governments to ensure respect for these rights. For the full Convention please visit www.un.org/womenwatch/daw/cedaw/.

34 Interview with a civil society activist in September 2006.

35 Interview with Minister of State for Agriculture and Forestry Ms Ann Ito, also see a List of senior officials of Sudan's first national unity government available at www. sacbc.org.za/docs/denis/gnu.doc.

36 Noeleen Heyzer, statement before the UN Security Council on 26 October 2006.

37 Interview with Ms Safa Alagib; a Gender/Darfurian activist who was involved in the Abuja Peace negotiations, this also came in another interview with a CS activist Ms Samia Ahmed.

38 See 'Women Priorities in Peace and Recovery in Darfur', recommendations presented in the seventh round of the Darfur peace negotiations in Abuja, Nigeria in 30 December 2005.

39 The 'Women's Priorities in the Peace Process and Reconstruction in Darfur' presented by women activists in the seventh round of Darfur peace negotiations stated a number of demands for representation of women in decision-making positions. For example, a 30 per cent representation at the state level and 50 per cent at the regional level (Darfur specifically). For the full report please see www.peacewomen.org/resources/Sudan/Womens_Priorities.doc.

40 Ibid.

41

Reaffirms the importance of appropriate expertise on issues relating to gender in peacekeeping operations and post-conflict peacebuilding in accordance with Resolution 1325 (2000), recalls the need to address violence against women and girls as a tool of warfare, and encourages UNMIS as well as the Sudanese parties to actively address these issues.

(UNSCR 1590/2005)

42 Interviews with UNMIS Gender Affairs Unit on 28 September 2006.

43 In particular the Beijing Declaration and Platform for Action and the Outcome Document of the special session of the General Assembly 53 (Beijing +5) as well as Security Council Resolution 1325/2000.

44 Interview with Gender Affairs Unit staff on 28 September 2006.

45 Gender-based violence (GBV)

refers to violence targeting women or men, girls or boys on the basis of their gender or sexual orientation. It includes, but is not limited to, sexual violence, which is often used as an instrument of terror and torture in armed conflict situations.

46 In Darfur UNMIS is developing cooperative strategies to help implement the Government of National Unity's National Action Plan on GBV in Darfur. Four entry points have been identified as priorities: awareness-raising on the 'Criminal Form Eight'; establishment of victim-friendly centres in the IDP camps; building the capacity of civil society organisations; and advocacy. While rape victims no longer need to complete the Criminal Form Eight, a medical evidence document, to receive emergency medical assistance, too little has been done to inform women and the police (both Sudanese and the African Union civilian police) of this change. In the past, women were often denied treatment because a physician was unavailable or unwilling to fill out such a form, and in some cases, they were subjected to abusive medical exams, for more information International Crises Group Africa Report No. 112 'Beyond Victimhood: Women's Peacebuilding in Sudan, Congo and Uganda', 2006. Available at www.crisisgroup.org/en/regions/africa/central-africa/112-beyond-victimhood-womens-peacebuilding-in-sudan-congo-and-uganda.aspx.

47 See Final Report: 'Ensuring a Sustainable Peace in Sudan: Assessing Steps Forward for Implementation of Security Council Resolution 1325 on Women, Peace and Security', a Strategy Session organised by the UNMIS Gender Unit, 20 December 2005, UNMIS Headquarters, Khartoum. Available at www.peacewomen.org/resources/Sudan/UNMIS_StrategySessionReport.doc.

48 Interview with a civil society leader on 12 September 2005, also an interview with a gender activist on 3 October 2005.
49 The researcher attended a workshop in September 2006 organised by the NCP members of the Parliament entitled 'The Impact of Foreign Presence on Women in Darfur' in transliteration: [*Athar al Wogood AL agnabi ala al maraa fi Darfur*]. The workshop clearly stated the following: that the purpose of the INGO presence in Darfur is to gather information without vetting, that they do so without considering local authorities and that both women and men in Darfur should be cautious in their dealings with these entities.
50 Interview with UNMIS staff on 20 September 2006.
51 UNSCR 1325 article 10 calls for taking special measures to protect women and girls from GBV particularly rape and other sorts of sexual abuse and violence in situations of armed conflicts.
52 UNFPA programme brochure, also an interview with staff.
53 A meeting with a UNFPA GBV officer on 13 September 2006.
54 See 'UNFPA supporting implementation of Security Council Resolution 1325 in Sudan' brochure.
55 UNFPA is putting on more efforts in adopting recommended policy framework on GBV and Sexually Transmitted Infections (STIs) including HIV/AIDS management and safe motherhood in addition to the efforts in increasing the capacity of its national partners in providing emergency RH services and information and support responsive coordination mechanisms, as the programme document stated.
56 UNFPA programme brochure.
57 AMIS is mandated according to the Peace and Security Council of 2004, to

> Contribute to a secure environment for the delivery of humanitarian relief and beyond that, the return of IDPs and refugees to their homes in order to assist increasing the level of compliance of all parties with the Humanitarian Ceasefire Agreement and to contribute to the environment of the security situation through-out Darfur.

The mandate is limited and weak and focuses on monitoring and observation rather than direct protection responsibilities, and the proactive steps that AMIS can take were limited to 'civilians whom it encounters under immediate threat and the imme-diate vicinity within capabilities' and providing 'visible military presence by patrol-ling and by the establishment of temporary outposts in order to deter uncontrolled armed groups from committing hostile acts against the population'.
58 J. Oyediran article 'Regional and International Mechanisms around Viol-ence Against Women[2]', in SIHA (Strategic Initiative for Women in the Horn of Africa) Network Report – Violence Against Women and Girls in Conflict and Post Conflict Situations Consultation Report June 2005, www.sihanet.org/index.php?option=com_docman&itemid=6.
59 Interview with a civil society activist 6 September 2006.
60 See www.amis-sudan.org.

10 Women and gender issues in peacebuilding

Lessons learned from Timor-Leste

Sumie Nakaya

Introduction

This chapter analyses violence against women in post-war Timor-Leste, especially in the context of institutional change in the transition from war to peace. The chapter focuses on violence against women not only because it persists in post-conflict states, despite the enhanced political participation and representation of women in decision-making, as the Timor example highlights, but also because civilian security is one of the fundamental requirements of the peacebuilding process. In particular, this chapter addresses three issues related to the political, economic and social dimensions of peacebuilding and the role of women in this process, particularly in the context of UN Security Council Resolution 1325 (UNSCR 1325). These include, first, the rule of law, including the reform of criminal codes, the police, the judiciary, and civil and family law; second, the peacekeeping economy and its impact on the sexual exploitation of women; and third, the reform of public administration. These areas are directly related to the role of UN transitional assistance in post-conflict states, including in Timor-Leste, where the policies and priorities of external actors could have an enduring impact on gender relations. Notwithstanding cultural and other local factors that affect the status of women, these institutional frameworks determine the scope of post-war violence generally, not only against women, because institutions established in the process of the post-war transition are based on the realignment of power among groups engaged in civil war violence.

The Timor-Leste case highlights particular challenges facing women and gender issues in peacebuilding. On the one hand, the end of the civil war and the ensuing transition to post-war democratization, with international assistance, can increase the representation of women in decision-making and state institutions. In July 2001, Timorese women won 26 per cent of the seats in the Constituent Assembly, even without electoral quotas being allocated to them. In 2007, 20 per cent of ministers and administrators within the executive branch were women. At the same time, gender-based violence (GBV) tends to remain pervasive in post-conflict states. In Timor-Leste, despite the massive mobilization and empowerment of women for the first democratic elections five months earlier, nearly 40 per cent of all reported crimes in December 2001 involved violence against women and girls, such as rape, attempted rape and sexual assault.[1] Statistics from 2004 indicate that GBV constituted more than half of the cases reported to the police and approximately one-third of the cases coming before the courts that year.[2]

At the same time, the Timor-Leste case study also highlights that women can be vulnerable in the rapid post-war transition toward political and economic liberalization that characterizes the current approach to peacebuilding.[3] This analysis is based on a literature review and an earlier trip to Timor-Leste as part of the global assessment supported by the UN Development Fund for Women (UNIFEM) of the impact of armed conflict on women and their correlative role in peacebuilding. In extensive consultations on gender issues with civil society, legislators, government officials and representatives of multilateral and bilateral donors, it was agreed that violence against women has emerged as one of the most pressing issues in Timor-Leste.

International interventions in the transitional period have several advantages. First, the international administration of local authority can generally apply high human rights and gender equality standards in accordance with international benchmarks, including the Convention for the Elimination of All Forms of Discrimination against Women (CEDAW), the Beijing Platform for Action (PFA), and UNSCR 1325. Second, as the international administration becomes the de facto government, it can exercise influence in the design of the state system, thereby advocating gender equality in constitutional, legislative, judicial and electoral reforms. The establishment of the Gender Affairs Unit in the UN Transitional Administration in East Timor (UNTAET) contributed to these goals by introducing mainstream gender perspectives in the UN mission's planning and management and in the interim national decision-making process in the National Congress for Timorese Reconstruction (CNRT).[4]

Those who were involved in the drafting of Resolution 1325 made a conscious effort to emphasize the political empowerment of women, calling for their participation in peace negotiations, peacebuilding and other macro-level institutional reforms in order to build on the socio-economic origins of other international instruments on gender equality. Given that Resolution 1325 was adopted in October 2000, shortly after UNTAET's arrival, the document was not widely known among Timorese women's groups or national political leaders at the time. When the Women's Congress was organized in Dili in June 2000, participants referred to the PFA when discussing issues pertaining to peacebuilding and women's role in this process. Resolution 1325 was subsequently utilized by women's groups to increase their participation in decision-making, including during the campaigning period for the 2001 elections.

Women coping with conflict

From 1975 onwards, the Indonesian military and militias reportedly raped, tortured and assaulted women and girls on a massive scale, although irreplaceable data detailing such atrocities was destroyed in the 1999 rampage.[5] Many women were abducted and brought to military-run brothels or taken as 'local wives' by military members, and wives of prominent leaders of the independence movement were targeted for punishment and surveillance.[6] Like many other conflicts, however, little was known about the gender dimensions of violence in East Timor (as the country was known at the time), at least until toward the end of the occupation. In November 1998, several East Timorese women's organizations brought a group of women victimized by violence to a public event in Dili, and their testimonials were later published in English and Tetum.[7]

The scope and nature of East Timorese women's movements prior to the arrival of UNTAET were defined in the context of resistance to the Indonesian occupation, and were therefore more clandestine-political and humanitarian than peacebuilding per se. The Popular Organization of Timorese Women (OPMT) was established in 1975 as part of the main resistance group in East Timor, Fretilin (Revolutionary Front for an Independent East Timor). The Organization of Timorese Women was also established in 1975 initially as an illegal organization, with the stated goals of raising political awareness, providing logistical support to resistance forces, fundraising to sustain resistance movements and disseminating information.[8] It is said that women constituted approximately 60 per cent of clandestine movements, acting as local representatives of the OPMT or gaining a certain status within Falintil (Armed Forces of National Liberation of East Timor) – the armed wing of Fretilin – except that there were no women in its command structure.[9] More service-oriented organizations emerged in the late 1990s, such as FOKUPERS (East Timorese Women's Communication Forum), founded in 1997 to provide psychosocial support to the victims of the conflict, including war widows, former political prisoners and their families. The organization East Timorese Women against Violence, established in 1998, seeks to collect data on victims of violence. After UNTAET's arrival in 1999, women's groups organized themselves to play a substantive role in the country's reconstruction. In June 2000, the First Congress of East Timorese Women was convened, bringing together 500 women in Dili, and it established the East Timorese Women's Network – consisting of 16 women's groups – to advocate a rights-based approach to development, justice and gender equality.

Despite their significant roles in the resistance movement and community-based coping with the crisis, national and international support for the participation of women in peacebuilding was scant in the early days of the transition, and the success of subsequent gender mainstreaming within the UNTAET framework was due in large part to the mobilization of the East Timorese women's groups. Women's participation in the intra-East Timorese dialogue, initiated in 1995 by the UN Secretary-General (not as a parallel track to the tripartite negotiation between Indonesia and Portugal under the auspices of the Secretary-General, but designed to complement it through the informal exchange of views among the Timorese from all sections of the political spectrum), was limited to only four out of the total of 38 East Timorese representatives. The women's groups had to lobby tirelessly for the establishment of the Gender Affairs Unit within UNTAET as well. The original proposal to create a prominent gender unit in a transitional government, made at the CNRT meeting in late 1999 (convened to discuss the structure of the transitional government), disappeared when the CNRT merged into the UNTAET framework, partly because 'the UN cadres involved did not see it as such a priority'.[10] The women's groups campaigned to reinstate the idea and place the unit within the Office of the Special Representative of the Secretary-General (SRSG), but they met a number of obstacles: primarily, it appeared that the unit was abolished due to budgetary constraints and, after further lobbying, a small unit was created in the Office of the Deputy SRSG under the governance and public administration pillar.

In post-conflict states, including in Timor-Leste, changing gender roles in families and the failure of the state to provide political, educational and socioeconomic opportunities tend to marginalize women, reversing the leadership roles that they played during the war as the heads of households, as primary sources of income or in liberation/opposition movements. Women in Timor-Leste played an active role in the 24-year resistance movement against the Indonesian occupation, assisting in Fretilin's clandestine activities logistically. They were also the main caretakers of communities while Fretilin members were engaged in guerrilla warfare, although their rights – political, economic and social – were never fully recognized in customary or Indonesian legal frameworks. Not only do the post-war formal institutional arrangements continue to treat women and gender issues marginally, but they also tend to co-exist with the existing informal structure of the social hierarchy that continues to govern post-conflict gender relations at the community level. The rest of this chapter examines the post-war institutional arrangements in Timor, Leste and what role, if any, UNSCR 1325 considerations had in these developments.

Rule of law

The rule of law is the primary, although not exclusive, method of combatting violence against women and the culture of impunity. The establishment of the judiciary is a priority for both peace maintenance, in which a functioning criminal justice system is the core feature of law and order,[11] and for the observance and implementation of statutory laws guaranteeing the rights of women. Gender equality and the protection of women under the rule of law encompass gender-sensitive reforms of basic and fundamental laws, including the constitution, criminal justice systems, and civil and family laws, as well as post-war justice, such as war crimes tribunals. Access to justice is also a critical aspect of the rule of law, particularly for women and the poor.

Constitutional reform

The new Timor-Leste Constitution has progressive language with regard to human rights and gender equality. It includes a provision protecting children born outside of marriage, thereby recognizing the citizenship of children born of rape or parented by international peacekeeping personnel.[12] This achievement resulted from a coalition of national and international organizations, such as Oxfam, the UNTAET Gender Affairs Unit and UNIFEM, as they established a Gender and Constitution Working Group to review various constitutional models (those of Portugal, Indonesia and Japan, among others) from a gender perspective and to involve local women in consultations on constitutional issues. Timorese women's groups subsequently formulated a ten-article Charter of Women's Rights.[13] The charter calls for the prohibition of prostitution, slavery and exploitation, as well as the upholding of the rights of women to equal access to education, employment, health care, personal security and political opportunities. It also advocates equal inheritance rights. The Constituent Assembly voted to accept the charter, with the exception of a proposal to prohibit the traditional system of bride price, or the dowry system. The Timor-Leste Constitution does not permit dual citizenship,[14] however, excluding Indonesian migrants to East Timor from the definition of 'original citizens', including women and children trafficked from Indonesia to East Timor prior to 1999.[15] The citizenship of minority women and children also remains ambiguous.

Penal codes

Legal systems in Timor-Leste (other than those embodied in the Constitution) are in a state of flux as a result of multiple co-existing legal traditions. This legal pluralism, common in many post-conflict states, involves traditional customary laws that substituted for the collapse of the judiciary during war, colonial/foreign laws and incoherent approaches adopted by the UN.[16] In Timor-Leste, there are three official laws: (1) Indonesian laws, including the Indonesian Penal Code, which were designated as a basic legal framework by UNTAET; (2) UNTAET regulations, including the Transitional Rules of Criminal Procedures; and (3) a broad set of international laws introduced by UNTAET, including the Convention on the Elimination of All forms of Discrimination Against Women (CEDAW) and the Convention on the Rights of the Child (CRC). This arrangement was introduced to avoid a legal vacuum in the initial phase of the transitional administration and was instituted with consideration for local lawyers who had obtained law degrees and training in the Indonesian legal system.[17] However, it was done without a thorough review, clarification or systematization of the three different legal systems. As a result, some of the UNTAET-issued regulations contradicted the Indonesian law-based framework.[18] Although UNTAET maintained that Indonesian laws are only applicable when consistent with international human rights laws, it was not endowed with the financial and operational capacity to undertake a comprehensive assessment of those legal gaps within its limited duration.[19]

For most day-to-day matters, particularly regarding criminal offences, the Indonesian laws continue to apply, despite the antagonism and mistrust among local populations toward any state apparatus of Indonesian origin. The Indonesian Penal Code does not provide adequate protection for women and children from sexual violence and exploitation. It defines a sexual offence as 'crimes against decency' and criminalizes adultery[20] but it does not recognize marital rape and attempted assault as crimes,[21] nor does it treat domestic violence as a distinct crime. It also does not regulate sexual crimes committed by the state.[22] UNTAET decriminalized adultery in 2001, but has not addressed other aspects of criminal laws on sexual violence.

In addition, UNTAET has permitted the continued use of alternative justice mechanisms at the local level.[23] In cases of sexual and domestic violence, these traditional justice mechanisms are commonly used at the *suku* (clan or sub-village) and village levels. Disputes at the community level, including reports of violence against women, are often resolved through mediation and compensation, such as the payment of a dowry to the victim's family, as agreed among village chief/elders and men representing the families of victim and offender.[24] As such, traditional definitions and treatment of violence against women and children are often incompatible with international standards. Amnesty International's report on the justice systems in East Timor notes the disparities:[25]

> The chronic delay in establishing an effective criminal justice system by UNTAET has reinforced an existing lack of confidence in formal justice systems and contributed to a continued reliance on alternative forms of justice.... Traditional justice and other informal mechanisms are being applied inconsistently without effective monitoring by, or full integration into, the formal judicial system.

Consequently, the inconsistent and incoherent adoption of different legal norms and traditions has created a great deal of confusion among local populations, as well as national and international law enforcement officials, and placed onerous burdens on the scarce resources of any local legal capacity. Despite its support on CEDAW, the Convention of the Rights of the Child (CRC) and other international human rights instruments, UNTAET seemed content to accept the role of traditional justice forms for 'minor crimes', without defining what constitutes a minor crime.[26] The UN Civilian Police Force (CIVPOL), entrusted with restoring and maintaining law and order until the local police services are fully established, are not familiar with the complex mix of various kinds of legal jargon, have received no training on the substance of these laws and do not know which laws to apply in particular circumstances.[27] In some instances, including those involving rape, CIVPOL deferred to traditional law, and no attempt was made to charge the case formally under Indonesian law or UNTAET rules.[28] Language barriers, lack of competence and professional misconduct have also undermined CIVPOL's efficacy.[29]

In response to the growing criticism concerning the lack of protection of women and children, UNTAET established the Vulnerable Persons' Unit (VPU) within CIVPOL, first in Dili and subsequently in other districts. VPU Dili has female officers and female translators dedicated to responding to violence against women and children, and works with the women's group FOKUPERS to provide shelter and psychosocial support to survivors of sexual violence. In other districts, however, women rarely knew of VPU, and often a single CIVPOL officer was simply appointed as a VPU focal point.[30]

Civil and family law

The reform of civil code and family law has also faced considerable delay. The task of reforming civil and family law has been complicated by the breakdown of family institutions during the war. Existing civil and family laws in Timor-Leste not only make divorce difficult, but also provide few civil remedies in cases of divorce resulting from domestic violence.[31] The Indonesian Marriage Law (1974) states that divorce may be carried out only before a court of law, and only after the court has endeavoured to reconcile the parties. Domestic violence falls under 'cruelty or mistreatment endangering life', suggesting that lesser violence is acceptable.[32] Although divorce may be the only viable option to escape from domestic violence, these legal barriers continue to constrain women from seeking divorce. Many women, without any prospects of remarriage, earning enough income or receiving state support, ultimately choose to stay in their marriages despite violence against themselves and their children.

War crimes tribunals and truth and reconciliation commissions

The pursuit of post-war justice strengthens the sense of justice and confidence in the rule of law, if the process is carried out properly. Legal proceedings on crimes committed during the war can promote transparency and accountability, improve the local rule of law, and contribute to collective memory in national catharsis and further reconciliation,[33] as post-war justice often focuses on a restorative approach that prioritizes the restoration of relationships rather than inflicting punishment.[34]

Timor-Leste began investigating and prosecuting 'serious crimes' in the Dili District Court, which involve cases of genocide, crimes against humanity, war crimes, torture and certain violations of the Indonesian Penal Code – including murder and sexual violence – that took place in 1999.[35] However, the Serious Crimes Unit, comprising predominantly international judges and staff,

> was viewed with much anger by East Timorese jurists, who felt that they had been excluded from the process and that the atrocity cases, which they had previously been dealing with, were being taken away from them by the international community.[36]

Furthermore, the Serious Crimes Unit does not address lesser crimes and crimes committed prior to 1999, which include a large number of cases involving rape, sexual slavery and the sexual assault of women and children perpetrated by Indonesian military and militias.

In search of a workable alternative, the Timorese proposed the establishment of a Commission for Reception, Truth and Reconciliation (CAVR), which was established by UNTAET in July 2001 (Regulation 2001/10). Unlike the Serious Crimes Unit, the CAVR is headed by seven national commissioners and staffed by Timorese, with the logistical support of a small number of international technical advisors.[37] The CAVR is intended to address lesser crimes committed between 25 April 1974 and 25 October 1999 by seeking truth and facilitating grassroots reconciliation. The commission began its work in 2002, and sought to ensure women's participation as commissioners and staff in both healing workshops and the CAVR's Urgent Reparations Programme, as well as in the formation of a special research team on women's issues and the holding of a national public hearing on women.[38] For instance, a Working Group on Victim Support consisted of seven members, four of whom were women, and 50 per cent of statement takers (including oral testimonies) were women. Fifty per cent of the district-level victim support staff and 30 per cent of regional commissioners were also women. Although it is difficult to verify whether women's representation in these mechanisms led to more female victims and witnesses submitting cases to the commission, by the end of its operations, the CAVR was able to provide priority reparations in the form of cash grants to 516 men (73 per cent) and 196 women (23 per cent) who sought compensation.[39]

Peacekeeping economy

The arrival of large-scale peacekeeping missions usually corresponds with an increase in sexual violence and the exploitation of women in two ways. First, the presence of large, foreign, externally supplied missions creates an inflationary economy that is particularly destabilizing in poor countries. The economic boom that was exclusively centred on construction, trade and the service sector aimed at foreign consumption can relegate women to primary employees in restaurants, bars, hotels and shops. Job security, however, is often non-existent, since any peacekeeping economy is necessarily unsustainable and bound to downsize. In Timor-Leste, the Dili-centred emergence of a US dollar-based economy in one of the world's poorest nation has created considerable urban–rural disparity. Although UNTAET officials recognized the impact of UNTAET's withdrawal on the local economy and women in the service sector, no concrete response was developed.[40] The vulnerability and exploitation of women in a peacekeeping economy are often exacerbated by the failure of peacekeeping missions to provide skills training, stable income-generating jobs, education and community development in rural areas. In this regard, UNTAET and its national counterpart, the East Timor Transitional Authority, made a systematic effort to recruit women to fill at least 30 per cent of all positions. As of August 2001, the 30 per cent goal had been achieved in the departments of education, health and foreign affairs.[41]

Second, the conduct of peacekeepers can also discount the legitimacy of the operations in the eyes of the local population because of the valid association with increased sexual exploitation of local women and children. In Timor-Leste, two members of the Pakistani army engineering battalion were sent home in disgrace after being found guilty of 'inappropriate behavior' involving Timorese women, and several Jordanian soldiers faced charges at a local court after an UNTAET investigation concluded that strong grounds for prosecution were found over alleged sexual misconduct. At the time of UNTAET's deployment, the UN did not have clear, coherent policies that guided or regulated staff inter-action with local populations, and it had no permanent mechanism to monitor, investigate and prosecute charges against peacekeeping personnel. Although vol-untary codes of conduct were established for peacekeepers – but not for civilian personnel in peacekeeping missions, nor for humanitarian and development aid workers – the sanctioning of the conduct of UN peacekeeping troops is left to the military courts or judicial systems of the sending states. The maintenance of professional conduct within each mission varies depending on the gender sensi-tivity of the mission's leadership at the highest level. UNTAET's relative success in gender mainstreaming is owed in large part to the leadership of the former SRSG, Sergio Viera de Mello, who held regular consultations with local women's groups and took steps to revoke the diplomatic immunity of peace-keepers when evidence of rape was confirmed in August 2001.[42]

Governance

Women's political empowerment and participation are not ends in themselves, but part of the post-conflict democratic process in which decision-making power is transferred from those making war to every citizen on a basis of equality. Women's contributions to this process stem not only from the fact that women constitute a sizeable constituency, if not the majority, but also because they have intimate knowledge of the diverse and complex needs of war-affected families and communities. Women and girls constitute the majority of single heads of households and they represent the needs of the war-affected families and com-munities that they cared for during the time of war. Thus, the participation of women from all kinds of backgrounds – refugees, internally displaced people, mothers, widows, girls, and minority and/or indigenous women – is critical for structural and social transformation during peace negotiations and post-conflict reconstruction. Yet women continue to be marginalized in post-war decision-making structures due to gender discriminatory policies and behaviours that pre-date the conflict.

One of the major safeguards available for greater representation in the elect-oral process is the introduction of quotas for women's participation. Statutory quotas require parties to recruit a certain number of women candidates in terms of a constitution or national legislation such as an electoral law, or of informal quotas voluntarily adopted by political parties.[43]

In Timor-Leste, women's groups demanded the introduction of quotas for the July 2001 elections, but the National Council (an interim legislative body pre-ceding the Constituent Assembly) passed the electoral regulation without refer-ence to the proposal. During the intensive negotiations between the National Council and several women's groups, UNTAET did not forcefully intervene in favour of quotas, as UNTAET's Political Affairs Division and the UN Depart-ment of Political Affairs in New York were reluctant to set a precedent that sup-ported quotas for UN standing policies. According to Timorese women and other sources, UNTAET's Political Affairs Division even lobbied against the quotas, particularly among National Council members.

Owing in large part to outreach and mobilization efforts spearheaded by women's groups, with the support of the Gender Affairs Unit, women were able to win 26 per cent of the seats in the National Assembly, despite the lack of quotas. To promote gender equality in post-conflict reconstruction, women have also called for the establishment of a national women's machinery. In Timor-Leste, heated discussions took place concerning the future location of the equivalent of UNTAET's Gender Affairs Unit after the July 2001 elections. The Gender Affairs Unit was part of the Transitional Authority's National Planning Office, and some argued that the gender office should be part of the Ministry of Justice. Ultimately, the position of advisor on equality was created, concurrently with an advisor on human rights, who reports directly to the head of cabinet.

Regardless of where these offices are located and to whom they report, their efficacy continues to be challenged by (1) their lack of budgetary and operational capacity to reach out to their constituency (women in rural areas), and (2) their lack of authority to influence national law-making and budgetary processes. As such, gender equality and respect for and protection of human rights are part of improving governance that is based on transparency and accountability. In Timor-Leste, the new government is under pressure from international financial institutions to reduce the size of its civil service and public expenditures. As a result, most assistance to the survivors of sexual violence and exploitation has been delivered by local women's groups funded and trained by international donors and NGOs. The need for training and strengthening the civil service in the areas of health and education is less emphasized.

Conclusion: future steps

To women, the 'post-war' period brings new threats from unresolved communal and domestic violence, from international peacekeepers, and from the contest between the new 'international standards' and 'traditional' or patriarchal law that may discriminate against women. In Timor-Leste, according to a court monitor, of 26 cases heard in October 2005, 14 (53 per cent) involved violence against women. The government drafted a new Penal Code, which was passed by the Council of Ministers as a decree law in December 2005, but the new criminal law reinforces gender-biased approaches, with light penalties for rape (a basic penalty of two to ten years). As a recent World Bank report argues:[44]

> These cases cannot be satisfactorily resolved in the traditional justice system, and the fact that cases of gender-based violence are being brought to court at all constitutes an improvement over the Indonesian era. However, given that crimes such as rape and domestic violence tend to be under-reported to start with, light sentences and the slow resolution of cases involving gender-based violence act as a further deterrent to female victims seeking justice.

UNTAET's success in mainstreaming gender in the peacekeeping context, including the introduction of an affirmative action policy for women in public employment and international standards, was driven by the combination of strong leadership within UNTAET (by the SRSG and the Gender Affairs Unit), local women's groups and some national leaders in the executive branch. Yet, the UN state-building intervention in Timor-Leste has demonstrated that women continue to receive inadequate protection under the rule of law, and in decision-making institutions and the peacekeeping economy. These challenges include: (1) the incoherent introduction of international human rights standards and the lack of consolidation with national and local judicial structures; (2) instituting political and economic liberalization without providing protection for vulnerable groups, including women; and (3) the weak capacity of the state apparatus. Resolution 1325, although it provides a policy framework to address gender issues in peacebuilding, does not directly address these concerns, and it will require readjustments in the current peacekeeping and peacebuilding practice to prevent and/or mitigate these risks.

Furthermore, the establishment of gender units in peacekeeping missions or national women's machinery, although intended to enhance gender equality in international and national decision-making processes, may have marginalized the issues related to women by creating a weak agency without adequate authority, capacity or expertise. It has thereby alleviated the responsibility of all other relevant institutions to take the needs of women into account within their mandates and activities. Thus, the bureaucratic institutionalization of gender issues is not a solution in itself, and supplementary measures need to be explored, including mandatory and regular 'gender audits' involving budgetary, personnel and operational performance reviews from a gender perspective, and the recruitment of a gender specialist in a senior position in every department of UN missions and interim/post-conflict governments.

UN approaches to post-conflict institutional reforms have been generally ad hoc, inconsistent and incoherent. To address this gap, some policymakers have proposed 'justice packages' for peace operations[45] that focus on the establishment of a functioning criminal justice system as a crucial priority if the gains of a peacekeeping operation are to be consolidated and a relapse into conflict avoided. No viable government or social order can be built without them, according to the advocates of these justice packages, and there will be situations where only the UN is capable of delivering them.[46] However, a normative gap remains in the treatment of domestic violence in international human rights instruments. While sexual violence is now recognized in the Statute of the International Criminal Court as a war crime and a crime against humanity, domestic violence is not distinctively recognized per se as prosecutable under international criminal law.[47] As a result, the definition of domestic violence in national criminal justice systems remains ambiguous in many countries, including Timor-Leste. While UNTAET has recognized the increase of domestic violence as a societal issue, its response in January 2002 to launch a nationwide advocacy campaign against domestic violence fell short of fulfilling the need for domestic violence legislation.[48] Domestic violence legislation has been drafted and put before parliament (at the beginning of 2005 it had not yet been passed, because it was awaiting the finalization of Timor-Leste's penal code).[49]

Finally, the promotion of governance, including democratization, transparency, accountability and civil society development, requires a regional approach. Much of Timor-Leste's reconciliation and reconstruction depends on future relations with Indonesia, particularly West Timor. International involvement in peacebuilding thus needs to develop regional approaches that take into account the political, legal, social and economic development of neighbouring countries.

Since 2001, Timorese women's groups have used Resolution 1325 as an advocacy tool that builds on their decades-long activism in the resistance movement. Resolution 1325 has not had a significant impact on improving service provisions for women, however, and funding for work on GBV has dropped since 2002, as few donors are willing to fund projects over the long term or to cover core operating costs of organizations providing critical counselling and medical services. The implementation of Resolution 1325 in a wider context of peacebuilding and institutional arrangements for the protection and empowerment of women continues to be a formidable challenge for both external and internal actors involved in transitions from civil wars to reconstruction.

Notes

1 'UNTAET Daily Briefing', 22 January 2002.
2 UNFPA, 'Gender-Based Violence in Timor-Lester', paper presented at the Consultative Meeting, Bucharest, 2005.
3 Roland Paris discusses the limitations of peacebuilding based on political and economic liberalization as follows:

> A single paradigm – liberal internationalism – appears to guide the work of international agencies engaged in peace building. The central tenet of this paradigm is the assumption that the surest foundation for peace, both within and between states, is market democracy, that is, a liberal democratic polity and a market-oriented economy. Peace building is in effect an enormous experiment in social engineering ... this paradigm, however, has not been a particularly effective model for establishing stable peace. Paradoxically, the very process of political and economic liberalization has generated destabilizing side effects in war-shattered states, hindering the consolidation of peace and in some cases, even sparking renewed fighting.'
> (R. Paris, 'Peacebuilding and the Limits of Liberal Internationalism',
> *International Security*, Vol. 22, No. 2, Fall 1997, p. 56.)

4 Gender Affairs Unit, UNTAET, *Report to the Department of Peacekeeping Operations on the Implementation of Security Council Resolution 1325*, Dili, 25 May 2001.
5 One of the forms of systematic violence against women during the occupation was the Indonesian national population control programme, *Program Keluarga Berencana* (the 'KB' programme), which reportedly conducted forcible injections of young women with hormonal contraceptives. KB birth control programmes were often carried out by members of the military, and therefore coercively, without the consent of the predominantly Catholic Timorese women (Medical Aid for East Timor, *Conditions of Women in East Timor*, www.aideasttimor.org/women.html).
6 *Joint Report of the Special Rapporteur on Extrajudicial, Arbitrary and Summary Executions and Special Rapporteur on Violence against Women on the Situation of*

Human Rights in East Timor, UN doc. A/54/660, December 1999. See also Oxfam Community Aid, 'East Timorese Women Demand Human Rights', July 1999; Medical Aid for East Timor, op. cit.

7 C. Gabrielson, 'East Timorese Women's Fight against Violence', *Institute of Current World Affairs Newsletter*, New Hampshire, January 2002.

8 T. Rebbøll, 'The Women of East Timor', paper presented at the East Timor conference, Stockholm, 21 May 2002.

9 I. Cristalis and C. Scott, *The Story of Women's Activism in East Timor*, London: Progressio, 2005, chap. 2.

10 E. Roynestad, 'Peace Agreements as a Means for Promoting Gender Equality and Ensuring Participation of Women', paper prepared for the UN Division for the Advancement of Women Expert Group Meeting, Ottawa, 10–13 November 2003, p. 4.

11 M. Plunkett, 'Reestablishing Law and Order in Peace-Maintenance', *Global Governance* January–March, Vol. 4, No. 1, 1998, p. 66.

12 Interview with Milena Pires, member of the Constituent Assembly and longtime gender specialist and advocate, Helsinki, 11 March 2002.

13 'Campaign to Support Women's Rights in the Constitution', *La'o Hamutuk Bulletin*, Vol. 2, No. 5, August 2001, www.etan.org/lh/bulletins/bulletinv2n5.html.

14 Constitution of Timor-Leste, sec. 3.

15 The US State Department *Human Rights Report* noted unconfirmed reports of trafficking of women and children from Indonesia to East Timor (US Department of State, Bureau of Democracy, Human Rights, and Labor, *Country Reports on Human Rights Practice 2001: East Timor*, Washington, DC, 4 March 2002).

16 In both Cambodia and Timor-Leste, legal pluralism also hampers the already scarce capacity of local legal sources. In Timor-Leste, the lack of translators and locally trained legal professionals familiar with both Indonesian law and international humanitarian law has delayed the proceedings of the courts established by UNTAET. When UNTAC designed Cambodian political and legal systems based on liberal democratic principles, the number of surviving legal professionals who had been trained under French rule and had some familiarity with the new UNTAC systems was estimated to be only between six and ten. Most of the Khmer lawyers had been trained in Vietnamese laws based on the socialist model, which limits the rights of free speech, press and assembly, and does not provide for the independence of the judiciary.

17 H. Strohmeyer, 'Policing the Peace: Post-conflict Judicial System Reconstruction in East Timor', *UNSW Law Journal*, Vol. 24, No. 1, 2001, p. 174.

18 J.J. Fox, 'East Timor: Assessing UNTAET's Role in Building Local Capacities for the Future', paper presented to Council for Asia Europe Cooperation on Comparing Experiences with State Building in Asia and Europe: The Cases of East Timor, Bosnia and Kosovo.

19 Judicial System Monitoring Programme, 'East Timor's New Judicial System', *La'o Hamutuk Bulletin*, Vol. 2, Nos. 6 & 7, October 2001.

20 S. Linton, 'Cambodia, East Timor and Sierra Leone: Experiments in International Justice', *Criminal Law Forum*, No. 12, 2001, p. 211.

21 K. Halliday, 'Women and Justice', *La'o Hamutuk Bulletin*, Vol. 2, No. 3. August 2001.

22 R. Coomaraswamy, *Mission Report to Indonesia and East Timor on the Issue of Violence against Women*, E/CN.4/1999/68/Add.3, January 1999.

23 Amnesty International, *East Timor: Justice Past, Present, and Future*, July 2001, p. 39 Available at www.amnesty.org/en/library/asset/ASA57/001/2001/en/b20bd656-d91a-11dd-ad8c-f3d4445c118e/asa570012001en.pdf.

24 'An Assessment of the UN's Police Mission in East Timor', *La'o Hamutuk Bulletin*, Vol. 3, No. 1, February 2002, p. 3. In one rape case, a perpetrator gave nine water buffalos to the victim's family.

25 Amnesty International, op. cit., p. 41.
26 Ibid.
27 *La'o Hamutuk Bulletin*, op. cit, p. 3.
28 Ibid.
29 A. Suhrke, A. Ofsta and A. Knudsen, *A Decade of Peacebuilding: Lessons for Afghanistan*, Center for Michelsen Institute, Bergen, 2 April 2002, p. 32; author's interviews in Timor-Leste, 10–16 July 2001.
30 Interviews in the districts of Occussi and Alieu, 11–12 July 2001.
31 R.S. Levi, *Cambodia: Rattling the Killing Fields*, Family Violence Prevention Fund, http://endabuse.org/programs/display.php3?DocID=97.
32 *Legal Profiles of Indonesia*, Islam Family Law Project, Law and Religion Program of Emory University, http://els41.law.emory.edu/ifl/legal/indonesia.htm.
33 S. Marks, 'Elusive Justice for the Victims of the Khmer Rouge', *Journal of International Affairs*, Vol. 52, No. 2, Spring 1999, p. 3.
34 W. Lambourne, 'The Pursuit of Justice and Reconciliation: Responding to Genocide in Cambodia and Rwanda', paper presented at the International Studies Association Annual Convention, Washington, DC, February 1999, p. 4.
35 Linton, op. cit. p. 211.
36 Ibid., p. 214.
37 For more on the commission, see its homepage, www.easttimor-reconciliation.org/index.htm.
38 Commission on Reception, Truth and Reconciliation in Timor Leste (CAVR), 'Women and Conflict National Public Hearing', CAVR National Headquarters, former Comarca Balide, Dili, 28–29 April 2003.
39 G. Wandita, K. Campbell-Nelson and M.L. Pereira, *Gender and Reparations in Timor-Leste*, International Center for Transitional Justice and International Development Research Centre, www.ictj.org/static/Asia/Timor/TimorLesteExecSum.pdf#search=%22gender%20and%20reparations%20in%20timor-leste%22.(accessed 19 September 2006).
40 Interview with chief of administration, Dili, 10 July 2001.
41 'Employment of Women in the East Timor Transitional Administration', *La'o Hamutuk Bulletin*, Vol. 2, No. 5, August 2001, www.etan.org/lh/bulletins/bulletinv2n5.html.
42 Interviews with Milena Pires, Sherrill Willington, the head of the Gender Affairs Unit, and women's groups, Timor-Leste, 10 July 2001.
43 International IDEA, 'The Effect of Electoral Systems on Women's Representation', *Women in Politics: Women in Parliament*, www.idea.int/women/parl/ch3c.htm, 04/09/01.
44 World Bank, *Strengthening the Institutions of Governance in Timor-Leste*, Washington, DC, April 2006, pp. 21–22.
45 Plunkett, op. cit. pp. 61–79; Thomas Carothers, 'The Rule of Law Revival', *Foreign Affairs*, Vol. 77, No. 2, March/April 1998, pp. 95–106.
46 Gareth Evans, cited in Carothers, op. cit.
47 Meanwhile, the 1992 recommendation issued by the CEDAW Committee, which supplements the 1979 CEDAW by correcting a previous lack of treatment for sexual violence, urges states to adopt legal measures, including penal sanctions, civil remedies and compensatory provisions, to protect women against all kinds of violence, including violence and abuse in the family.
48 *Secretary-General's Report of UNTAET to the Security Council*, January 2002; UNTAET press releases, 22 January 2002.
49 On the other hand, the Vienna-based UN Commission for Crime Prevention and Criminal Justice drafted a resolution in 1997 to enhance gender equality in the area of criminal justice systems, which was approved by the UN General Assembly in December (UN doc. A/52/86). This resolution and its annex entitled 'Model Strat-

egies and Practical Measures on the Elimination of Violence against Women in the Field of Crime Prevention and Criminal Justice' provide guidance on a wide range of issues, including criminal procedures, police powers, sentencing and correction, and victim support and assistance, and should be considered for implementation in UN transitional administrations (International Centre for Criminal Law Reform and Criminal Justice Policy, *Model Strategies and Practical Measures on the Elimination of Violence against Women in the Field of Crime Prevention and Criminal Justice*, Vancouver, 1999).

Part III
Regional case studies

11 The African Union and implementation of UNSCR 1325

Bineta Diop

Introduction

Africa was the source and venue for the establishment of the type of principles and policies articulated in UNSCR 1325 even before the emergence of this UN resolution on women. The Fifth Regional Conference on Women held in Dakar, Senegal, constitutes one of the first steps at the regional level that is in line with the adoption of UNSCR 1325. In November 1994, the Conference adopted the African Platform for Action, which was in effect:

> a synthesis of regional perspectives and priorities as well as a framework for action for the formulation of policies and implementation of concrete and sustainable programmes for the advancement of women [...] that aims to accelerate the social, economic and political empowerment of all women at all levels and at all stages of their lives.[1]

The main principles of the African Platform for Action were taken up in 1995 and incorporated into the Beijing Declaration and Platform for Action (PFA) adopted by the Fourth World Conference on Women. The issue of women affected by conflict in Africa was highlighted in this process by the United Nations Development Fund for Women (UNIFEM) through the African Women in Crisis (AWIC) programme.

The Windhoek Conference, held in Namibia in May 2000, organised by the UN Department of Peacekeeping Operations (DPKO), is another initiative concerned with the gender issue in wartime, which influenced the development of UNSCR 1325. The conference ended up with a declaration that contributed to the adoption of UNSCR 1325. The declaration mainly expressed regret that women had been denied their full role in United Nations peace support operations, both nationally and internationally, and that the gender dimension in peace processes had not been adequately addressed. It further emphasised the need to include the principle of gender equality in UN missions, in order to ensure the effectiveness of peace support operations.[2] The NGO Working Group on Women, Peace and Security was formed in May 2000 to advocate for a United Nations Security Council resolution on women, peace and security. Through the use of 'Arria Formula'[3] meetings, women's organisations had the opportunity to bring the gender and women's issues to the United Nations Security Council and to denounce the violations of women's rights by States. Security Council Resolution 1325 was unanimously adopted under the Namibian Presidency of the Security Council on 31 October 2000 and the NGO Working Group on Women, Peace and Security started to work for the full implementation of the Resolution at the international level.

This chapter discusses the African Union's efforts to implement UN Resolution 1325 (UNSCR 1325) and assesses the progress recorded as well as the challenges that remain.

UNSCR 1325, a weapon for peace in Africa

The Resolution 1325 of the United Nations Security Council, as the first legal instrument to address exclusively women's concerns relating to peace and security, has provided a justification and a framework which enable stakeholders to protect women and support their struggle for their equal participation in conflict prevention, peacebuilding, post-conflict reconstruction and their human rights.

UNSCR 1325 is a weapon used by African women towards peace. It provides African women with a legitimate platform to hold African states accountable for the respect of women's empowerment, gender equality and mainstreaming in peace and security policies and plans, and to demand adequate protection to women and girls during and after conflicts. At a continental level, the advocacy of civil society organisations has contributed to the respect by African Union member states of their commitment towards UNSCR 1325. The African Union (AU) has taken steps to domesticate UNSCR 1325 within its legal framework and its architecture.

The domestication of UNSCR 1325 by the AU

UNSCR 1325 was adopted nearly two years before the establishment of the AU. The transformation of the continental organisation from the Organization of African Unity (OAU) to the AU in 2002 was an opportunity to address the issues articulated in the main pillars of UNSCR 1325 – on prevention, protection, participation and relief – in its legal framework and key policy frameworks.

UNSCR 1325 and the AU legal framework: AU Constitutive Act and Statutes

From the establishment of the AU in July 2002, member states have indicated their commitment to gender equality and women's empowerment. Indeed, the first AU Summit adopted the gender parity principle mentioned in Article 4 of the AU Constitutive Act as follows: 'The Union shall function in accordance with the principle [of] promotion of gender equality.' Furthermore, the AU Statutes stipulate more actions that the member states need to promote in order to promote gender equality. The parity principle was implemented by the AU by electing five female commissioners out of ten to the AU Commission in 2003 and this has continued to be the case.

Protocol to the African Charter on Human and People's Rights on the Rights of Women in Africa

The important role played by the civil society in the maintenance of peace and security and the process of post-conflict reconstruction in Africa was recognised by the OAU as well as the AU.[4] The creation of the African Women's Committee on Peace and Development (AWCPD), by the OAU and the United Nations Economic Commission for Africa (UNECA) as a women's peace mechanism, is a good example.[5] The AWCPD later became the African Union Women's Committee (AUWC) within the AU. The AUWC has expert capacity to advise the Chairperson of the Commission and allows women from the grassroots level to bring their voices into the prevention, management and resolution of conflicts in Africa, through civil society organisations. Therefore, in July 2003, civil society organisations under the leadership of Foundation for Community Development (FCD) Chairperson, Ms Graca Machel, advocated within the AWCPD for a stronger commitment of the AU to gender mainstreaming and empowerment and for the adoption of a legal instrument that protects women's human rights in Africa.

Their advocacy efforts were fruitful when AU member states further demonstrated their commitment to gender and women issues with the adoption at the Second African Union Summit in Mozambique of the Protocol to the African Charter on Human and Peoples' Rights on the Rights of Women in Africa (known as the Maputo Protocol). The Maputo Protocol contains 32 articles relating to the protection of women's human rights in Africa, including among others specific protection for women in armed conflict and provision for women's rights to peace and sustainable development. The Protocol entered into force in 2005 after being ratified by 16 member states. The implementation of the Protocol contributes to the overall implementation of the principles within UNSCR 1325.

Solemn Declaration on Gender Equality in Africa (SDGEA)

In 2004, the AU adopted the Solemn Declaration on Gender Equality in Africa (SDGEA), which affirmed the commitment of member states to gender key issues, including among others:

- Implementation of gender-specific economic, social and legal measures on HIV/AIDS;
- Gender-mainstreaming of peace processes;
- Gender-based violence;
- Education of girls;

- Enforcement of the *Protocol to the African Charter on Human and Peoples' Rights on the Rights of Women in Africa.*

This instrument is intended to promote gender equality and women's empowerment at the highest political level. It stipulates that it would ensure:

> the full and effective participation and representation of women in peace processes including the prevention, resolution, management of conflicts and post conflict reconstruction in Africa as stipulated in UN Resolution 1325 (2000) and to also appoint women as Special Envoys and Special Representatives of the African Union.[6]

The adoption of the SDGEA and the inclusion of UNSCR 1325 in particular is indicative of the recognition given by the AU to strengthen African women's engagement in peace and security issues. It now remains to be seen how all of this has translated into meaningful action.

UNSCR 1325 and the African Union Peace and Security Architecture

The African Union Peace and Security Architecture (APSA) is the main framework for the maintenance of peace and security on the African continent. APSA represents a set of structures established for the prevention and resolution of conflict in Africa and for addressing identified threats to African security. At the core of the APSA is the Peace and Security Council (PSC). Article 3 of the Protocol related to the PSC sets out far-reaching objectives with regard to the anticipation, prevention and resolution of conflict in Africa. As outlined in the Protocol, the PSC's functions will include promotion of peace; security and stability in Africa; early warning and preventative diplomacy; peacemaking; peace support operations; peacebuilding and post-conflict reconstruction; and humanitarian action and disaster management.[7] The PSC is supported by a Continental Early Warning System (CEWS); a Panel of the Wise; an African Standby Force (ASF); and a Peace Fund. The early warning system is expected to anticipate conflicts and crisis and provide appropriate information for conflict prevention, while the Panel of the Wise is to advise the Chairperson and provide support for conflict prevention. The ASF is to be deployed in situations where conflicts and crisis have escalated to situations where there is a potential threat to peace and stability in a country and the region.

The Women Gender Development Directorate (WGDD)

The Statutes of the Commission of the AU stipulates in its Article 8 that the Chairperson is ultimately responsible and accountable for gender mainstreaming within the Commission. In order to facilitate this mandate, a mechanism has been established in the Office of the Chairperson to coordinate all activities and programmes of the Commission related to gender issues.[8] It is used to advance the principle of gender equality and the principles of the SDGEA through gender mainstreaming. The WGDD and the AUWC work closely on issues of peace and security. We will now examine how these efforts are implemented in practice and whether and how they feature in the peace and security work of the AU.

Peace missions

In its activities, the AU attempts to respect the principles of UNSCR 1325 in implementing the gender parity principle and gender equality. The African Union Gender Directorate (AUGD) and AUWC have organised peace missions to Ivory Coast and Darfur, to support women's participation in conflict resolution, reconciliation and the democratization process for sustainable peace. Members of the mission met with representatives from governments and civil society organisations, especially women's networks.

Peace mediations

Recognition is being given to the added value that women could bring at the negotiation table as well as mediation support of civil society organisations on many aspects. The AUGD and UNIFEM brought a team of Sudanese women to participate in the Abuja Inter-Sudanese Peace Talks in 2006 and seconded a Gender Expert to the Mediation Team. However, this is done on an ad hoc basis; few women are nominated to positions of mediators or special envoys. At a national level, the participation of women in official peace processes remains a major challenge. As a result, women have had to find other ways to ensure that their voices are heard and to participate at the peace table. The experience of the Sixth Clan in Somalia is one such example. In order to participate at the negotiation table and attend a conference for peace and reconciliation, Somali women decided to create their own clan, as the conference's participation was based on the five principal clans' organisation. This represented for the Somali women the first step of gender representation in a peace process in Somalia. Similarly, the caucus of Congelese women during the Sun City peace talks that brought more than 30 per cent of women was another example of women's involvement in peace negotiations.

Peacekeeping missions

At the international level, the United Nations Mission in Liberia (UNMIL) had an all-women unit constituted exclusively of more than 100 female peacekeepers from India. The main mandate of the contingent was to work as an armed police unit to help monitor peace in Liberia. The female-composition of the unit has provided hope for thousands of women who suffered from all forms of sexual violence during the conflict.[9] In practice, however, their presence has been largely symbolic and it is perhaps still too soon to see in concrete terms the impact of their contribution to peacekeeping.

At the continental level, the African Union Mission in Sudan (AMIS) was at its origin a peacekeeping mission aimed at stabilising the situation in Dafur. With regard to the principles articulated in the SDGEA and UNSCR 1325, one can highlight the United Nations Development Programme (UNDP) training, in partnership with AMIS, where 29 AMIS Women Desk Officers have been sensitised on issues related to sexual and gender-based violence.[10] Civil society has often provided advice to the AU Commission for the training and empowerment of women for greater involvement in conflict prevention, protection, resolution and management, as well as the training of military personnel on gender issues.[11] Dafur offered a chance to expand this sort of collaboration. Because of the lack of resources to adequately protect civilians and humanitarian workers, AMIS became an observer mission.[12] In the end, AMIS was folded into what became a hybrid mission incorporating AU troops and UN troops, known as the United Nations–African Union Mission in Dafur (UNAMID).[13]

Panel of the Wise

Within the AU architecture, the Panel of the Wise constitutes five eminent persons to represent the five regions of the continent on conflict prevention issues. Two members out of the five are women, namely Elisabeth K. Pognon, President of the Constitutional Court of Benin and Brigalia Bam, South Africa's Independent Electoral Commission chief.

Overall, there has been no real connection between the efforts to promote women's participation in peace and security processes on the continent and the implementation of APSA's main activities. The gender work of the AU by and large remains implemented separately from the Union's peace and security work despite the solid legal and normative framework, which outlines a clear role for women. As a result, it has been difficult to translate these norms into practice. Instead, efforts to ensure the inclusion of women into peace and security processes has been largely ad hoc and not the result of making women's participation an established part of the peace and security architecture of the AU.

Implementing UNSCR 1325 in Africa

The main challenge is how to bring UNSCR 1325 to the people in ways that it can be relevant to the day-to-day lives of citizens. We discuss in this section some of the efforts being made to implement UNSCR 1325 beyond the Commission of the AU and the APSA.

Technical support

The AU, through its Women, Gender and Development Division, provides support to its member states in encouraging them to implement UNSCR 1325. This is done through provision of advice on policy development and creation of linkages to enable member states to learn from each other on initiatives being undertaken at the national level on gender and peace issues. The AU also sources for support from donor partners in order to enhance the implementation of the Resolution, for instance, they had consultations with Denmark, which launched an 'Africa Program for Peace' in which the implementation of UNSCR 1325 has been mainstreamed.

A joint strategy between the AU and the European Union (EU) was also adopted during the second Africa–EU Summit in Lisbon in December 2007. In the strategy, the AU and the EU committed themselves to the implementation of UNSCR 1325 as well as to strengthening efforts to mainstream gender in all strategies, policies, programmes and actions to promote the participation of women in decision-making and peace processes. This strategy gave impetus to the need for more focused implementation of the Resolution at the regional level. The 27 February 2009 AU–EU panel in New York on the implementation and monitoring and evaluation of UNSCR 1325, not just in Africa but also in Europe, was another means of continued collaboration between the two continents.

Liaison with regional bodies

The AU's recognition of the Regional Economic Communities (RECs) as building blocks for the operationalisation of the APSA, provides space for strategic alliances between member states and regional bodies in Africa. The regional approach provides added value in terms of direct linkage with member states while advancing policy formulation and implementation at the regional level. The Economic Community of West African States (ECOWAS) and the Southern African Development Community (SADC) as well as the Mano River Union and the Great Lakes Conference have put in place policies and programmes monitoring gender, peace and security. Some networks that have done the same are the Mano River Women's Peace Network (MARWOPNET), Women in Peacebuilding Network (WIPNET) and the Women Peace and Security Network Africa (WIPSEN-Africa). See the chapter on ECOWAS for further discussion of these issues.

The obligation of reporting and achievements towards the SDGEA

Under Article 12 of the SDGEA, member states 'commit [themselves] to report annually on progress made in terms of gender mainstreaming and to support and champion all issues raised in [the Solemn] Declaration, [including the implementation of the UNSCR 1325], both at the national and regional levels'.[14] In adopting the SDGEA and in expressly mentioning UNSCR 1325, member states of the AU have committed themselves towards its implementation. This reporting obligation is intended to assist member states to fulfil their responsibilities. However, it has been shown that only 19 AU member states out of 53 had submitted their annual reports during the 2007–2009 Summits.[15] And of those that submitted reports only Cameroon, Namibia and South Africa presented in their annual reports some achievements in the implementation of the

SDGEA.[16] In Cameroon women's applications for positions in the United Nations System and the AU have been privileged. As a result, in 2003, a Cameroon woman was elected as judge at the International Criminal Tribunal for Rwanda; another one was elected Trade and Industry Commissioner in the AU. Namibia reported that the National Defence Force made a resounding success of the implementation of UNSCR 1325 by deploying women in peacekeeping operations. South Africa has also deployed a number of women to participate in the UN and the AU-sponsored peacekeeping missions and has involved senior women at decision-making levels in peacekeeping missions in the continent on a regular basis.

Assessing overall progress

In March 2009, women from around the world met in Liberia for the International Colloquium on Women's Empowerment, Leadership Development, International Peace and Security. This offered an opportunity to assess progress on the implementation of UNSCR 1325. Participants sought to identify the successes and failures of measures adopted for its implementation. They observed that many countries do not feel committed enough to follow the recommendations of the Resolution. Among other things, the International Colloquium presented recommendations through the Monrovia Call to Action on UNSCR 1325, including, for example, to:

- Set up a monitoring and evaluation international and national entity for all the 1325 work in the world and in the countries with national action plans;
- Create enabling mechanisms to ensure women's equal and full participation in peace negotiations, mediations and all peace processes;
- Incorporate UNSCR 1325 provisions in all peacekeeping mandates;
- Appoint women to serve as Special Representatives and Deputy Special Representatives of the Secretary-General.

Interestingly, in Africa, only Ivory Coast, Liberia and Uganda had launched their National Action Plans (NAPs) in 2008 while Rwanda, Burundi and DRC had developed NAPs by the end of 2009.[17] As discussed earlier, there is not yet an institutionalised process in the AU to systematically ensure the full and equal participation of women in peace negotiations, mediation and peace processes at the highest levels. AU peacekeeping mandates will also benefit from the systematic inclusion of women beyond dealing with issues of violence against women.

Assessing the AU's own performance on gender equality

The GIMAC network has established indicators and mechanisms for evaluating the implementation of the AU's SDGEA through the production of shadow reports that are submitted at AU's Heads of State and Government Summits bi-annually. Interestingly, one set of indicators of whether the AU is indeed making progress on its commitment to women's participation and gender equality is the representation of women in the AU's own institutions. Tables 11.1 and 11.2, which categorise AU staff by grade and sex, tell their own story about the value that the organisation places on gender equality. While this is no doubt an improvement when compared to its predecessor, the OAU, it is at best an indication that the AU's commitment to gender equality is still work in progress.

Table 11.1 Staff of the AU by grade and sex

Grade	Number			Rate (%)	
	Men	*Women*	*Total*	*Men*	*Women*
Chairperson	1	0	1	100	0
Deputy Chairperson	1	0	1	100	0
Commissioner	3	5	8	37.5	62.5
D1	12	6	18	66.7	33.3
P6	4	3	7	57.1	42.9
P5	35	13	48	72.9	27.1
P4	20	12	32	62.5	37.5
P3	69	16	85	81.2	18.8
P2	52	22	74	70.3	29.7
P1	5	1	6	83.3	16.7
GSA	95	100	195	48.7	51.3
GSB	127	28	155	81.9	18.1

Source: Roselyn Musa, *Evaluation on the Implementation of the Solemn Declaration on Gender Equality in Africa*, GIMAC, 2009.

Table 11.2 Staff of AU organs and associated institutions by sex

AU organ and its other institutions	Number		Rate (%)		
	Men	*Women*	*Total*	*Men*	*Women*
Assembly	52	1	53	98	2
Executive Council	43	10	53	81	19
PRC	50	3	53	94	6
AUC	424	206	630	67.3	32.7
Peace and Security Council	14	1	15	93	7
PAP (Bureau)	3	2	5	60	40
ECOSOCC (Bureau)	8	12	20	40	60
The Court of Justice	9	2	11	n/a	n/a
African Commission on Human and People's Rights	4	7	11		

Source: Roselyn Musa, *Evaluation on the Implementation of the Solemn Declaration on Gender Equality in Africa*, GIMAC, 2009.

Conclusion

UNSCR 1325 is no doubt a powerful tool for women and African women in particular. However, much remains to be done in order to realise its potentials. Perhaps most of all there is a need for a stronger political will at international, regional and national levels. Furthermore, the implementation of UNSCR 1325 is laden with other challenges, not least the absence of accountability and reporting mechanisms and a lack of knowledge and awareness on UNSCR 1325 at a grassroots level. Although UNSCR 1325 has been translated so far into more than 20 African languages, more should be done to bring its provisions down to the people.[18] In this regard, women's NGOs and civil society play a significant role in giving more visibility and awareness to UNSCR 1325 and in promoting the adoption of NAPs on its implementation.[19]

Notes

1 African Platform for Action, *African Common Position for the Advancement of Women*, Adopted at the Fifth African Regional Conference on Women, Dakar, Senegal, 16–23 November 1994.
2 Windhoek Declaration, The Namibia Plan of Action on 'Mainstreaming a Gender Perspective in Multidimensional, Peace Support Operations', Windhoek, Namibia, 31 May 2000.
3 An *Arria Formula* meeting (named after Mr Arria who proposed it), is a meeting held outside the Security Council chamber and not chaired by a current chair of the Security Council, to allow an opportunity to hear the views of non-state members, who would otherwise not be able to bring issues directly before the Council.
4 S. Mottiar and S. Van Jaarsveld, 'Mediating Peace in Africa: Securing Conflict Prevention. Strengthening the Mediation and Conflict Prevention Aspects of the African Peace and Security Architecture', a research report based on a seminar organised by ACCORD and the Ministry of Foreign Affairs of Finland, held in Addis Ababa, Ethiopia, March 2009, p. 22.
5 African Platform for Action, op. cit.
6 'Solemn Declaration on Gender Equality in Africa', Declaration adopted at the Third Ordinary Session of the African Union, Addis Ababa, Ethiopia, 4–6 July 2004, p. 2.
7 African Union, Protocol Relating to the Establishment of the Peace and Security Council of the African Union, Article 3, 2002.
8 Article 12(3) of the Statutes of the AU Commission. Available at www.africa-union.org/ Structure_of_the_Commission/WOMEN,%20GENDER%20AND%20DEVELOPMENT. htm.
9 See reports available at www.unmil.org.
10 United Nations Sudan Information Gateway, 'Humanitarian Action in Darfur', Weekly Bulletin No. 11, 18 October 2007. Available at www.unsudanig.org/docs/ Humanitarian%20Action%20in%20Darfur%20Weekly%20Bulletin%20-11.pdf.
11 Mottiar and Van Jaarsveld, op. cit., p. 22.
12 A.V. Mansaray, 'AMIS in Darfur: Africa's Litmus Test in Peacekeeping and Mediation', African Security Review, vol. 18, no. 1, 2009, p. 37.
13 Ibid. p. 45.
14 'Solemn Declaration on Gender Equality in Africa', op. cit., p. 3.
15 R.Musa, *Evaluation on the Implementation of the Solemn Declaration on Gender Equality in Africa*, GIMAC, 2009, p. 16.
16 Musa, op. cit., pp. 26–27.

17 The regional consultation was funded by the Government of Finland and organised by Femmes Africa Solidarité and the Executive Secretariat of the International Conference of the Great Lakes Region. For further information please see www.fasngo.org/index.html.
18 UNSCR 1325 has been translated into languages from the five regions of the continent, namely Arabic, Somali, Lingala, Wolof and Zulu. For more information see www.peacewomen.org/1325inTranslation/index.html.
19 So far, Ivory Coast, Liberia and Uganda have launched their NAPs in 2008 and 2009 respectively, while Burundi and Rwanda are in the development phase.

12 The gender dimensions of the ECOWAS peace and security architecture

A regional perspective on UNSCR 1325

Awa Ceesay-Ebo

Introduction

Two challenges confront UN Security Council Resolution 1325 (UNSCR 1325) in terms of its regional application. The first is that despite its significance and global relevance, the even more important need to operationalize and contextualize it remains, particularly in the regions that are most affected by conflict. Among other things, this involves ensuring that each region develops its own particular programme for achieving the goals set out in the resolution. In this regard, and in the West African context, it is important to link the Economic Community of West African States (ECOWAS) peace and security architecture with UNSCR 1325. The second major challenge is to ensure that any such strategic linkage recognizes and integrates the energies of ordinary women working at the grassroots level in communities and villages in the various regions of the world. Therefore, in West Africa, while recognizing the leadership role of educated and elite women, there is a need to acknowledge the role of ordinary West African women and to ensure that any policy agenda that is drawn up reflects their interests, perceptions and priorities.

This chapter is structured into four parts. The first part discusses the role of women in peace and security processes, while the second enumerates the main elements of the ECOWAS peace and security architecture and assesses the extent to which these comply with UNSCR 1325. The third part identifies the challenges facing the implementation of UNSCR 1325 in the West African context, while the final section concludes the chapter and puts forward some options for addressing the challenges.

Women in regional and international peace processes

On the whole and as a general trend, the reality of peace processes has been that those who take up arms are the main actors in peace negotiations, which unwittingly creates the impression that peace agreements are rewards for the havoc that has been wreaked and the lives that have been taken. Thus, the more atrocious the human rights abuses, the more space belligerent actors seem to occupy at the peace negotiation table. The peace processes in Liberia and Sierra Leone confirm this. Rebel groups who had been responsible for despicable acts against their own populations, particularly against women, featured as the main parties to peace agreements. Even though women have regularly organized for peace at various levels (community, national, regional and global), they are rarely visible in the official peace processes instituted after conflict. A central assumption of this chapter is that peace processes that marginalize, ignore and/or exclude women are unlikely to lead to sustainable peace. Such processes lack the input and support of a large section of the population and amount to at best a partial search for peace. Such exclusionary (so-called) peace agreements contribute to the resumption of violent conflict. The inclusion of the perspectives of women in peace processes and in related decision-making is therefore not a mere human rights imperative for women to be involved in decisions and processes that affect them directly and indirectly, critical as this may be. Crucially, the engagement and inclusion of women in discussions and decisions on peace is a necessary condition for sustainable peace and security. In other words, it is not a normative appeal, but a necessary condition for peace.

UNSCR 1325 has evolved as the main global instrument for addressing questions relating to peace and security from a gender perspective. It is pertinent to examine the extent to which it has permeated the activities and thinking of peace and security initiatives in various parts of the world. In this regard, West Africa presents a useful case study through which the implementation of UNSCR 1325 can be measured. In the discussion that follows, therefore, an attempt is made to measure the ECOWAS peace and security architecture against the provisions and demands of UNSCR 1325.

The end of the Cold War and the related marked decrease in external strategic interest in Africa has both necessitated and facilitated the emergence of regional peace and security initiatives, with the West African subregion being a pioneer in this regard. At the continental level, it has been noted that the regime of the Organization of African Unity (OAU) paid little attention to the issue of women in peace and security, or in governance generally. Maria Nzomo notes that 'in terms of gender representation in the OAU, African women including women's organizations were virtually absent from its organs and held no position of influence during its 39 years of existence'.[1] Nonetheless, the establishment of the African Women Committee on Peace and Development (AWCPD) by the OAU and UN Economic Commission for Africa (UNECA) in 1998 was commendable. The AWCPD functioned mainly more from outside than within the OAU.[2]

The African Union (AU) – the organization that replaced the OAU in 2002 – on the other hand, has from the onset recognized the pivotal role of women. Accordingly, at the Durban Summit of July 2002, the AU took major decisions that provide the institutional basis for mainstreaming gender within the organization. It is a positive coincidence that the process leading to the formation of the AU occurred around the same time as the negotiations regarding what eventually emerged as UNSCR 1325. In a recent assessment of the AU's position on gender, the president of the AU Commission noted the following:[3]

The African Union has provided a legal framework that provides for gender equality and women's empowerment. The Constitutive act of the Union, the African Charter on Human and People's Rights, the Protocol to African charter on Human and People's Rights on the Rights of Women in Africa and the Solemn Declaration on Gender Equality in Africa all provide for the attainment of gender equality and women's empowerment in Africa. From the onset, the African Union recognized the centrality of gender equality and women's empowerment to the attainment of sustainable human development and security on the continent.

Accordingly, following the decisions of the Durban Summit, the AU Commission has a 50 per cent representation of women. In addition, a Gender Directorate has been created in the Office of the AU Chairperson.

At the level of West Africa, the end of the Cold War marked the start of the first Liberian civil war. This civil war and subsequent conflicts in the subregion exposed the challenges faced by women in conflict and post-conflict settings.[4] Conflicts in Liberia, Sierra Leone, Guinea-Bissau and Côte d'Ivoire have displayed the demands they place on women, the multiple roles that women play and the challenges that they face while such conflicts are under way.[5] While gender-disaggregated data has been generally lacking, there is overwhelming empirical evidence of the links among gender, conflict and the search for peace and security. In response, regional normative instruments have evolved that seek to address the issue of women in peace and security in both preventative and post-conflict peacebuilding.

The ECOWAS peace and security architecture and UNSCR 1325

As detailed in Table 12.1, UNSCR 1325 calls for action in three key related areas, which are discussed below.

Participation of women in decision-making and peace processes

The first four paragraphs of UNSCR 1325 focus on women's participation and representation in decision-making and peace processes, including in peacekeeping and other field-based operations. Paragraph 1 specifically 'urges member states to ensure increased representation of women at all decision-making levels in national, regional and international institutions and mechanisms for the prevention, management, and resolution of conflict'.

In consonance with the provisions of UNSCR 1325, the ECOWAS Mechanism directly addresses the participation of women in decision-making generally, and in peace processes in particular. Article 40 provides that 'ECOWAS shall recognise, encourage and support the role of women in its initiatives for conflict prevention, management, resolution, peace-keeping and security'. Furthermore, the ECOWAS Council of the Wise (previously named the Council of the Elders)

Table 12.1 Measuring the ECOWAS peace and security architecture against UNSCR 1325

UNSCR 1325 benchmarks	ECOWAS mechanism[a]	Good governance protocol[b]
Increased representation of women in national, regional and international organizations and mechanisms on conflict (paras. 1–6)	Council of Elders (the Wise) to include women (art. 20)	States are 'to take all appropriate measures to ensure that women have equal rights with men to vote and be voted for in elections, to participate in the formulation of government policies and the implementation thereof and to hold public offices and perform public functions at all levels of governance' (art. 2.3). 'ECOWAS election observation missions shall include women' (art. 14).
The protection of women in armed conflict, including the adoption of mechanisms that ensure the protection of and respect for the human rights of women and girls (paras. 9–13)	'Member States shall provide assistance to vulnerable persons, including children, the elderly, women' (art. 44). 'ECOWAS shall recognize, encourage and support the role of women in its initiatives for conflict prevention, management, resolution, peace-keeping and security' (art. 40.4).	'Member States agree that the development and promotion of the welfare of women are essential factors for development, progress and peace in the society. Consequently, they undertake to eliminate all forms of discrimination and harmful and degrading practices against women' (art. 40). 'The Executive Secretariat shall put in place all necessary structures within its establishment to ensure the effective implementation of common policies and programmes relating to the education and the promotion of the welfare of women and youth' (art. 43).
The inclusion of gender perspectives and training in peacekeeping (paras. 15–17)	'A policy to promote women's education at all levels and in all fields of training shall be adopted and implemented in each Member State and at the level of ECOWAS' (art. 30.4). 'Member States shall guarantee women equal rights with men in the field of education…. They shall also ensure the elimination of stereotyped concepts of roles of men and women at all levels and in all forms of education' (art. 30.5).	

Notes
a Protocol Relating to the Mechanism for Conflict Prevention, Management, Resolution, Peace-Keeping and Security (ECOWAS Mechanism), adopted at Lomé, 10 December 1999.
b Protocol A/SP1/12/01 on Democracy and Good Governance Supplementary to the Protocol Relating to the Mechanism for Conflict Prevention, Management, Resolution, Peacekeeping and Security (Good Governance Protocol), adopted at Dakar, 21 December 2001.

is an important component of the ECOWAS peace and security architecture. It is composed of eminent personalities from various segments of society who deploy their good offices and experience to play the role of mediators, counsellors and facilitators on behalf of ECOWAS for the purpose of managing and resolving conflicts in West Africa. While the executive secretary of ECOWAS (now the president) compiles a list of such individuals annually for the approval of the Mediation and Security Council, the ECOWAS Mechanism expressly states that such a list shall include women (art. 20). However, no specific quota is laid down. Out of a total of 15 members, currently three are women.[6]

Beyond conflict, however, there is a need to recognize that the inclusion of women in governance generally is an essential strategy for conflict prevention and building the necessary conditions for sustainable development. In this regard, it is pertinent to note that the Good Governance Protocol provides for the equal rights of women to vote and be voted for, and to participate in the formulation and implementation of government policies by holding public offices (art. 2.3). Specifically in terms of election monitoring – a cardinal aspect of establishing the legitimacy and transparency of electoral processes – the Good Governance Protocol states that

> the Executive Secretary shall appoint the leader and the members of the Observer/Supervisory Mission, who shall be independent persons and nationals of Member States other than the Member State conducting the elections. The Members of the Mission shall include women'
>
> (art. 14).

Again, no specific quota is laid down regarding the representation of women.

There appears to be a marked gap between normative provisions and actual implementation. Within the ECOWAS Commission itself, only two of the seven current commissioners are women. No woman has been executive secretary (now president) of the ECOWAS Secretariat (now Commission) since its inception in 1975. Although a more detailed study will be needed to determine the extent of compliance with UNSCR 1325 within ECOWAS states, there are some encouraging developments. It is indeed commendable that West Africa boasts of the first and, so far, only elected female African president (Liberia), and virtually all ECOWAS states have female ministers (including a female vice-president in the Gambia). However, two significant observations are worthy of note in this regard. With few exceptions (such as the case of the former Nigerian foreign affairs minister), female ministers in West Africa are often located in 'non-strategic' portfolios. Therefore, while women's participation in decision-making has certainly witnessed quantitative improvements, the extent of qualitative changes can be easily exaggerated. Second, while a specific assessment of women's participation in governance on a country-by-country basis may not be feasible in the present exercise, available secondary data indicates that, even in terms of sheer numbers, West Africa compares unfavourably with other regions in Africa (see Figure 12.1).

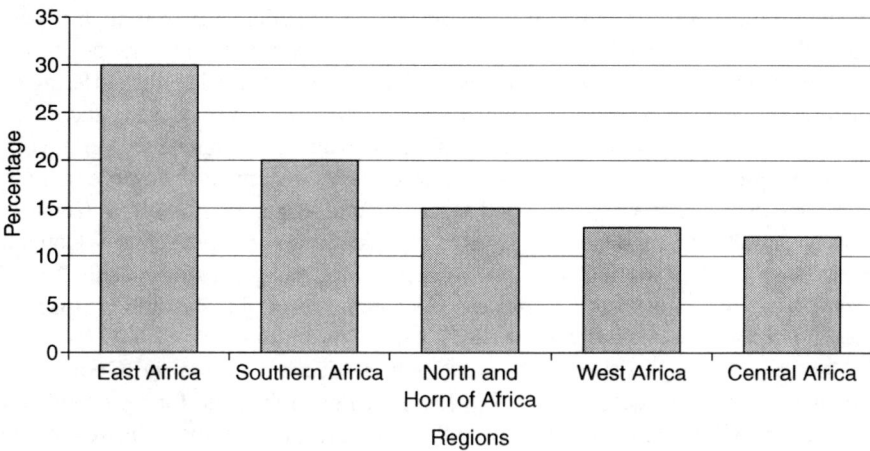

Figure 12.1 Regional representation of women in Africa (source: Kemi Ogunsanya, 'Gender Peace and Security in Africa', presentation at the Gender and ESDP Course, Budapest, 18–20 April 2007).

In East Africa, women occupy some 30 per cent of all posts in government, while the equivalent figures are 22 per cent in Southern Africa, and 16 per cent in North Africa and the Horn of Africa. The corresponding figure for West Africa is 14 per cent, which is only marginally better than the situation in Central Africa. There is no minimal quota for women's participation, which remains at the discretion of the respective ECOWAS states. While the ECOWAS peace and security instruments may therefore, in normative terms, comply to a large extent with the provisions of UNSCR 1325, it would appear that there is much room for improvement in terms of meeting such normative standards in practice.

Protection of women, including in armed conflict

Paragraph 9 of UNSCR 1325 'calls upon parties to a conflict to respect fully international law applicable to the protection of women and girls'. Paragraph 10 further calls for the adoption of special measures to protect women and girls from gender-based violence (GBV) in situations of armed conflict. There is ample evidence from the Liberian and Sierra Leonean civil wars that both state and non-state combatants routinely disregarded, and, indeed, actively abused the rights of women and girls. The phenomenon of 'bush wives', referring to women who were captured to serve as sex slaves for combatants; the indiscriminate amputation of limbs; and despicable acts of disembowelling pregnant women suggest a wide gap between the provisions of UNSCR 1325 and actual practice during conflicts in West Africa.

There can be little doubt, however, that at the level of legal and normative instruments, ECOWAS as a regional organization displays the utmost respect for international law dealing with the protection of women's rights. Virtually all ECOWAS normative and legal instruments expressly recognize the need for the protection of women during armed conflict and in post-conflict situations. Even though it pre-dates the adoption of UNSCR 1325, the ECOWAS Mechanism, in its preamble, recognizes the need 'to develop effective policies that will alleviate the suffering of the civil population, especially women and children'. In the same vein, the Good Governance Protocol notes in its preamble that 'women's rights have been recog-nized and guaranteed in all international human rights instruments'. In the emerging additions to the ECOWAS peace and security architecture, the ECOWAS Conven-tion on Small Arms states expressly that it '[takes] into account Security Council Resolution 1325 on women peace and security which recognizes the specific role of women in Peacebuilding'.[7] However, such enthusiasm for Resolution 1325 is scarcely reflected in the body of the Small Arms Convention itself.

Various sections of the ECOWAS Conflict Mechanism and the Good Gov-ernance Protocol (as detailed in Table 12.1) recognize the need for the protection of women within and after armed conflict. In the final analysis, however, the reality in West Africa is that states are only a part of the security complex. Therefore, while states and regional organizations such as ECOWAS are mindful of international law provisions dealing with the protection of women, the same cannot be said for the numerous non-state actors (such as armed groups) that are constant features in West African conflicts.

Paragraph 13 of UNSCR 1325 highlights the need to take account of women ex-combatants' needs in disarmament, demobilization and reintegration (DDR) programmes (art. 13). However, ECOWAS peace and security instruments do not directly address the special needs and concerns of women and girls in DDR programmes. While the paucity of data and information makes it virtually impossible to discuss the extent to which women's special needs were met in ECOWAS peace missions, the general impression is one of a shortfall in this regard. Even in UN missions, as has been noted in the case of Sierra Leone, abducted women in the fighting forces (i.e. 'bush wives') were excluded from the DDR programme and were regarded as official dependants of male combat-ants, thus having no rights of their own. In both the Liberian and Sierra Leonean DDR processes, gender advisors (now a regular feature of UN peace support operations) were not present at their inception, resulting in the marginalization of gender dimensions in DDR planning.[8] In the case of Liberia, however, the involvement of 'women associated with fighting forces' (a more respectable name for 'bush wives') has received greater attention, and some 22,000 women were integrated into the DDR programme.

First-hand accounts have indicated, however, that the initiatives of women's groups in the DDR process often received a condescending reception. The pro-posals of Liberian women's groups were rejected in the early stages of the DDR process in that country on the grounds that they were not considered to be 'experts'. Instead, the programme brought in 'experts' from other contexts like Kosovo and Sierra Leone, but did not include Liberian women's voices in its planning. The women who tried to get involved in the DDR process were told to 'go home and take care of the children'.[9]

Gender perspectives and training in peacekeeping

Paragraphs 4 and 5 of UNSCR 1325 relate to the need for gender perspectives and training in UN peacekeeping missions. In this regard, while it has been noted that, thanks mainly to UNSCR 1325 and the Secretary-General's Strategic Plan of Action, the number of gender advisors rose from two in 2000 to ten by September 2005. However, the absence of ECOWAS peace missions for much of this period makes a comparison impossible. Relevant UN missions include all the peace missions in West Africa: the UN Mission in Liberia (UNMIL), the UN Integrated Office in Sierra Leone (UNIOSIL) and the UN Operation in Côte d'Ivoire (UNOCI). In addition, gender mainstreaming in the UN reporting systems and programmatic implementation mechanisms is increasingly visible. If we focus on UNMIL, for example, the Office of the Gender Advisor has made a marked difference. A gender policy has been established for the Liberia National Police, while a gender curriculum and training manual has been developed for the Police Academy. A Women's NGO Secretariat has been established with UN support. Also noteworthy is the production of various gender resources and materials, including the integration of gender into the country's Poverty Reduction Strategy Paper and the development of gender-based training materials for UNMIL personnel.[10] Also, for the first time in the history of the UN, an all-female police unit has been deployed to UNMIL since January 2007.[11]

It is, however, easy to exaggerate the pace of progress in mainstreaming gender within UN peacekeeping as a whole. In the first five years after the adoption of UNSCR 1325, only 25 per cent of the total civilian personnel serving in UN missions were women. The percentage in the police was 5 per cent, and 1 per cent in the armed forces.[12] These figures have increased only marginally at the ten-year mark.

In the ECOWAS Mechanism there is no provision regarding the training of peacekeeping and armed forces personnel on the special needs of women, or on the requirement for the inclusion of women in DDR programmes. Beyond general statements such as in Article 44 of the Mechanism (see Table 12.1, above), there is no mention of special measures to be adopted in armed conflicts to protect women from GBV and of the responsibilities of states to prosecute those responsible for violations.

There are, however, encouraging indications that ECOWAS is upgrading its gender instruments and institutional approaches to peace and security. The prospects for gender mainstreaming in regional integration generally, and in peace and security in particular, are positive. At the 26th Session of the Authority of Heads of State and Government held in Dakar in January 2003, an institutional mechanism for mainstreaming gender in the ECOWAS region was put in place. A Gender Division was created within the Executive Secretariat (now known as the Commission) and the West African Women's Association was transformed into the ECOWAS Gender Development Centre. The objectives of the gender development programme, among other things, are to mobilize women and empower them to be active participants in the regional integration process, mainstream gender in ECOWAS institutions and member states, and develop networks and partnerships with relevant agencies for technical and financial support for the ECOWAS gender mainstreaming programme. The meeting of the Council of Ministers held in July 2004 strengthened the gender programme by adopting the Gender Policy document, the administrative structure of the ECOWAS Gender Development Centre, a strategic plan framework, and guidelines on the structures and mechanisms of ECOWAS gender management systems.

Currently, the ECOWAS framework on gender is receiving a boost. Within the Gender Division, a training manual on gender and child protection issues during complex emergencies is under development. More strategically, 'Women, Peace and Security' is one of the 14 components of the ECOWAS Conflict Prevention Framework (ECPF), which was adopted by ECOWAS in 2008.[13]

Box 12.1 ECOWAS conflict and prevention framework: women, peace and security component[14]

The objective of the Women Peace and Security component of ECPF shall be to promote women's role and contribution to centre stage in the design, elaboration, implementation and evaluation of conflict prevention, resolution and peace-building initiatives while strengthening regional and national systems for the protection and advancement of women.

To enhance the visibility and impact of women in peace and security, the following activities shall be prioritised:

a   The Department of Human Development and Gender and the Gender Center, in collaboration with identifiable networks of women organizations in West Africa to study the gendered impact of conflicts on women and map out their role in the emerging ECOWAS security architecture.

b   Adopt a regional policy to combat discrimination against women in all its forms, including in inheritance, pay differentials, female genital mutilation (FGM), arranged marriages and girl-child labor.

c   Develop programmes to enhance the capacity of women organizations in project design and implementation and support them with targeted financial and equipment packages.

d   Develop targeted programmes to enhance the leadership, negotiation and dispute resolution skills within women organizations.

e   Adopt an ECOWAS policy to include women in the leadership of factfinding and peace missions, and in peace negotiations.

f   Establishment of 'Young Women's Fellowship' program with the collaboration of institutions of higher learning and the private sector in ECOWAS and other regional institutions working on peace and security.

g   Mainstream gender in all aspects of the ECOWAS peace architecture.

h   Put women organizations at the forefront of community and crossborder peace initiatives, reintegration processes, as well as programs to combat human trafficking, HIV/AIDS and STDs.

i   Adopt affirmative policies to enhance girl-child education.

Women's organizations, contributions to peace and security in West Africa

Civil society has also been active in the task of engendering peace and security, with UNSCR 1325 often featuring as a point of reference. A group of women's organizations focusing on peace and security issues have emerged in the last decade, all of which increasingly seek to operationalize UNSCR 1325. The organization Femmes Africa Solidarité (FAS) was created in 1996, and in its early years it played an active role in engaging women in conflict management and resolution. The Mano River Women's Peace Network (MARWOPNET) is a network of more than 100 civil society groups, particularly women's associations, located in Guinea, Sierra Leone and Liberia, launched as an FAS initiative in 2000. Its aim is to advance the role of women in promoting peace, security and development in the Mano River subregion.[15]

The Women in Peacebuilding Network (WIPNET) was created in 2001 as a programme of the West African Network for Peacebuilding[16] to mobilize women, build their capacity and encourage collaboration among them to build lasting peace and promote human security in West Africa. WIPNET's focus is on the integration of women's concerns and their participation in policy formulation and implementation regarding peace and security issues in the subregion. Its main objectives include the development of policy recommendations for mainstreaming women's issues in peace and security; strengthening links among policymakers, technocrats and women's groups; strengthening the capacity of rural/grassroots women in peacebuilding at the community and national levels; building strategic partnerships with women's networks in other regions; and sustaining women's participation in formal peacebuilding in West Africa. In November 2004, WIPNET held a consultation with women's groups and the ECOWAS Gender Unit to develop a policy framework for mainstreaming women's issues in peace and security in West Africa. WIPNET has also been active in the localization of training methodologies and it has translated its specialized training manual and UNSCR 1325 into seven local/indigenous West African languages. In November 2005, the Fourth Annual WIPNET Regional Conference was dedicated to the theme of 'Revisiting United Nations Security Council Resolution 1325: Opportunities and Challenges for the Future'.

The Women Peace and Security Network – Africa (WIPSEN-Africa) was formally launched at the Strategic Reflection Forum for Women in Peacebuilding with the theme 'Institutionalizing Women Peace and Security in Africa', which was held at the Kofi Annan International Peacekeeping Training Centre in Accra, Ghana, on 21–24 May 2007.[17] According to its blog, WIPSEN-Africa is a pan-African network with a core mandate to institutionalize women's peace and security in Africa. WIPSEN-Africa is both women-led and women-focused, and envisions a 'violence free, non-discriminatory continent that fosters peaceful coexistence, equality, collective ownership and the full participation of particularly women in decision making on peace and security'.[18]

Broader in scope, the West African Civil Society Forum (WACSOF) was created in 2003, arising out of 'the need to create an institutionalized dialogue between regional civil society organizations ... and the ECOWAS Commission (formerly the Executive Secretariat)'.[19] Gender is one of WACSOF's programme areas.[20] As part of its recommendations to the ECOWAS Council of Ministers Meeting held in Ouagadougou, Burkina Faso on 18–19 December 2006, WACSOF called for the implementation of UNSCR 1325 and urged 'the implementation of the ECOWAS Gender Policy and the ratification of the Protocol to the African Charter on Human and People's Rights on the Rights of Women'.[21]

In a nutshell, therefore, UNSCR 1325 has featured, and is increasingly featuring, on the West African peace and security landscape both within the peace and security architecture and in the activities and programmes of civil society organizations. However, gender peace and security mainstreaming in West Africa is not far beyond infancy, and several challenges remain on the path to achieving the goals of UNSCR 1325.

Challenges of implementing UNSCR 1325 in West Africa

The resilience of established mindsets

In the final analysis, what UNSCR 1325 seeks is a change in the mindsets of all the actors engaged in peace and security in the direction of gender mainstreaming and inclusion. Seeking a fundamental change in attitudes, social practices and ways of thinking that are centuries old is necessarily a long-term project that requires sustained efforts. This is particularly so when the very institutions on which the success of UNSCR 1325 depends continue to be dominated and directed by men. A degree of resistance is therefore to be expected. In this regard, however, it is important that UNSCR 1325 has, ultimately, the political objective of altering power relations between men and women.

The increase in intra-state armed conflict, often deliberately targeting civilians and typically featuring armed non-state groups, means that state-based instruments such as UNSCR 1325 are insufficient to protect women, as these non-state groups often deliberately disregard such normative instruments. UNSCR 1325 therefore faces the dilemma of several other international legal and normative documents that are state-based and therefore of limited practical value on the ground. For instance, despite the UN Security Council's many strategic initiatives to promote gender equality and support the empowerment of women, its attention to gender issues is not systematic. Since the adoption of UNSCR 1325 in 2000, as of 30 June 2006, only 55 of 200 (i.e. 28 per cent) country-specific Security Council resolutions included language on women or gender.[22] With specific regard to West Africa, women's representation remains marginal in ECOWAS institutions. Unlike the AU, which has agreed on a 50 per cent quota for women at the level of AU commissioners, ECOWAS does not have such a quota. As earlier indicated, among the latter's seven statutory commissioners, only two are women. In addition, beyond standards setting at the macro level, accompanying benchmarks and timelines are not specified for the achievement of the objectives of UNSCR 1325.

UNSCR 1325: necessary, but not sufficient

The sheer distance between norms and practice on gender and the depth of the marginalization of women in social organization and governance in Africa means that a lot more is required than the provision of adequate legal frameworks, useful and desirable as these may be. The widespread and continued flagrant discrimination against women and girls; the use of rape as a weapon of war, torture and dehumanization; the mere act of lip service exhibited by public office holders to gender equality and women's empowerment concerns and the concomitant lack of genuine political will on the part of governments to commit to the implementation of the instruments they have signed; persistent gender inequality and injustices; and the reinforcement of patriarchy within typically male-dominated peace and security structures are some of the factors responsible for the persistent gaps between the goals of UNSCR 1325 and their realization in West Africa. In addition to UNSCR 1325, therefore, governance and legal reforms that address discriminatory laws against women are necessary at both the regional and national levels. As noted elsewhere, while international law may seek to address gender inequalities, social norms do not necessarily advance in line with these changes, and women often remain politically and economically disadvantaged. The tension between discriminatory customary law and state or international law must also be recognized in post-conflict reconstruction strategies.[23]

Grassroots imperatives of UNSCR 1325

Undoubtedly, UNSCR 1325 is a watershed political framework for addressing the challenges faced by women, particularly in post-conflict reconstruction. In reality, however, a wide gulf often exists between the perspectives and priorities of ordinary, mostly uneducated and rural women, on the one hand, and educated elite African women who lead the gender debate and who (ostensibly on behalf of ordinary African women) enter into dialogues with international organizations and donors, on the other. The challenge, therefore, is to ensure that strategies for localizing and contextualizing UNSCR 1325 in West Africa are based on and reflect the energies and priorities of people at the grassroots level in the region's villages and communities.

Conclusion and recommendations[24]

This chapter uses UNCSR 1325 as a template for addressing peace and security in West Africa from a gender perspective. The chapter is not, and does not claim to be, a comprehensive assessment of the role of women in peace and security in West Africa. In any event, such an exercise is an ongoing process, the scope of which is far beyond the reach of a single analysis. The chapter's modest contribution is that of an approach for measuring the implementation of global legal and normative instruments in specific regional contexts. Given the fact that UNSCR 1325 is only as good as its implementation, its use as a yardstick for gender-based regional assessments is recommended for other parts of Africa and beyond.

The chapter has noted that the main ECOWAS peace and security instruments largely reflect and comply with UNSCR 1325. The more recent instruments such as the ECOWAS Conflict Prevention Framework (ECPF) and Small Arms Convention make specific reference to this resolution. In terms of implementation, however, the chapter observed that several gaps remain. The ECOWAS bureaucratic decision-making structure still reflects a deficit with regard to the representation of women. An overwhelming percentage of posts are still held by men, without any specific quota for the increased participation of women or even a timeline in this regard.

The interface between UNSCR 1325 and the ECOWAS peace and security architecture and experiences raises several issues, for which the chapter puts forward the following specific proposals. First, the principles of UNSCR 1325 should be integrated into ECOWAS peace support operations. ECOWAS has an impressive record of innovative regional peacekeeping missions as seen in interventions in Sierra Leone, Guinea-Bissau and Côte d'Ivoire. This will become institutionalized through the ECOWAS Standby Force (ESF). With the adoption of UNSCR 1325, deliberate steps should now be taken to ensure that subsequent missions comply with this resolution. As with UN missions, future ESF missions should include gender advisors, in addition to other gender mainstreaming approaches detailed in UNSCR 1325. Special representatives of the ECOWAS president should include women.

Second, women should be represented at the highest levels in ECOWAS. The ECOWAS Commission should introduce a quota system to guarantee women effective participation in decision-making related to peace and security and other aspects of regional integration. Within the larger ECOWAS Commission bureaucracy, affirmative action policies should be further entrenched to encourage the interest of women in working for the organization, particularly in the field of peace and security.

Third, the absence of relevant data must be addressed. Gender-specific analysis, information and data are necessary to paint a clearer picture of the challenges facing women, particularly during and after conflict. Such an approach would enhance planning for ESF operations. Fourth, ECOWAS states should adopt national action plans for the implementation of UNSCR 1325, which should flow from and comply with a regional ECOWAS action plan.

Finally, there is a need for more coherent and sustained civil society advocacy. Civil society organizations should sustain sensitization campaigns and programmes for the localization of UNSCR 1325 in order to improve on the region's understanding of gender and to bring the resolution closer to the majority of ordinary, particularly rural, African women.

Notes

1 M. Nzomo, 'From OAU to AU and NEPAD: Regional Integration Processes in Africa and African Women', keynote address, Regional Strategy Meeting on Women's Political Participation and Gender Mainstreaming in AU and NEPAD, Nairobi, 27–31 October, 2003, p. 3.
2 Ibid.
3 Ibid.
4 A.O. Konare, 'Statement in Celebration of International Women's Day', 8 March 2007.
5 See Meredith Turshen and Clotilde Twagiramariya (eds), *What Women Do in Wartime: Gender and Conflict in Africa*, London: Zed Books, 1998.
6 It is estimated that as many as 40 per cent of Liberian women were raped during the 14-year civil war. See Refugees International, 'Liberia: Major Effort Needed to Address Gender-based Violence', 16 January 2004, www.refugeesinternational.org/content/article/detail/932/.
7 As of 2010, the three women currently on the ECOWAS Council of the Wise are Theresa Leigh Sherman (Liberia), Elizabeth Alpha-Lavalie (Sierra Leone) and Sira Diop (Mali).
8 Preamble, *ECOWAS Convention on Small Arms Light Weapons, Their Ammunition and Other Related Material*, 2006, www.iansa.org/regions/wafrica/documents/CONVENTION-CEDEAO-ENGLISH.PDF.
9 T. Bouta *et al.*, *Gender and Peacekeeping in the West African Context*, report of the Stakeholders' Workshop held at KAIPTC, Accra, 1–3 December 2004, p. 19.
10 L. Gbowee, 'Women Building Peace through Disarmament, Demobilization and Reintegration', paper presented at the Beijing+10 Review Conference, 9 March 2005, www.womenwarpeace.org/issues/ddr/ddrpanelcsw05.pdf.
11 For further details of activities of the UNMIL Office of the Gender Advisor, see 'Outcomes of Gender Mainstreaming by the Office of the Gender Advisor: UNMIL 2004–2006,' http://unmil.org/documents/OGA_Achievement_2004_2006.pdf.
12 See UN News Centre, www.un.org/apps/news/story.asp?NewsID=21391&Cr=Liberia&Cr1.
13 M. Edfast, 'Operation 1325 and Resolution 1325: An Overview', October 2006.
14 The components of the ECPF are Early Warning; Preventive Diplomacy; Democracy and Political Governance; Natural Resource Governance; Cross-Border Initiatives; Security; Women, Peace and Security; Micro-Disarmament; Youth Empowerment; the ECOWAS Standby Force; Human Rights and the Rule of Law; and Humanitarian Assistance. See ECOWAS Commission, *Draft ECOWAS Conflict Prevention Framework*, as revised at the Experts' Meeting on the ECPF, Banjul, the Gambia, 24–28 June 2007.
15 'The ECOWAS Conflict Prevention Framework', Regulation MSC/REG.1/01/08, January 2008, pp. 41–3. For the whole Framework, please see www.ecowas.int/publications/en/framework/ECPF_final.pdf.
16 See www.peacewomen.org/1325inaction/index.html.
17 See www.wanep.org/programs/wipnet.html, accessed 2 October 2007.
18 This part of the paper is based on the forum report. See Tema Agera and Awa Ceesay-Ebo, *Report of the Strategic Reflection Forum for Women in Peacebuilding: Institutionalizing Women Peace and Security in Africa, Hosted by WIPSEN-Africa, Held at the Kofi Annan International Peacekeeping Training Centre, Accra, Ghana, 21–24 May 2007*. See also www.wipsen-africa.org/.
19 WIPSEN-Africa, Mission Statement. Available at www.wipsen-africa.org/wipsen/about/ (accessed 23 November 2009).
20 See www.wacsof.org/background.html.

21 Other programme areas are Peace and Security, Food, Agriculture and Environment, Youth, Regional Integration, Economic Development, Trade and Investment, Democracy, and Good Governance and Human Rights.
22 See Recommendations of the West African Civil Society Forum (WACSOF) to the ECOWAS Council of Ministers Meeting in Ouagadougou, Burkina Faso, 18–19 December 2006, www.wacsof.org/info/WAFSOC%20FORA%20COMMUNIQUE/ WACSOF_4th_Forum_Communique%5B1%5D.doc.
23 UN Security Council, *Report of the Secretary General on Women Peace and Security*, UN doc. S/2006/770, 27 September 2006, p. 9.
24 Y. Clarke and H. Scanlon, *Women and Peacebuilding in Africa*, report of the seminar hosted by the Centre for Conflict Resolution and UNIFEM, Cape Town, 27–28 October 2005.

13 A look at UNSCR 1325 in SADC

Nyaradzo Machingambi-Pariola

Introduction

This chapter looks at the implementation of UN Security Council Resolution 1325 (UNSCR 1325) at the regional level by focusing on the achievement of UNSCR 1325 aspirations by the Southern African Development Community (SADC), the Regional Economic Community of 14 Southern African states.[1] Originally known as the Southern African Development Co-ordination Conference (SADCC) the Declaration and Treaty establishing SADC which replaced the Co-ordination Conference was signed at the Summit of Heads of State or Government on 17 August 1992, in Windhoek, Namibia.[2] The aim of SADC is to create a Community providing for regional peace and security, and an integrated regional economy. As a regional institution it laid the basis on which regional planning and development can be pursued in southern Africa. Furthermore, SADC forms one of the building blocks of the African Union (AU).

Africa's Regional Economic Communities or RECs, as they are now commonly known, were created with the aim of harmonising and strategising the achievement of development and economic integration for the region. They represent a critical pillar through which member states can be held to account for their international commitments and obligations such as those acquired through UNSCR 1325. This chapter will also look at the different means and ways SADC has used to advance the issue of gender equality in the region particularly in the area of peace and security. It examines what opportunities exist at the regional level to drive the UNSCR 1325 agenda and the constraints that exist at this level. It also looks at the relevance of SADC structures, policy instruments and mechanisms in terms of what they mean for the promotion of gender equality in southern Africa and for the implementation of UNSCR 1325 in particular.

The Southern African context

Southern Africa has undergone significant changes over the last two decades, with the conclusion of civil wars in Mozambique and Angola, and democratic transitions in Namibia and South Africa. The region now faces the critical challenge of nurturing post-conflict transitions through the promotion of peacebuilding, post-conflict reconstruction and entrenching inclusive and participatory systems of governance.[3] However, the picture emerging reflects the difficulties inherent in democratic consolidation, as it is a process that requires political commitment and vigilance. Some countries such as South Africa, Botswana and Mauritius have made strides towards democratisation with positive indicators such as transparent and participatory democratic structures, which are the building blocks of democracy.[4]

Several other countries however have remained weak and unable to establish participatory democracy and constitutionalism. Institutions of governance in these countries have been compromised, fuelling corruption, human rights violations and disregard for the rule of law.[5] Economic mismanagement and corruption have fostered the impoverishment of citizens and created uncharacteristically high levels of poverty. The inadequate provision of public health services, combined with the HIV/AIDS pandemic, have further removed economically active individuals from participating in the development of their countries.[6] This situation further undermines efforts to promote development, and places an even greater burden on badly managed economies[7] and impacts severely on the human security of SADC citizens, especially women and children.

Southern Africa also faces enormous human security challenges, which include but are not confined to HIV/AIDS, poverty, socio-economic inequalities, gender inequality and governance challenges. It has some of the highest HIV/AIDS statistics in the world, with an average prevalence rate of 25 per cent and poverty is widespread with about 60 per cent of people in the 14 SADC countries currently living below the poverty line.[8] The two cross-cutting issues of HIV/AIDS and poverty are impacting negatively on the stability and development of the sub-region. SADC's security framework acknowledges the need to address human security challenges, and the organisation has developed an impressive list of protocols and declarations to address some of these human security challenges, which must be followed by effective implementation mechanisms.[9]

SADC's challenges in the difficult areas of peace and security took on a new urgency with the establishment of the AU in Durban, South Africa, in 2002. Harmonising SADC's activities with those of the AU has become an urgent priority, along with advancing continental capacity in peace and security.[10] The adoption of the AU Protocol on Peace and Security, and the establishment of the 15-member Peace and Security Council (PSC) in July 2004 underscored the need for African sub-regional organisations to play an active role in the AU's peace and security agenda. This is because in the AU's evolving security architecture, sub-regional organisations such as SADC are seen as the building blocks and pillars for future co-operation, particularly in the establishment of the African Standby Force (ASF), scheduled to become operational by 2010.[11]

The AU and the New Partnership for Africa's Development (NEPAD) have also given sub-regional organisations new impetus to focus on democracy and governance and to address regional conflicts.[12] These developments provide opportunities and present challenges to sub-regional organisations such as

SADC, including making substantive inputs into the structures and work of the AU's organs and articulating clear regional positions.[13]

Gender equality in SADC

The SADC region recognises gender equality as a fundamental human right and an integral part of regional integration and economic growth and development.[14] SADC member states' commitment to gender equality is demonstrated through accession to and ratification of frameworks that promote women's human rights such as the Convention on the Elimination of All Forms of Discrimination Against Women (CEDAW), which became an SADC-ratified Protocol in 2004, the Solemn Declaration on Gender Equality in Africa (SDGEA) through which they have reaffirmed their commitment to, among others, gender equality as enshrined in the Constitutive Act of the African Union Article 4, the Dakar Platform of Action (1994), the Beijing Platform of Action (1995), United Nations Resolution 1325 on Women, Peace and Security (2000), and the Protocol to the African Charter on the Rights of Women in Africa (2003).[15]

Furthermore a Draft SADC Gender Policy was developed to provide a sound, authoritative, coherent and strategic mechanism for achieving the objectives of the SADC Declaration on Gender and Development.[16] The policy is intended to facilitate the implementation of the SADC Gender Commitments as it includes similar standards, indicators and timeframes, which will be the driving force to motivate all member states to move towards the achievement of the set targets.[17] The SADC region has made significant progress in the implementation of these commitments and has witnessed improvements in the development of national policies, structures, guidelines, action plans and programmes addressing gender inequalities, raising awareness in gender analysis and mainstreaming at both national and regional levels.[18]

Despite this progress, however, implementation still fell short of the stated commitments and improvements are needed to face emerging threats such as the increasing poverty, HIV/AIDS, escalating levels of gender violence and human trafficking in the region.[19] Major challenges remain on gender inequality and, in particular, violence against women, who are particularly vulnerable to the HIV/AIDS pandemic, and constitute half of the estimated three million infections in Southern Africa. Human trafficking, which adversely affects the security of women and girls, is also seen to be on the increase, with major inroads on this illicit trade yet to be made by SADC member states.[20]

SADC security policies and mechanisms

Ongoing governance challenges, including the need to consolidate democracy, weak electoral and oversight processes in some instances, and tensions around political power sharing,[21] the feminisation of poverty and HIV/AIDS are the main issues that affect the security of women in Southern Africa. In this context, SADC has developed and consolidated its peace and security plan through two key policy instruments, the Regional Indicative Strategic Development Plan (RISDP) of 2001 and through its Strategic Indicative Plan for the Organ (SIPO) on Politics, Security and Defence Co-operation.[22] Both aim to promote security and development in southern Africa and to provide a framework for a comprehensive, holistic approach to building human security; strengthening democratic governance; and fostering economic integration in the region,[23] all of which should lead to improved human security for women in SADC.

SIPO has devised strategies for development in four broad sectors: politics; defence; state security; and public security.[24] The SIPO document, which is primarily concerned with operationalising the 'hard' security provisions of the Protocol on Politics, Defence and Security Co-operation, also makes welcome reference to human security threats such as poverty, HIV/AIDS, gender-based violence and governance issues,[25] which are critical human security issues in the sub-region. The objective of SIPO is to provide a broad framework on which more specific strategies to address SADC's human security challenges can be further developed. Civil society actors have however criticised the provisions of SIPO for stressing 'hard' security issues while lacking clearly defined mechanisms to address human security challenges effectively.[26]

SIPO seeks to promote democratic values and regional co-operation in the evolution of common political values and institutions; to control cross-border crime through co-operation in intelligence and law enforcement; to establish early-warning and common indicators for conflict prevention; and to develop regional capacity to prevent conflict and to engage in peacekeeping.[27] These provisions could be used to further the goals of UNSCR 1325. For instance, with regards to SIPO's aim to create early warning systems for conflict prevention, UNSCR 1325 recognised women's potential in contributing to the prevention of conflict by pushing for their inclusion in the creation of all these mechanisms as it recognised that women are the most reliable source of information in their communities, on issues such as mounting tensions and signs of instability, not to mention signs of gender violence, and recognised that if their views are taken into account, they can play a decisive role in providing early warning of conflict.[28]

The RISDP focuses on managing and mitigating HIV/AIDS and other health problems; maintaining and creating food security (including measures to strengthen preparedness and early response); addressing social policies; creating an enabling environment for development; and addressing both inequality and gender disparities,[29] all of which are critical for enhancing the security of women in southern Africa. The RISDP restructures the goals of SADC into four thematic clusters, as well as providing general direction and timeframes. RISDP aims to improve SADC's strategies and direction toward 'good political, economic and corporate governance entrenched in a culture of democracy, full participation by civil society, transparency and respect for the rule of law'.[30] Goals include poverty eradication, socio-economic development and regional integration/partly as a means toward chapter four's focus on gender equality, including in governance. RISDP aims for substantive equality and gender mainstreaming, which should contribute to the achievement of qualitative transformation of structural gender inequities, which UNSCR 1325 envisages. The rights of the African woman to happiness, success and political life were reaffirmed by this agreement.[31]

In addition to SIPO and the RISDP, SADC has adopted a number of other documents: the Maseru Declaration on HIV/AIDS of 2003 to address the political, social and economic impacts of HIV/AIDS; the Declaration on Gender and Development of 1997, which seeks to establish a policy framework for mainstreaming gender into all of SADC's activities; and the SADC Principles and Guidelines Governing Democratic Elections of 2004, to govern election processes in southern Africa. Though some successes have been recorded in a number of these specific areas, practical experience points to poor implementation and a disappointing monitoring record by SADC members.[32]

Opportunities for UNSCR 1325 advancement in SADC

While UNSCR 1325 seems mainly seized with the issue of engendering UN peacemaking processes, it does stress the need for UN member states to promote the increased representation of women[33] at all 'decision-making levels in national, regional and international institutions and mechanisms for the prevention, management, and resolution of conflict'. The inclusion of women basically encompasses the issue of governance, which is critical to addressing security threats for SADC women. As one commentator aptly put it,

> The main thrust of the resolution regards the participation and involvement of women in our collective efforts for the maintenance and promotion of peace and security, the protection of women and girls from human rights abuses which constitute the most abhorrent and condemnable aspect of present-day conflict and the mainstreaming of gender perspectives in issues directly related to conflict and post-conflict situations.[34] Those are the main subjects dealt with by resolution 1325 (2000), which the Security Council, the United Nations system, States, civil society and other actors must address in order to advance the fundamental role that women can and should play in ensuring a more peaceful, just and equitable world.[35]

One of the main opportunities that exist for SADC to implement UNSCR 1325 in terms of mainstreaming a gender perspective into all aspects of SADC citizens' lives is the critically acclaimed signing by the SADC Heads of State of the SADC Protocol on Gender and Development on 17 August 2008. This instrument is hailed as an important step towards the empowerment of women, the elimination of discrimination and achievement of gender equality and equity in SADC. It breaks new ground globally by incorporating and enhancing all existing commitments, thus creating synergy and harmonising the various reporting processes.[36]

The Protocol also takes account of all the commitments made by member countries in the various continental and international instruments; but also enhances these by taking account of gaps that have been identified in the existing instruments and in their implementation. The Protocol incorporates all existing targets and also sets realistic, achievable targets where these do not exist. These targets include raising the current target of 30 per cent women in decision-making by 2005 to gender parity in all areas of decision-making by 2020, in line with the AU position, through a phased and incremental approach.[37] The Protocol is accompanied by an action planning framework and institutional structures that would ensure regular and effective reporting benchmarking, monitoring and evaluation, and appropriate sanctions for non-compliance.[38]

In the context of peace and security, the Protocol stipulates that States Parties shall endeavour to put in place measures to ensure that women have equal representation and participation in key decision-making positions in conflict resolution and peacebuilding processes by 2015, in accordance with Resolution 1325.[39] Furthermore, the Protocol specifies that States Parties shall during times of armed conflict, take such steps as are necessary to prevent and eliminate incidences of human rights abuses, especially of women and children and ensure that the perpetrators of such abuses are brought to justice before a court of competent jurisdiction.[40] This is a recognition of the fact that sexual violence in conflict situations is inextricably linked to gender inequality and that there is therefore a need to advocate more strongly for the equal participation and full involvement of women in all efforts for the maintenance and promotion of peace and security.

Another key opportunity is the emergence of the AU's peace and security architecture within which SADC forms a building block and through which SADC has to establish a Southern African Standby Brigade (SADBRIG) as part of the AU's African Standby Force (ASF), which will undertake traditional peacekeeping operations, as well as observer missions and peacebuilding activities. SADC is in the process of establishing an interim planning unit for the Southern African Brigade within its secretariat in Gaborone, Botswana. SADC members have also committed the requisite 3,500 troops to the brigade, and have agreed on a peace support doctrine for the region.[41] SADBRIG must establish a training toolkit for its brigade on the gendered impact of conflicts and it must ensure that a gender resource manual has been developed to assist in the training of peacekeeping operatives prior to their deployment.

UNSCR 1325 implores member states to mainstream a gender perspective into peacekeeping operations and calls for specialised training for all peacekeeping personnel on the special needs and human rights of women and children in conflict situations. Gender training is critical for peacekeeping forces and the training content and methodology should ensure that trainees are 'conscientised' and not just 'sensitised' on gender equality and its relevance to building sustainable peace.[42] To ensure that training takes into account gender relations peculiar to the local context, adequate consultation with local actors at all levels of peacekeeping and peacebuilding is important, a critical factor that SADBRIG needs to take into account.

Resolution 1325 has also emphasised the incorporation of HIV/AIDS aware-ness into pre-deployment and in-mission training programmes, building on UNSCR 1308 of 2000, which acknowledged the particular vulnerabilities of international peacekeeping personnel to HIV/AIDS.[43] These should be incorpo-rated into all SADBRIG gender training tools. With plans to create the AU's ASF, it is important that these policies are mainstreamed into all continental deployment initiatives. Gender advisers and HIV/AIDS policy advisers must establish close working partnerships in peacekeeping missions and incorporate gender-training aspects into HIV/AIDS training.[44]

Since Africa's regional armies will face increasing challenges as they engage in multi-dimensional peacekeeping operations, SADC should engage more effectively in strengthening regional participation in UN and AU peace opera-tions. This represents another opportunity for it to mainstream gender into its operations as the involvement of international and regional actors in peacekeep-ing and peacebuilding efforts in Africa has created the conditions for an integ-rated approach to developing a continental peace and security architecture.[45] The UN must institutionalise mechanisms for achieving 1325 in its co-operative agreements with the regional organisations to facilitate the achievement of their gender equality agenda.

Challenges that impact on SADC's ability to implement 1325 and advance gender equality in the field of peace and security

SADC has acknowledged the gender dimensions of human and political insecu-rity in southern Africa by identifying gender as a key issue cutting across its pro-grammes. Gender issues are addressed in several SADC instruments, including the 1992 SADC Declaration[46] and Treaty; the 1997 SADC Declaration on Gender and Development; the 1998 Addendum on the Prevention and Eradica-tion of Violence against Women and Children; and the RISDP of 2001.[47] SADC member states are also party to a range of international agreements that highlight the importance of human rights and gender equality.

Notwithstanding these commitments, however, recent experiences raise ques-tions about the ability of the sub-regional body to effectively implement these policies as SADC peacekeepers, militaries, mission leaders, negotiators and police officers in southern Africa appear to have limited capacity to address gender issues in their activities, and knowledge is generally poor of international and continental obligations, such as UNSCR 1325.[48] The SADC secretariat also unfortunately lacks resources to successfully co-ordinate the implementation of its gender strategy, although the organisation recently committed to ensuring the effective involvement of women in peacebuilding processes and conflict situ-ations.[49] These specific challenges faced by the SADC Gender Unit in imple-menting UNSCR 1325 are indicative of this problem of effective implementation of international instruments. There is thus a need for more action and leadership on gender issues within SADC's politics, defence and security sectors.

A key problem with commitments over gender issues is that they are generally non-systematic and non-binding. Thus, the gap between policy and practice often compromises the efforts of member states. Furthermore, there has been inconsistency in the implementation by member states of SADC's Gender and Development Declaration.[50] There has also been slow progress in promoting the domestication of international instruments, including Resolution 1325, by the organisation.[51] Political will is also often lacking for the implementation of agreements and, in this regard, principles of 'good governance' are critical. Moreover, the contradictions that often exist between customary law and modern codified law when it comes to women's rights are not addressed in SADC's constitution, nor have they been sufficiently identified.[52] This deficiency is a critical shortcoming in a region where gender inequality and, in particular, violence against women remains a major challenge.

The SADC Civil Society Forum observes that while the SADC region has not experienced major inter-state wars since the collapse of the Cold War and demise of apartheid in South Africa, intra-state conflicts and instability still persist, thereby posing a serious threat to peace and security.[53] The Forum is concerned that many SADC countries tend to prioritise state security over human security yet the letter poses a major challenge for peace in the region today. Human insecurity is exacerbated by economic inequality, endemic health crisis, unabated poverty and hunger.[54]

The Forum further notes that the SADC region is still vulnerable to violent intra-state conflicts affecting civilian populations. There is also a continued proliferation of small arms and light weapons circulating throughout the region. These weapons are often used in fuelling violent criminal activities.[55] The regional security architecture in SADC still remains nascent and challenges for conflict prevention, management and transformation are daunting.[56] The Forum notes that escalation of intra-state conflicts generates political instability and compromises security. In many SADC countries violent conflicts tend to intensify around elections with adverse effects for democracy, peace and security.[57]

Some proposals for improvement

In November 2005, the AU Protocol of the African Charter on Human and Peoples' Rights on the Rights of Women in Africa came into force. This Protocol provides a legal framework that commits African leaders to the principle of gender equity and sets out key protection mechanisms for African women.[58] The document further seeks to address violations of African women's rights, outlines a framework for the protection of women in armed conflict, and provides provisions to address gender-based violence.[59] Thus far only four SADC countries have ratified it, namely Lesotho, Namibia, Malawi and South Africa. Ratifying this Protocol would be a progressive step for these countries in terms of advancing context-sensitive gender equality for southern African women.

The Protocol builds on efforts to promote the participation of women in decision-making and gender equity at the level of African institutions over the last five years, through such instruments as the AU's 2004 Heads of State Solemn Declaration on Gender Equality in Africa (SDGEA). This declaration commits AU members to ensure full and effective participation and representation of women in peace processes, including the prevention, resolution and management of conflict and post-conflict reconstruction efforts,[60] which coincide neatly with the aspirations of Resolution 1325.

An effective realisation of women's rights also requires the existence of inclusive programmes involving the AU such as its African Peer Review Mechanism (APRM) of 2004. The APRM could be used to gauge the ratification and implementation of the Protocol. Implementation within states should serve as one of the APRM's criteria for assessing and monitoring the progress of African governments in promoting and protecting human rights.[61] Such programmes should furthermore address the implementation of the Protocol in conjunction with UNSCR 1325 and the AU SDGEA.[62]

In southern Africa, the increase of women in decision-making in the years since the Beijing conference has been more rapid than anywhere else in the world. As a region, southern Africa is second only to the Scandinavian countries. Despite the many gaps, there seems to be an unstoppable march towards women's equal participation in decision-making. Around the region, the 50/50 campaign is being embraced, buoyed by the recent AU position and evidence that some countries in the region are ready to move on. In this regard the parliaments of Rwanda, South Africa and Mozambique currently rank among those in the 17 top parliaments in the world in the area of women's representation.

Despite this welcome increase in the number of women in decision-making positions, adequate capacity-building initiatives, which capture the unique needs of African women, are also necessary.[63] There is a need to recognise the unequal power relations that still exist in public life in southern Africa and the discrimination that women continue to face when vying for and occupying public office. While the achievement of a critical mass of women in power is vital, it is also necessary that institutions transform themselves in order to be conscientised over gender concerns within peace and security issues.[64]

In order for SADC to achieve its desired success in the region's human security areas, greater synergy with the AU and other RECs needs to be cultivated. SADC also needs to work with the UN, the EU and other key actors to achieve the goals of its SIPO on Politics, Defence and Security of 2004, and its RISDP of 2001. SADC faces challenges of threats to human security, such as the eradication of poverty, particularly in terms of the UN Millennium Developmental Goals' aims of halving poverty by 2015; violence against women and children globally; and effective regional economic integration.[65] An integrated plan of action is needed, along with a streamlined list of priorities in respect of human security.

SADC needs to focus on the gender aspect of its peace and security instruments and processes, especially regarding the implementation of its RISDP and SIPO. This could be done through improving the capacity of its personnel to address gender issues.[66] These SADC key policy instruments including its 2001 Protocol on Politics, Defence and Security Co-operation, and its Mutual Defence

Pact of 2004 need to be further developed into more coherent programmes of implementation and monitoring.[67] The internal capacity of the SADC gender unit should also be strengthened, as well as its linkages with member state structures, for the promotion of gender-inclusive democratic developmental states. Gender biases in economic policy should be removed as well as discriminatory mechanisms and/or cultural practices as they exacerbate poverty and retard development.[68] Similarly, the AU policy on gender equality and women's rights can be a valuable instrument through which SADC can measure its progress.

Conclusion

There is an urgent need for SADC to develop effective implementation and monitoring mechanisms, and to translate its ideals into practical strategies that would contribute to deepening its gender equality agenda. There is a need for SADC to consolidate the RISDP and SIPO, the two complementary documents providing 'regional expression' to the AU/NEPAD principles, which were adopted to steer and operationalise SADC's shared vision of the advancement of women into a concrete programme of action.[69] This is because despite the region having acceded to the many international and regional instruments that protect the rights of women and children as well as promoting gender equality, there are major gaps and constraints that are hindering progress.

The status of women in southern Africa and the plight of the girl child is such that women continue to be the poorest, the unemployed, the abused and disadvantaged in terms of limited access to productive resources, opportunities, health, education, training, etc. The high HIV prevalence rates in women and burden of care further increases their vulnerability and risk of infection of the girl child. The emerging gender issues and concerns – specifically human trafficking and increasing levels of gender-based violence need to be urgently addressed. Thus the gap between commitment and implementation remains a concern, contradictions exist between customary laws and representation of women remains below target (20 per cent regional average) and high levels of poverty among women and girls remains a major obstacle for gender equality.

There needs to be a consensus, to escalate the interventions on gender equality that significantly improve the quality of life of the marginalised women and children in the region. The pace is slow, implementation inconsistent and capacity low with limited resources. The concrete and practical interventions pronounced in the regional Gender Policy guidelines on the one hand and the legal muscle provided by the Protocol on the other, should give impetus to the implementation of gender issues and make gender mainstreaming real.

Notes

1 These comprise Angola, Botswana, Democratic Republic of Congo (which is also a member of ECAS for Central African States), Lesotho, Madagascar, Malawi, Mauritius, Mozambique, Namibia, Seychelles, South Africa, Swaziland, Zambia and Zimbabwe.

2 'History and Present Status', SADC, South African Department of Foreign Affairs, 2004. Available at www.dfa.gov.za/foreign/Multilateral/africa/sadc.htm (accessed 12 January 2010).

3 N. Mashumba and C. Scott, 'Whither SADC? Southern Africa's Post-Apartheid Security Agenda', Policy Seminar Report, Centre for Conflict Resolution, 18–19 June 2005, Vol. 5, p. 30.

4 Ibid., p. 32.

5 Ibid.

6 Ibid., p. 30.

7 Ibid., p. 30.

8 Ibid., p. 10.

9 Ibid., p. 10.

10 Ibid., p. 24.

11 C. Saunders and D. Nagar, 'Security and Development in Southern Africa', Policy and Advisory Seminar Group Report, Centre for Conflict Resolution, 8–10 June 2008, Vol. 27, p. 13.

12 Mashumba and Scott, op. cit., p. 25.

13 Ibid.

14 SADC Declaration and Treaty 1992. Available at www.sadc.int/index/browse/page/119 (accessed 23 November 2009).

15 Briefing Notes on the Draft SADC Protocol on gender and development and the Draft SADC Gender Policy. Available at www.iss.co.za/uploads/SADCGENDER15JUL08.PDF (accessed 19 November 2008).

16 Ibid.

17 Ibid.

18 Ibid.

19 Ibid.

20 Saunders and Nagar, op. cit., p. 21.

21 Ibid., p. 23.

22 Ibid.

23 Ibid.

24 Ibid., p. 13.

25 Mashumba and Scott, op. cit., p. 11.

26 Ibid.

27 Saunders and Nagar, op. cit., p. 23.

28 Angolan Statement on Women, Peace and Security, Security Council Open Debate on Women, Peace and Security: A Compilation of Statements, Compiled by the NGO Working Group on Women and Security, 28 October 2004, p. 5.

29 Saunders and Nagar, op. cit., p. 24.

30 RISDP. Available at www.sadc.int/english/documents/risdp/summary.php (accessed 24 November 2009).

31 Gender and Governance in SADC 2008–2009, Southern Africa Gender Protocol Alliance, Gender Advocacy Program, p. 5.

32 Mashumba and Scott, op. cit., p. 11.

33 UNSCR 1325 calls on member states to ensure that gender is mainstreamed throughout all conflict prevention and peacebuilding activities, and reaffirms women's rights to be involved in decision-making and to access and take on leadership positions. For the detailed report see S/Res/1325 www.un.org/events/res_1325e.pdf.

34 Angolan Statement on Women, Peace and Security, op. cit., p. 5.

35 Ibid.

36 'Rationale for a SADC Protocol on Accelerating Gender Equality,' Audit commissioned by the SADC Gender Unit and the SADC Parliamentary Forum, p. 1. Organisations that contributed to the audit include: Gender Links, the Gender and Media Southern Africa (GEMSA) Network, the Media Institute of Southern Africa (MISA),

Women in Law in Development in Africa (WILDAF), SARDC/WIDSAA and SAFAIDS.

37 Ibid.

38 Ibid.

39 'SADC Protocol on Gender and Development', Southern African Development Community, 2008. Availble at www.sadc.int/attachment/download/file/247.

40 Ibid.

41 Saunders and Nagar, op. cit., p. 8.

42 Y. Clark and H. Scanlon, 'Women and Peacebuilding in Africa', Policy Seminar Report, Centre for Conflict Resolution, 26–27 October 2005, Vol. 9, p. 17.

43 Ibid., p. 22.

44 Ibid.

45 Saunders and Nagar, op. cit., p. 9.

46 Gender equality and the empowerment of women is one of the founding principles of SADC and is enshrined in our SADC Treaty (1992). For further reading please see the official SADC website www.sadc.int/index/browse/page/119.

47 Saunders and Nagar, op. cit., p. 9.

48 Ibid.

49 Ibid., p. 26.

50 Ibid.

51 Ibid.

52 Clark and Scanlon, op. cit., p. 26.

53 'Democratic governance and Regional Economic Integration', communiqué by the SADC Civil Society Forum, The Southern African Development Community Council of Non-Governmental Organizations (SADC-CNGO), 14–16 August 2006, p. 2.

54 Ibid.

55 Ibid.

56 Ibid.

57 Ibid.

58 Clark and Scanlon, op. cit., p. 21.

59 'Protocol to the African Charter on Human and Peoples' Rights on the Rights of Women in Africa', The African Union Commission on Human and Peoples' Rights, 2003. Available at www.achpr.org/english/_info/women_en.html (accessed 13 January 2010).

60 Clark and Scanlon, op. cit., p. 21.

61 L. Stone and A. Mindzie, 'Women in Post-Conflict Societies in Africa', Policy Seminar Report, Centre for Conflict Resolution, 6–7 November 2006, Vol. 20, p. 9.

62 Ibid.

63 Ibid., p. 21.

64 Ibid., p. 22.

65 Saunders and Nagar, op. cit., p. 7.

66 Ibid., p. 22.

67 Ibid., p. 11.

68 Ibid.

69 Mashumba and Scott, op. cit., p. 37.

14 Turning policies into action?

The European Union and the implementation of UNSCR 1325

Karen Barnes

The EU recognises the close links between the issues of peace, security, development and gender equality. Therefore, there is not only the need to promote the participation and the protection of women in conflict situations and peace building but also the need to ensure that these actions are supported by wider development considerations, such as the promotion of women's economic security and opportunities and their access to health services and education. This is particularly important in the light of the long-term negative impact that violent conflict has on the development of a country or a region and the need to plan for a multidimensional human security as the basic condition for attaining long term peace and development.[1]

European countries have been some of the most active supporters of UNSCR 1325 since its adoption in October 2000. They have pushed for action to be taken at the UN level, developed their own national action plans (NAPs) for implementation and have funded various initiatives in conflict-affected countries. As the global leader in funding for development assistance and an increasingly important actor in crisis management and peacebuilding, the EU could play a key role in leveraging support for the mainstreaming of UNSCR 1325 and gender issues into peace and security processes. Nevertheless, until 2008, it was slow to articulate a coordinated policy approach in relation to UNSCR 1325 or to integrate the provisions of the Resolution into its planning and programming. This chapter will first present an overview of the evolution of the EU's policies in relation to women, peace and security issues. It will then turn to an assessment of some of the key areas where the EU has an added value in relation to the implementation of UNSCR 1325, as well as highlighting some of the ongoing obstacles. Finally, the chapter will conclude by considering some of the factors that enabled UNSCR 1325 to find its way onto the EU's policy agenda.

The EU and women, peace and security issues

The EU is an important actor on the ground in conflict-affected regions through its development and humanitarian assistance programmes, through the role of EU member states in peacekeeping missions or its own EU-led missions, and due to its position in influencing international regional security policies. Furthermore, the EU is able to act across all areas of defence, diplomacy and development, which means that it can theoretically engage in all aspects of the peacebuilding process and in all areas relevant to UNSCR 1325.

Since the adoption of the Resolution in October 2000, the EU has developed a number of instruments, policy documents and resolutions that are either related to or mention women, peace and security issues. The first European Parliament (EP) resolution on these issues entitled 'The participation of women in peaceful conflict resolution'[2] was adopted in November 2000, shortly after UNSCR 1325. Similar to UNSCR 1325, the language in the EP resolution and accompanying report was vague, calling on member states to take certain actions rather than requesting them to do so. Since then, this has been followed by several more resolutions and reports by the EP, but generally little concrete action was taken by the EU from 2000 to 2005, aside from statements during the annual debates on UNSCR 1325 held in the Security Council every October.

In 2005, momentum around women, peace and security issues finally began to increase at the EU. In 2005, the Council released a document on the implementation of UNSCR 1325 in the context of European Security and Defence Policy (ESDP) missions which was followed up by a checklist that sought to make the Resolution operational. This represented the first real policy commitment at the EU that specified action on UNSCR 1325. These commitments were subsequently tested during the EUFOR RD Congo[3] mission in 2006, which represented a turning point for the integration of gender issues into the EU's peacekeeping missions. It was the first time that a gender advisor had been deployed and it resulted in a number of valuable lessons learned and documentation of good practices.[4] For example, the gender advisor developed a workplan for integrating gender issues into the work of the mission, engaged with local women's organisations, and was able to carry out gender trainings and create a network of gender focal points throughout the mission.[5] After her return, the mission's gender advisor, who had been seconded by the Swedish Armed Forces, was seized on by UNSCR 1325 advocates, and she presented her experiences in a wide variety of forums at the European level, often to audiences with security sector officials. This enabled the sharing of good practices and lessons learned with a broad audience and, perhaps more importantly, enabled the articulation of how UNSCR 1325 could advance operational effectiveness in language that the military could understand.

There were a number of events held during 2006 and 2007 relating to women, peace and security issues in Brussels and other European capitals, mostly organised by civil society networks such as the European Peacebuilding Liaison Office (EPLO) and with the key aim of raising awareness about UNSCR 1325 and advocating for greater accountability for implementation by the EU and its member states. In 2008, momentum around the implementation of UNSCR 1325 grew markedly during the Slovenian and French presidencies, and key individuals within the Council and the Directorate-General for External Relations (DG RELEX) began to push the agenda forward. In early 2008, the Slovenian presidency (January–June 2008) commissioned a study to highlight the EU's strengths and weaknesses in relation to women and armed conflict.[6] This report provided a detailed analysis of the EU's approach to women and armed conflict and outlined the key spheres of action with the relevant policy frameworks and funding instruments. It also made a number of recommendations and identified ten potential short-term next steps. The latter were designed to set out some clear and realistic steps that could be taken in the three to six months following publication of the report to build momentum and encourage a more systematic response to the implementation of UNSCR 1325. The report was well-received by both EU officials and member states, and its findings were presented widely including to the Council working groups. It became the main resource used by those both inside and outside the EU to advocate for action on UNSCR 1325, and ended up being published at a very strategic moment when its ability to influence the EU-level debates on UNSCR 1325 was maximised.

The French presidency of the EU (July–December 2008) built on the Slovenian initiative, and made the issue of violence against women (VAW) one of its presidential priorities. During its presidency, a review of member state actions in relation to Platform E of the Beijing Platform for Action (PfA)[7] was carried out. This review drew attention to the fact that many gaps in implementation of the PfA's recommendations remained, and that there was little strategic prioritisation of women, peace and security issues by the EU member states.[8] The French presidency also produced a report outlining four indicators relating to VAW that it proposed could be applied to assess implementation of Platform E.[9] The culmination of these efforts was the adoption on 8 December 2008 of the *Comprehensive Approach to EU Implementation of United Nations Security Council Resolutions 1325 and 1820 on Women, Peace and Security* (CA) by the Council of the European Union.[10]

The CA outlines some common definitions and principles based on international and EU-specific lessons learned in relation to gender and peacebuilding, and aims to bring about greater coherence and impact among the EU's crisis management initiatives and reconstruction and development work in this area. In this document, the EU outlines the 'three-pronged approach' that it commits to adopting in its work in this area: integrating women, peace and security issues in its policy and political dialogue with partner governments; mainstreaming a gender approach in its policies and activities; and supporting strategic actions targeting the protection and empowerment of women.[11] The adoption of the CA signified an increased level of commitment and understanding of these issues within the EU, as well as outlining a comprehensive and coordinated framework for the institutions in terms of UNSCR 1325 and 1820. However, the major limitation in this framework is that it lacks any clear articulation of the kinds of action that the EU institutions are going to take, and does not include an in-built monitoring or accountability mechanism to measure implementation.

Responding to the need for a holistic framework, the CA outlines some common definitions and principles based on international and EU-specific lessons learned in relation to gender and peacebuilding, and promotes greater

Box 14.1 Selected key policy commitments guiding the EU's response to women, peace and security issues

EU Plan of Action on Gender Equality and Women's Empowerment in Development (2010)	An operational document that highlights activities for 2010–2015 focused on achieving the MDGs and other gender-related international policy commitments. The plan seeks to coordinate and strengthen gender equality policies in development cooperation, particularly in areas where the EU has a comparative advantage. Supporting partner countries in fully implementing UNSCR 1325, 1820, 1888 and 1889 is highlighted as one such area. Notably, it commits that 'By 2013 at least 60% of EU Delegations in fragile, conflict or post-conflict countries develop a strategy to implement the EU Comprehensive approach from the perspective of the sectors they are involved in and development co-operation'.
EU Comprehensive Approach to the EU implementation of SCR 1325 and 1820 (2008)	Outlines some common definitions and principles based on international and EU-specific lessons learned in relation to gender and peacebuilding, and promotes greater coherence and impact among the EU's crisis management initiatives and reconstruction and development work in this area. The CA outlines the three-pronged approach that the EU commits to adopting:integrating women, peace and security issues in its policy and political dialogue with partner governments; mainstreaming a gender approach in its policies and activities; andsupporting strategic actions targeting the protection and empowerment of women. The CA also highlights actions the EU will take in regard to training, exchange of information, and the issues it will consider in the context of its programmes at the country and regional level, in a variety of thematic areas.
EU guidelines on violence against women and girls and combating all forms of discrimination against them (2008)	These guidelines stress the fact that women and girls face an increased risk of violence during situations of conflict. Among other things, they call for capacity-building in bilateral and multilateral programmes, notably through the provision of assistance for developing NAPs for the implementation of SCR 1325.

Document	Description
Implementation of UNSCR 1325 as reinforced by UNSCR 1820 in the context of ESDP (2008) and check list to ensure gender mainstreaming and implementation of UNSCR 1325 in the planning and conduct of ESDP Operations (2006, updated in 2008)	These documents relate to the integration of a gender perspective in all aspects of the EU's crisis management activities, from the planning to the reporting and lessons learned. Strategic and operational measures are identified, and the more recent updates incorporate the provisions of SCR 1820 as well as 1325. The documents provide guidelines on how to integrate gender issues into fact-finding missions, concept of operations, training, reporting, and a wide array of other dimensions of ESDP missions.
EC Communication on Gender Equality and Women's Empowerment in Development Cooperation (2007)	This document gives a common vision for the EU on gender equality in development cooperation. It 'calls on the Commission and Member States to develop and fully implement appropriate measures, such as concerted and harmonised national action plans for the implementation of Resolution 1325, integration of provisions of Resolution 1325 in CSPs, DDR and post-conflict reconstruction, peace-building and development'.
European Consensus on Humanitarian Aid (2007)	This document recognises the importance of supporting women's participation in humanitarian aid responses and the incorporation of protection strategies against sexual and gender-based violence in all aspects of humanitarian assistance.
Roadmap for Equality between Women and Men (2006–2010)	The Roadmap builds on previous policies and strategies and accelerates the EU's efforts to achieve gender equality. One of the six priority areas is the promotion of gender in the external and development policies.
European Consensus on Development (2005)	The document commits the EU to mainstreaming gender equality as a cross-cutting issue, and also states that the EU 'will maintain its support to conflict prevention and resolution and to peacebuilding by addressing the root-causes of violent conflict, including poverty, degradation, exploitation and unequal distribution and access to land and natural resources, weak governance, human rights abuses and gender inequality' (section 92).

coherence and impact among the EU's crisis management initiatives and recon-struction and development work in this area. The CA framework could reduce the lack of coherence, coordination and complementarities that characterises efforts to integrate gender issues into peace, security and development responses across the EU's institutions, pillars and their respective instruments. This docu-ment also committed the EU to establishing a 'Women, Peace and Security Task Force', to act as a platform for information-sharing, as well as to facilitate coordination between the different EU institutions.

There was a small window of political opportunity to push the CA through the Council and, as a result, there was little time to consult with civil society or other stakeholders. The gender cluster of the Initiative for Peacebuilding (IfP) was invited to give comments at a late stage of the drafting, but this was not the more extensive consultation that some of those involved in the CA had initially hoped for.[12] Following the release of the CA, attention shifted in 2009 to the need to develop indicators and a way of assessing implementation of the CA, and by extension of UNSCR 1325 and 1820. A key event in this process was a roundtable organised by IfP with representatives from across the EU institutions, and the resulting synthesis paper that suggested some possible indicators that could be used in the EU context.[13]

In September 2009, the EC organised the first ever training for staff in delega-tions and Brussels on 'gender, conflict, peace and development'. The training was delivered by International Alert over three days, and introduced EC officials to a range of theoretical, policy and practical issues linked to the implementation of UNSCR 1325 and 1820 and the application of a gender perspective in its peacebuilding and conflict prevention work.[14] Clearly such trainings only target a small number of individuals and do not necessarily have a broader impact across the organisation, but they do indicate recognition of a need for greater capacity and expertise in this area among EU officials.

In 2009, the EU and AU delegations at the UN in New York also collaborated on two events, highlighting the role of regional institutions in advancing the res-olution and in taking action on women, peace and security issues. Finally, during 2009, the EU also positioned itself to play a key role in the run up to the tenth anniversary of UNSCR 1325. As a follow-up to the international conference 'Women, Stabilising an Insecure World' of 6 March 2008, Benita Ferrero-Waldner, the European Commissioner for External Relations and European Neighbourhood Policy, together with 40 other international women leaders, called on the UN Secretary-General to convene in 2010 a ministerial-level meeting to review implementation of UNSCR 1325 and reinvigorate commit-ment to tackling outstanding issues.[15]

Implementation of UNSCR 1325 by the EU

The varied roles and responsibilities of the institutions and the different dimen-sions of EU action and instruments results in a complex landscape for the imple-mentation of UNSCR 1325. However, the EU is particularly well-placed to take action on a number of levels. The EU could drive the development and sharing of regional and context-specific expertise in the area of women, peace and security issues. The CA mandates such exchanges of good practice among member states, and the meeting organised by the Council on 2 October 2009 on NAPs is one example of this kind of activity.[16] There is significant expertise within the EU region, both in terms of civil society organisations and networks such as EPLO and IfP, as well as national-level initiatives such as the Irish Joint Consortium on Gender-Based Violence (GBV) that brings together government and civil society in Ireland to develop more systematic responses to GBV in the context of UNSCR 1325. These groups can be valuable resources for enhancing implementation of women, peace and security commitments, and their expertise could be harnessed at the regional level. With the incorporation of a specific indicator relating to supporting partner countries in developing NAPs included in the operational framework for the EU Plan of Action on Gender Equality and Women's Empowerment in Development (2010–2015), the EU is also positioning itself to provide technical advice and support outside of the European region.[17]

The EU should also seek to integrate the CA and other commitments relating to women, peace and security across the range of peace and security initiatives that it undertakes. The inclusion of gender advisors in ESDP missions is a positive step forward, but more needs to be done to prioritise gender issues in the mandates of these missions, and adequate training should be given to all military and civilian staff. The lack of capacity on gender issues is something that has also been highlighted in the context of the EU's external relations instruments more broadly.[18] Indeed, while there have been important steps forward in regards to incorporating gender into the EU's crisis management responses, 'more efforts need to be made to integrate gender-related issues in ESDP policy-making, not as a separate issue, but as an aspect that permeates all action.'[19]

VAW is one area that the EU has consistently prioritised within its efforts to implement UNSCR 1325. This can partly be explained by the presence of several key member states such as France and Belgium who have pushed to have the issue on the EU's agenda. For example, the Government of Belgium, the European Commission and the United Nations Population Fund (UNFPA) launched the Brussels Call to Action to Address Sexual Violence in Conflict and Beyond in June 2006,[20] and the EU itself adopted its guidelines on VAW in 2008. The EU could therefore continue to speak out on this issue, and ensure that issues related to VAW are tackled prominently in the context of the EU's crisis management and peacekeeping activities. It should, however, be noted that there is the risk that the protection dimensions of UNSCR 1325 become emphasised over the participation elements, negating women's agency during conflict and peacebuilding and emphasising their role as victims. However, the CA offers a strong and holistic framework that recognises the agency of women and their vital contributions to peacebuilding processes and specifically mentions the interaction between the protection and participation pillars of UNSCR 1325:

> There is a close link between the prevention of sexual and gender-based violence (SGBV) and the opportunities made available to women to participate politically, to achieve a sustainable livelihood and to feel secure in their communities during and after conflict.[21]

The EU could also use its position as a regional body to collaborate with other organisations such as the AU and NATO that play important roles in regional peacekeeping and peacebuilding. Regional-level relationships are an important entry point in addressing conflict and security concerns, and these can also create platforms for engagement between regional bodies. Since processes such as peacekeeping initiatives, mediation efforts and election monitoring are often regionally organised or led, the EU could take the lead in mainstreaming gender and sharing good practice and lessons learned with other regional bodies. For example, analysis on women's participation as candidates and voters in elections is now systematically included in EU Electoral Observer Missions. Finally, as a major donor, the EU could actively ensure that promotion and implementation of UNSCR 1325 is a compulsory element of projects that are funded through its instruments in conflict-affected regions, for example by making it necessary that they include a component of consultation with local women's groups and civil society organisations.

There are a number of ongoing obstacles that limit the impact of the EU's efforts to implement UNSCR 1325 in a coherent and systematic way. While the CA does represent a relatively comprehensive approach to the issues, it still exists in the margins of the EU's peace and security policy. Gender issues do not feature strongly in the European Security Strategy, there are few women in senior positions within the institutions, and the resources allocated for implementing the CA are negligible. This demonstrates the fact that while the political rhetoric has placed UNSCR 1325 and the CA in a central role, in reality this does not translate into concrete action by the institutions. It must, however, be recognised that the CA is a relatively new policy document, and it will take time for it to be operationalised and to have an impact on the EU's structures and processes.

Overall, there has been very little accountability for the implementation of UNSCR 1325 at the UN, regional or national levels, and this has repeatedly been cited as a major obstacle to progress in integrating gender issues into conflict prevention, peacebuilding and reconstruction efforts. The CA commits the EU to strengthening its reporting mechanisms, and could potentially provide the basis of a framework for accountability. Indeed, these frameworks are key to ensuring that EU policy commitments such as the CA are translated into reality and concrete implementation of projects and programmes. For example, gender and conflict analysis should inform the work of the EC and its delegations, and should be seen as a process that actively engages, involves and empowers women and men in conflict-affected contexts. However, recent research has found that gender has rarely been mainstreamed into the EC's Country Strategy Papers, particularly in the context of programming choices.[22]

Another important level where the CA will need to be implemented is at country-level where the EC Delegations have the opportunity to work closely with local stakeholders, including women's organisations. The EC funding instruments can be used to support capacity-building, service provision and programmes to empower women to participate more effectively in peacebuilding and development activities. However, there is often a lack of coherence between the policy rhetoric in Brussels and the reality of the context the EC delegations are working in, and major human resource constraints in countries such as Liberia have had a major impact on the ability of the EC to implement UNSCR 1325, through the CA or otherwise, on the ground. Projects such as the 'EC/UN Partnership on Gender Equality for Development and Peace' are one way of building up the knowledge networks, expertise and capacity building in-country that can enable more coherent responses to post-conflict needs.[23] UNSCR 1325 and the CA call on international actors to engage more systematically with local women's groups and networks in conflict-affected contexts and the EU missions and EC delegations could play a critical role in this regard.

What factors drove the EU to address women, peace and security issues?

Having reviewed the EU's record in the implementation of UNSCR 1325, it is striking how much progress has been made in the past few years. The EU benefitted from the experience of the UN in the early years following the adoption of UNSCR 1325, making processes such as recruiting gender advisors into peace-keeping missions much easier. Several EU member states had also already articulated clear commitments to UNSCR 1325 through their NAPs, some of which mandated action at the EU level.[24] These factors certainly helped to chart a path for the EU. However, it is useful to highlight some other factors that contributed to the EU's actions in this area.

First, UNSCR 1325 provided an internationally-agreed commitment that could be drawn on for political leverage within the EU context. All EU member states had already agreed to the principles of the Resolution, and so this existing commitment was used by those inside the EU institutions, some member states and civil society organisations to advocate for action. Had this resolution not existed, it would have been more difficult to provide the rationale for including gender issues in the EU's peace and security issues.

Second, committed individuals within the EU institutions played a key role, lobbying from the inside and generating buy-in from the higher levels of decision-making. Given that so few human and financial resources were allocated to these issues, much of the groundwork for the CA and subsequent activities was due to the efforts of an advisor working in the office of Riina Kionka, the Personal Representative for Human Rights at the Council of the EU, and the focal point on gender and conflict within DG RELEX. Benita Ferrero-Waldner's role was also particularly important in terms of getting the issue onto the political agenda at the highest levels. However, this is not a sustainable strategy for pushing forward women, peace and security issues within the EU, and a more significant investment of resources will be needed before capacity and impact can visibly increase.

Third, the history of UNSCR 1325 would not be written were it not for the networks of women's rights activists and practitioners who advocated for a resolution, and so their impact at the European level must not be under-estimated. Civil society groups focusing on national-level implementation exist within many EU member states, and these groups played an important role in developing links with key individuals inside the EU institutions, organising events, raising awareness and producing research and policy briefings advocating for more attention to be paid to women, peace and security issues. More recently, the IfP also played a catalytic role, providing crucial additional capacity and a dedicated team of gender experts who had a mandate to support the EU in its UNSCR 1325-related activities. By choosing to fund this network, the EC in particular was able to benefit from the insights of a range of civil society organisations working on these issues, since IfP also collaborated closely with the gender, peace and security working group of EPLO.

Finally, there was also a shift in focus after 2005, as UN member states began to take on their commitments to UNSCR 1325 at the national level. As part of this shift, they also began to see regional organisations as mechanisms for implementing the resolution, and they began to place more emphasis on coordinated action by the EU institutions, and so some member states pushed for the EU to take more action.

It is promising that the EU has begun to take its commitments on women, peace and security more seriously at a rhetorical level, particularly given that it has only taken these issues on board relatively recently, but the real challenge will come in turning these commitments into resources, impact and change on the ground. The policy frameworks are now largely in place, there is a significant body of lessons learned and research that can inform future EU action in this area, and the discourse on security at the EU is now broadening to create more space for gender-related security concerns. It is, however, less clear if the EU will invest the necessary financial and human resources to operationalise these policies and lessons. The tenth anniversary will provide continued momentum and focus for the EU's efforts, but the organisation has a long way to go before it can truly be said to place women, peace and security at the heart of its development and peacebuilding responses.

Notes

1 Council of the EU, *Comprehensive approach to the EU implementation of the United Nations Security Council Resolutions 1325 and 1820 on women, peace and security*, Brussels, Belgium: The Council of the EU, 2008a, para 15, p. 9.
2 European Parliament Resolution on 'Participation of women in peaceful conflict resolution', (2000/2025(INI)), 30 November 2000. www.europarl.europa.eu/sides/getDoc.do?pubRef=-//EP//TEXT+TA+P5-TA-2000-0541+0+DOC+XML+V0//EN&language=EN (accessed 13 April 2010).

3 EUFOR RD Congo was the name given to the EU military operation in the Demo-cratic Republic of the Congo in support of the UN Mission in that country (MONUC).

4 Giji Gya, Charlotte Isaksson and Marta Martinelli, *Report on ESDP missions in the Democratic Republic of the Congo (DRC)*, Background paper for the conference 'From Commitment to Action – The EU Delivering to Women in Conflict and Post-Conflict', Brussels, 10 October 2008. www.unifem.sk/uploads/doc/09-01-30_ ESDP&DRC_Final%20report%20complete.pdf.

5 EU Operation headquarters, Operation Commander Lieutenant General Karlheinz Viereck, *Final Report on Gender Work inside EUFOR RD Congo*, Potsdam, 15 December 2006. www.honvedelem.hu/files/9/8008/eu_operation_headquarters_final_ gender_report_eufor_rd_con.pdf.

6 Andrew Sherriff with Karen Barnes, *Enhancing the EU response to women and armed conflict, with particular reference to development policy*, Study for the Slove-nian Presidency of the EU, Maastricht and Brussels: European Centre for Develop-ment Policy Management, 2008.

7 Platform E refers to women and armed conflict, and is one of the twelve pillars of the Beijing Platform for Action. New York: UN/Division for the Advancement of Women, 1995. Available at www.un.org/womenwatch/daw/beijing/platform/. The Madrid European Council of 1995 called for an annual review of implementation of the Beijing Platform for Action by EU member states and institutions. In 1998, the Council decided that this review should be accompanied by the development of quan-titative and qualitative indicators. The method to establish the indicators was to issue a questionnaire to member states and the EC, and elicit from the recommendations and priorities of those bodies a set of indicators to assess implementation of Platform E.

8 Council of the EU, *Review of the implementation by the Member States and EU insti-tutions of the Beijing Platform for Action – Indicators concerning women and armed conflicts. Draft Council Conclusions*, Addendum 2 to the Note, Brussels: EU, 2008b.

9 Ibid.

10 Council of the EU, 2008a, op. cit.

11 Council of the EU, 2008a, p. 11, para 18. For a more detailed analysis of the CA, see Karen Barnes, *Turning Policy into Impact on the Ground: Developing indicators and monitoring mechanisms on women, peace and security issues for the European Union*, Synthesis Report, London, Initiative for Peacebuilding, 2009.

12 Meeting with official from the Council, November 2008. The Initiative for Peace-building is an EC-funded consortium of ten non-governmental organisations led by International Alert with the objective of developing and harnessing international knowledge and expertise in the field of conflict prevention and peacebuilding. Gender is one of the six thematic focus areas of the consortium. For more information, see www.initiativeforpeacebuilding.eu.

13 Barnes, 2009, op. cit.

14 The author led the design and delivery of this training while she was a senior pro-gramme officer at International Alert responsible for gender and peacebuilding issues.

15 Benita Ferrero-Waldner was the European Commissioner for External Relations and European Neighbourhood Policy from 2004 to 2009.

16 The summary report of this meeting can be viewed at www.consilium.europa.eu/ ueDocs/cms_Data/docs/hr/news230.pdf. IfP and EPLO jointly organised a workshop with civil society representatives from 18 European countries prior to the official EU meeting on NAPs. The purpose of the civil society workshop was to identify and pri-oritise recommendations to member states and the EU institutions on developing NAPs and implementing UNSCR 1325 and 1820. These recommendations can be viewed at www.eplo.org/documents/Recommendations1325.pdf.

17 European Commission, *EU Plan of Action on Gender Equality and Women's Empow-erment in Development (2010–2015)*, Commission Staff Working Document, SEC

(2010) 265 final, March 2010, p. 16. http://ec.europa.eu/development/icenter/repository/SEC_2010_265_gender_action_plan_EN.pdf (accessed 5 May 2010).

18 G. Gya, 'Gender Mainstreaming and Empowerment of Women in EU's External Relations Instruments', study conducted by the Directorate-General for External Policies of the Union, 2009, p. 12. For the full report please see www.isis-europe.org/pdf/2009_artrel_306_09-04-epstudy-gender-ext-rel-gya.pdf (accessed 13 April 2010).

19 Wendy Harcourt, *Gender and Fragility: Policy Responses*, paper prepared for the Conference on 'Moving Towards the European Report on Development 2009', organised by the European Report on Development in Florence, Italy, 21–23 June 2009.

20 See www.unfpa.org/emergencies/symposium06/index.htm.

21 Council of the EU, 2008a, op. cit., p. 2.

22 Sheriff with Barnes, op. cit., p. 37.

23 The EC/UN Partnership, an initiative of the EC, UNIFEM and the ILO, aims to support national partners to fulfil their international obligations on gender equality, and is being implemented in 12 countries, four of which are conflict-affected (the DRC, Indonesia, Nepal and Papua New Guinea). For more information on this project see www.gendermatters.eu.

24 For details on which NAPs specify action at the EU level, see a table compiled by EPLO comparing the various plans across Europe: www.eplo.org/documents/CT.pdf.

Part IV
Conclusion

15 Conclusion

'Funmi Olonisakin and Eka Ikpe

Introduction

UNSCR 1325 no doubt marks a significant step toward the pursuit of gender equality in the realm of peace and security. At a minimum, it makes a strong case for elevating the concerns and agenda of women to the fore of the international security agenda. And in so doing, it provides a framework to guide the policies and programmes of critical actors particularly at national and regional levels in order to realize a qualitative shift in the conditions and roles of women. However, as Barnes argues in the second chapter of this volume, the Resolution does not directly address itself to the deep-seated issues at the root of gender inequality, including patriarchy, notions of masculinity and militarized power. Nonetheless it provides a basis for conversations around structural roots of gender inequality particularly in places that are receptive to the ideas of prevention, protection and participation that underlie UNSCR 1325. The case studies in this volume reflect the extent to which this has been achieved.

In this concluding chapter, we attempt to pull together the main strands of the country and regional studies discussed in the preceding chapters to provide guidance on whether and how UNSCR 1325 has made a real impact on the ground. In order to do this, we return to some of the key questions and issues raised in the introductory chapter. Three of these sets of questions will form the focus of this concluding chapter. The first and primary question underpinning all others is whether the eight country cases and four regional case studies provide any significant evidence that UNSCR 1325 can be used strategically to drive systemic change at the national and regional levels. If so, how does it drive that change? How do different national and regional actors use UNSCR 1325? Second, does the presence of international actors make a difference in terms of advancing gender equality? Does the presence of a peace mission help or hinder this process? Third, what lessons can be learned from the alternative local mechanisms that already exist in these contexts? What is the relationship between formal peace operation structures and informal local structures? Do peace operations undermine or reinforce local initiatives?

In the introductory chapter, we presented the main thematic issues explored in this volume while highlighting the variability in the country case studies.

Using the above questions as a broad guide, we shall now explore the main trends that emerged from the analysis of these thematic issues across the various national and regional contexts and the difference, if any, made by the variability.

Does the presence of international actors make a difference in terms of advancing gender equality?

There is often a high expectation that international actors can make a difference to the situations on the ground in conflict-affected settings. This is no different when it comes to the situation of women and the struggle for gender equality. What is more, UNSCR 1325 heightens this expectation. This is understandable, particularly when the conditions on the ground are overwhelmingly skewed against local actors. In places like Kosovo, for example, where patriarchal social hierarchies have constituted a huge stumbling block to the advancement of women, it is to be expected that an assertive international presence can combine with local efforts to create opportunities for the promotion of gender equality and a measure of structural change to sustain any gains for women. The presence of peace support operations ought to create windows of opportunity to make such change happen.

Clearly, the timing of international presence determines whether and how external actors can effectively contribute to the efforts to advance gender equality. The case studies in this volume reveal several patterns. First, whether international presence predated UNSCR 1325 (as was the case in Rwanda, Kosovo and Sierra Leone) or vice versa (as in Nepal), this made varying degrees of impact in terms of supporting the energy of women on the ground to promote gender equality. But in none of the cases did international presence fundamentally transform the situation of women. The real added value is the ability of international actors to facilitate local action through the provision of resources and moral support.

The second pattern is that UN presence other than peace operations has turned out to be more relevant to the concerns of women than the peacekeeping presence. This was the case, for example, in Liberia, Nepal and Sudan, where the United Nations Population Fund (UNFPA) had a practical effect on the ground through active implementation of UNSCR-related activities. Yet, these types of operational successes did not always translate into high-level political engagement to promote systemic change. Thus, failure of the UN political office on the ground to systematically engage on UNSCR 1325 invariably left unfilled gaps, which made it difficult to upscale the efforts of civil society and UN operational agencies. This underscores the importance of mutual interdependence between UN political and operational actors on the one hand, and between international and local actors on the other.

Peace support operations and UNSCR 1325 in action: the impact on the ground

The extent to which peace missions make a real difference in terms of advancing gender equality in their areas of operation is one of the key issues that this volume sought to investigate. In this regard, the extent to which UNSCR 1325 is understood and used by peace operations to actively seek to influence local actors and or to transfer principles and structures for advancing gender equality has been an important focus. In the cases where a peacekeeping mission is present, is the local population more aware of and sensitive to UNSCR 1325 than they were prior to the arrival of the UN? The analyses of some countries with peacekeeping presence for a sustained period – Liberia, Sierra Leone and Sudan – makes it possible to draw broad conclusions about the extent to which peace operations influenced local actors and processes to deliver the change that UNSCR 1325 intended.

Transmitting UNSCR 1325 from headquarters to the field level and to the national context

The type of guidelines transmitted from UN headquarters to the field level for implementation in peace operations is an important starting point for understanding how UNSCR 1325 is understood and internalized in the area of operation. Some of the country studies reveal whether or not the level of UNSCR 1325 implementation that occurs in the field-level contexts is consistent with what is intended in the original directives. Do actors at the field-level transmit the ideas within UNSCR 1325 to the national context where governments hold ultimate responsibility for advancing gender equality?

Overall, peace operations have been less influential than expected in terms of impact on their area of operation concerning application of UNSCR 1325. This study reveals a number of factors that can influence the transfer of UNSCR principles from headquarters to the field and national level. One is the explicit inclusion of UNSCR 1325 in the mission mandate. This not only provides legitimacy and space for action on the ground, it allows for the inclusion of this issue in priority setting and resource allocation. In Sierra Leone, where the United Nations Mission in Sierra Leone's (UNAMSIL) initial mandate did not include UNSCR 1325, the agenda of gender equality was slow to take off, at least within the mission and in terms of its engagement with the Sierra Leonean society on this issue.

Another factor is the attitude of and dynamism shown by the mission leadership to the issue of gender equality and the central messages contained in UNSCR 1325. The presence of UNSCR 1325 does not necessarily make a fundamental difference if the leadership do not actively seek to implement it as indicated in Sudan and Nepal. At best, the attention of the mission is focused on the mechanics of fulfilling the 'items' contained in its mandate and reporting on these items accordingly. The cases where a combination of these factors exist in peace operations – explicit mandate and committed leadership on UNSCR 1325 – are the exception rather than the norm. However, the presence of one or the other is better than none at all with marginal results in the field. One example is the measure of success achieved by the United Nations Transitional Administration in East Timor (UNTAET) through the introduction of an affirmative action policy for women in public employment and international standards. As Nakaya points out in this volume, this was made possible in part by the combination of factors – strong leadership of the Special Representative of the UN Secretary-General (SRSG) and the Gender Affairs Unit within UNTAET, and in local women's groups, and among some national leaders in the executive branch. That this was achieved at all despite the challenges posed for the achievement of gender equality by the overall governance environment demonstrates that some structural change is possible even in the most difficult operational environments.

Where mission leadership has not been keen on UNSCR 1325, there has been little willingness to engage by national authorities; and civil society is not as galvanized for action as it could be. Nepal is one example of an actively engaged civil society, whose activities were up-scaled through the support of the UN agencies and international NGOs (INGOs), which were present on the ground long before the arrival of the peace mission. However, the much needed political influence at the highest levels was missing not just because of the later arrival of the mission, but also because when that mission finally arrived, it did not see the need to duplicate the work already being done by UN agencies on UNSCR 1325. Yet there was a clear political gap for the mission to fill.

In Sierra Leone, Kosovo and Sudan, the influence of the mission on the national level was marginal even when UNSCR 1325 was included in the mandate. Engagement with national actors and institutions on 1325 was limited at best and the impact made was negligible. In Kosovo, as Hall-Martin points out in this volume, government establishments such as the Agency for Gender Equality largely ignored the concerns expressed by women's groups on security-related issues – a situation which is blamed in part on the lack of political will by international actors to promote gender equality.

Similarly in Sierra Leone, while civil society has been active, the government has been very weak in addressing issues of gender equality and this, as Barnes indicates, has been a major stumbling block for the effective application of UNSCR 1325 at the national level. The active engagement of civil society in Sierra Leone was not necessarily due to UNAMSIL's presence. Indeed, civil society's awareness of UNSCR 1325 was low during UNAMSIL's deployment. In Sudan, the United Nations Mission in Sudan (UNMIS) has equally made marginal impact on issues of gender equality with limited interaction with local actors and a government (in the North) that appears suspicious of internationally driven agendas.

These outcomes go beyond mandate and leadership issues. The extent to which UNSCR is applied in a peace operations environment is also the result of a range of other complex factors and processes. Desirable as the idea might be, the intentions and spirit of UNSCR 1325 will not be transferred to the field and national settings in a seamless manner. Different factors within and outside the control of the UN system invariably combine to make for an awkward transition and translation. We focus on two factors here. One is the approach of the peace mission to gender equality, particularly in relation to its understanding and interpretation of security in the operational environment. The other concerns local dynamics in the area of operation.

How is UNSCR 1325, and gender equality more broadly, understood within peace missions?

The idea that peace operations provide security to local communities and to women in particular is widespread but the reality on the ground hardly supports this. Gender equality is not paramount on the agenda of peace missions. Typically, gender equality is considered a long-term agenda that can be put on the back burner or compromised for more pressing security concerns. Despite the presence of gender units and gender advisors in peace missions, and in particular the individual heroism of some gender advisors, peace missions seem to have had only a marginal impact on the national contexts in which they operate. The country studies in this volume reveal a discord between the underlying conceptions of security within peace missions and those that inform the imperative of gender equality, which drives UNSCR 1325.

This apparent discord has led to missed opportunities to pursue the women's agenda with conviction or vigour within peace operations even where this is explicit in the mandate of the mission. The United Nations Interim Administration in Kosovo (UNMIK), for example, was well placed to lead the process of gender mainstreaming and the conditions on the ground were ripe for this. But UNMIK and women's organizations had different interpretations of security. While UNMIK focused on issues of protecting the territory from external threats women's groups were naturally preoccupied with the security challenges women faced as groups and individuals. Although the two should not necessarily be mutually exclusive, the failure of the mission to recognize this and to creatively adapt to the needs of the environment makes the point. As a result, women's civil society has been far more effective in the application of UNSCR 1325 in comparison to UNMIK, which adopted a gender-neutral view of security.

Similarly, UNAMSIL accorded less than adequate attention to gender mainstreaming and implementation of UNSCR 1325 in Sierra Leone, while civil society adopted a holistic approach to the pursuit of their agenda. In the chapter on Sierra Leone, Barnes describes what she refers to as the 'structural marginalization of gender issues' in UNAMSIL, where the location of the gender role in the mission and inadequate resources allocated to this role determined the degree of impact made in the mission let alone outside it. However, as the experience of Timor-Leste indicates, gender mainstreaming can be successfully undertaken, where mission leadership – in this case, the SRSG and the Gender Unit – is able to adapt a broader view of security and commit to promoting gender equality.

For both UNAMSIL and UNTAET, the fact these missions predate UNSCR 1325 by about one year tended not to matter over time, because there were opportunities subsequently, to implement the Resolution within the missions and in the national context. Similarly, the argument often employed by peacekeeping personnel for not paying adequate attention to gender, which is that in complex emergencies often characterized by armed conflict and/or humanitarian tragedy, considerations for application of gender and other related instruments (children) often take a back seat. While this might be true during some of the emergency conditions experienced in Sierra Leone, for example, in 2000, when about 500 UNAMSIL peacekeepers were kidnapped, the mission had five years afterward to turn its attention to these issues. This is almost always the case in every peace operation.

Interestingly, however, peace missions have tended to do better at implementing necessary aspects of gender mainstreaming within the mission rather than outside it, particularly when this is an explicit part of their mandate and reporting requirement. Peace operations have shown a consistency when it comes to establishing gender units, deploying gender advisors and undertaking recurrent activities such as provision of training for peacekeeping personnel. These activities appear to be better suited to the needs of large bureaucracies of which a typical UN peace mission is a part. Translating these into systematic engagement with local and national actors in dynamic environments tends to present a challenge for peace operations personnel. Indeed, the tendency to gravitate toward 'one size fits all' approaches is huge within UN missions. The costs of adapting to the needs and structures and processes of the different locales seem to far outweigh the benefits for time-bound missions which roll from one mandate period to another. Success is therefore often limited to instances where personnel demonstrate individual creativity and resilience.

As mentioned in the introductory chapter, the relationship between the peace mission and the communities where they are deployed is not unidirectional. In the effort to advance gender equality, it is clear that local culture, dynamics and power relations have the potential to influence the success of international actors on the ground. Places such as Sudan, for example, where local suspicions of internationally driven initiatives has been high, create a peculiar set of challenges for efforts to drive change on the ground.

Alternative strategies for implementing UNSCR 1325

What lessons can be learned from the alternative methods of advancing gender equality at the local level?

In all the countries and regions that formed a part of this study, civil society actors had been actively advocating for the rights of women and for the recognition of their contribution to peacebuilding as well as their potential contribution to official peace and security processes. As discussed in the chapter on Sierra Leone, 'an extensive network of resources and expertise' existed in civil society and predate UNSCR 1325.

And these groups also actively undertook UNSCR 1325-related activities even when they were not aware or familiar with the Resolution. In addition, women's groups had a more robust understanding of gender and security than that of international actors operating in the country. While the latter focused almost exclusively on women, the former had a gendered approach, which took men's perspectives into account and was a core strategy in their pursuit of gender equality. In a similar vein, Kosovo, Rwanda, Sudan and Nepal had active women's movements at various stages before and after UNSCR 1325. And in all cases, the experience of war strengthened women's activism and their commitment to the pursuit of gender equality. In fact, in Rwanda, there has been a 'UNSCR 1325 style' highly successful process of women's participation at strategic levels with limited recourse to the Resolution. This situation presents a strong set of lessons for the implementation of UNSCR 1325, key of which is the invaluable role of sound women's networks in pushing both protection and participation issues.

There can be no doubt that much of what was achieved by women even without the presence of peace operations in terms of empowering women and promoting gender equality was achieved at the informal, grassroots level. The preceding chapters contain various examples of the wide-ranging ways in which women contribute to armed struggles (as seen in Nepal) and to the making of peace across local divides and across national boundaries (Mano River). However, peace missions have tended to pay little or no attention to these informal contributions of women and no linkages are made between the mission and these efforts. In the process, valuable local efforts and approaches are relegated to the background and overshadowed by officially recognized and externally driven initiatives.

With few exceptions, failure to systematically link up formal activities on gender mainstreaming has had the effect (even if unintended) of obscuring valuable local ideas and approaches to gender equality. In Kosovo, promising and dynamic indigenous peacebuilding efforts were marginalized when UNMIK took over administration of the country and made little or no effort to link the informal and formal peacebuilding structures so as to generate a multiplier effect. UNMIS too did not build on the women's peacebuilding activities that existed prior to its deployment as it gave priority to the formal peace arrangements between the parties to the Comprehensive Peace Agreement (CPA). Similarly in Liberia UNMIL did not take advantage of the knowledge base of the women's networks that were central to advocating conflict resolution. And in Nepal, where the active participation of women had been a critical part of the people's movement, it was a struggle to ensure women's participation in the post-conflict governance arrangements.

Implementing UNSCR 1325 outside of the context of peace operations

The focus of this volume on contexts where peace support missions were deployed as well as places without peacekeeping presence makes it possible to assess the impact of locally driven initiatives and externally led efforts to promote gender equality. We sought to find out whether the impetus for advancing gender equality could be successful if it originates from a place other than a UN peace mission. The experiences of Nigeria and regional organizations are instructive in this regard. Rwanda is an exceptional case in which the war and the presence of the peace mission long predates the Resolution and gender equality was driven entirely on the inside. The success of the efforts within Rwanda were the result of a concerted effort by society as well as the government to respond to their specific needs on the ground. Actors outside of the peace operations environment clearly have the potential to complement the role of the peace missions but they also present their own distinct challenges.

What are the challenges encountered in implementing UNSCR 1325 outside of the context of peacekeeping operations?

The process of advancing gender equality in countries that have not experienced a UN peace mission differs from those that have had access to UN resources and mechanisms, but only to a degree. Are there noticeable differences in the extent to which UNSCR 1325 is implemented, or any significant differences in the way that it is translated to the national context? Countries like Nigeria, that are not officially recognized as being in conflict, remain on the margins of the ongoing discourse regarding UNSCR 1325 and this no doubt affects the effort to operationalize the Resolution on the ground. As the case of Nigeria demonstrates, there is no real urgency or willingness on the part of state actors and institutions to apply UNSCR 1325 despite the obvious need on the ground, particularly in conflict-affected areas. Indeed, the invocation of the Resolution by a government minister might have been an accident of history. The country's contribution to international peacekeeping and, in this regard, the demands of the peacekeeping environment (such as the need for women peacekeepers in Darfur) yielded positive results for the UNSCR 1325 agenda, while contributing to improving the country's image in international peacekeeping after having suffered a poor reputation in the past. The real effort in implementing UNSCR 1325 has come from civil society, which has demonstrated gallantry at times in mobilizing action on behalf of women in difficult conflict environments in the country such as in the Niger Delta.

The strategic importance of a country like Nigeria is not lost on many observers and Ikpe's chapter in this volume draws attention to this. Its role as a regular troop-contributor to international peacekeeping has an influencing potential, whether positively or negatively, on the environment of the peace operation. At a minimum, imbibing the values of UNSCR 1325 will not only reap rewards abroad in terms of the success of peace operations and a boost in the country's image, it will also potentially have a knock-on effect on the conduct of the armed and security forces at home.

Regional organizations

Situations like that of Nigeria, where, despite the absence of UN presence, the country plays an important regional and peacekeeping role, underscore the importance of regional organizations in the implementation of UNSCR 1325. Indeed, the roles played by various regional organizations and actors are of particular significance to the debate on the implementation of UNSCR 1325.

Clearly, the UN will not be present in every context. The most obvious terrain where UN peace operations can aim to make impact through concerted action over a sustained period is in conflict and post-conflict situations, particularly those on the agenda of the UN Security Council, where international presence and intervention has been negotiated or sanctioned. Beyond this, there are insufficient entry points and opportunities for UN engagement in other situations even if some of the UN's operational agencies are present. This is especially the case in societies undergoing transitions from long-term authoritarian rule, where state actors remain in control of the internal processes with limited engagement of international actors. In this regard, regional organizations, particularly those involved in the maintenance of regional peace and security, have a significant added value because of their regional reach as well as the potential to set standards and disseminate good practice.

On reflection, much has been done by regional bodies in setting norms on approaches to women, peace and security in their respective regions and in some instances at the broader international level. Six key trends emerge from the discussions on the African Union (AU), European Union (EU), Southern African Development Community (SADC) and the Economic Community of West African States (ECOWAS) in this volume, which present a picture of regional experiences on driving UNSCR 1325. First, all the organizations have succeeded in setting up instruments that directly relate to the objectives of UNSCR 1325. These include, for example, the AU's Maputo Protocol, the EU's CA, SADC's Protocol on Gender and Development and the ECOWAS Conflict Prevention Framework, ECPF – all which provide a degree of domestication of the Resolution in these various contexts. Second, many of the activities around the preparation, adoption and implementation of these instruments have also demonstrated broad and inclusive engagement by the regional organizations with civil society representatives. Third, these organisations have also been effective in joining energies and working together as well as learning from differing contexts to their own. The trends are, however, not all positive. Clearly, there have been challenges in reality, in meeting the expectations of UNSCR 1325.

Fourth, there has been a leaning toward emphasizing the protection of women provisions of the Resolution above the requirements for strategic participation of women in peace and security matters. Fifth, core peace and security policy issues remain insulated from debates on women, peace and security such that the latter is ghettoized as a separate issue. This is demonstrated by the near universal problem of poor representation of women in senior decision-making capacities on peace and security within the organizations themselves. Last, although some gains have been made at the regional level on UNSCR 1325, there has been far less success in terms of implementation at the national level in member states. This is not surprising giving that in many cases, the region relies on voluntary domestic accession by member states. This strongly resonates with the perennial problem that is encountered in the implementing of the Resolution, relating to the dire lack of accountability and monitoring mechanisms.

Can UNSCR 1325 be strategically used to drive systemic change?

To be certain, UNSCR 1325 is underlined by good intentions and a commitment on the part of key international actors to facilitate structural change in ways that will make a qualitative shift in the conditions of women particularly in situations of armed violence. In reality, however, weaknesses inherent in the Resolution itself, and in the structures and methods through which the Resolution is being translated into action on the ground, in addition to other obstacles, seriously limit its impact. As indicated at the beginning of this chapter, UNSCR 1325 does not go far enough to explicitly tackle deeply rooted challenges to the advancement of women. Perhaps the expectation of the creators of the Resolution was not to overhaul the systems that sustain the abuse of women, but rather to create pockets of resilience and groups of actors that can champion a process of achieving structural change. This in itself is an ambitious and desirable agenda.

Beyond this, it was always going to be impossible to guarantee the reach and impact of the Resolution beyond states affected by armed conflict, particularly those in which the UN is present. Not unusually, it is difficult to ensure the commitment of every member state to the Resolution. Therefore, the role of actors that can drive change in their regional and national contexts including regional actors and civil society becomes all the more crucial. But the UN has not naturally gravitated toward these potential champions for the implementation of UNSCR 1325. Rather, its natural inclination, which is not inconsistent with the Resolution, is to ensure implementation through its own structures. Several of the country studies in this volume reflect a good degree of UN system-wide engagement with UNSCR 1325 although obvious coordination challenges remain. And in this regard efforts to mainstream gender into the peace operations are evident even if this remains work in process.

However, a real challenge is presented in the translation of the principles and values of UNSCR 1325 from UN actors to the local and national context, where real change for women and for gender equality is much needed. The evidence here suggests that the existence of peace operations in these areas has not led to a bridging of gaps between internal and external UNSCR 1325-related initiatives. There have been no tangible gains in terms of translating and transferring women's achievements in peacebuilding in the informal realm, to the formal. This is compounded by the masculinist culture of the peace operations environment, which places the focus of most missions on state-centric security provision and a token response to the gender dimensions of security and the particular concerns of women. In such an environment, there is limited expectation that the mission will link with and seek to upscale local efforts to drive the implementation of UNSCR 1325.

This natural tendency in peace operations raises the question as to whether they are best placed to deliver the implementation of UNSCR 1325 on the ground beyond ensuring gender mainstreaming within the mission even if in mechanistic ways. The temptation to engage in bean-counting exercises, such as focusing on numbers of women in positions rather than quality or indeed shifts in structural conditions that marginalize women, is high. Furthermore, the targeting of women for programmes rather than seeking gender equality is a far more attractive proposition for peace missions. Under these circumstances, one is left with little else but to conclude that the continuing marginalization of women and failure to upscale their achievements from the informal level is a function of the incompatibility between the desired goal of UNSCR 1325 and the mechanisms through which the UN has sought to realize this goal.

Aside from this challenge, UNSCR 1325 could be strengthened by dealing with a range of obstacles that prevent its successful implementation in various contexts. Three factors are crucial in this respect. The first is the lack of accountability and monitoring. The ongoing efforts at the United Nations to implement UNSCR 1889 are a major step in this regard. Second, there is a need for more resources, particularly financial resources targeted at gender-related activities. Third, particular attention should be focused on women's civil society organizations and peacebuilding work at the community level. Last, in order to effectively address these issues, systematic attention should be paid to the collection of better data, information and analysis of the gender dimensions of the situation and needs on the ground as a standard part of all aspects of planning, implementation and evaluation of peacebuilding activities. Ten years after the adoption of UNSCR 1325, that the world community has embarked on a comprehensive review of the application of UNSCR 1325 holds some promise that concrete measures will be taken to address the gaps in implementation in ways that transform the lives of women.

Index